CLO

CLOUDS HILL

Vance Wood

© Vance Wood, 2020

Published by Warrior

A CIP catalogue record for this book is available from the British Library.

ISBN: 978-0-9929613-9-8

This is a novel. Any references to historical events, real people or real places are used fictitiously. Other names, characters, places and events are products of the author's imagination.

Book layout and cover design by Clare Brayshaw

Prepared and printed by:

York Publishing Services Ltd
64 Hallfield Road
Layerthorpe
York YO31 7ZQ

Tel: 01904 431213

Website: www.yps-publishing.co.uk

For the dreamers of the day

CHAPTER ONE

It is typical of Lawrence that he cycles from Bridlington to Clouds Hill. Mere mortals would choose a less challenging mode of transport to take them home, following their retirement, but Lawrence sees it as an adventure, a test of his resolve and instinct for survival. In fact, he positively hastens his goodbyes. The handshakes only linger when friends and colleagues insist, and, even then, he does not return their squeeze but lets his hand die in theirs, so that they understand his wish to be off to his heavenly cottage.

"I'll write," he promises, and they believe him, having seen him write so many letters.

In his final days, as he tries to leave his affairs at the RAF in order, he becomes conscious that he is letting go, that his energy is escaping him as air from a punctured tyre.

"And what plans do you have, old chap?" he is asked, the day before he leaves.

Lawrence replies, "Oh, you know, this and that," but he cannot, he laments, be more precise. Yes, he has a vague wish to continue to write – he knows it is impossible to try to emulate Hardy, Forster, Graves, or Shaw – but what and how elude him. And he sees they see that is unlike him, this lack of planning.

"Playing your cards close to your chest, eh?" persists one, slightly awkward at Lawrence's lack of openness.

"Something like that."

So they gather to wave him off on his bicycle. He presses on his pedal, and he is away to a rousing cheer that becomes applause lasting till he is out of sight. They return to their workshops and offices, but do not speak of what they have just witnessed.

Travelling light has always been Lawrence's style, and he chooses to go without spare inner tubes. If I have a puncture, then I shall mend it, he decides. In his pocket, he carries a tin of trusty rubber patches, glue, and chalk. A thousand times he has mended punctures, and his inner tubes record his determination not to spend money on new ones if he can avoid it. His salary, from now on, will be half of what it was, and he has already decided to drastically cut the number of letters he writes. He will send a card to everyone, to let them know, so that they do not worry that they have offended him, or fear for his health.

In his pocket, he carries money enough for refreshment and overnight accommodation. He stops at a teashop he knows. Once, on his Brough, he was purring through Bawtry, and bought a pot of tea and a fruit scone. The waitress was polite and friendly, and though she looked at his handsome face as if she recognised him, she answered his questions about the village enthusiastically, and, when he left, having tipped her more generously than he had intended, she said, "Do call in and see us again, some time, if you're passing."

"I will," he said.

And he does, though the waitress is no longer working there. He enquires after her, and her replacement, a much older, more clipped, woman replies, "Left ages ago. Got in the family way, and was asked to leave. Can't have our customers embarrassed."

Poor girl! thinks Lawrence. She was twice as genuine as you, but all enjoyment of my stop-off is now lost, so I will press on.

There is still a long way to go, and he knows he must rest. He has already chosen an inn. That has been the advantage of the Brough: it has allowed him to familiarise himself with huge swathes of the country.

Usually, he likes to absorb all the landscapes and landmarks of interest, but such is the effort required to keep pedalling that he passes them without noticing, and he wonders how he manages to be where he is.

This time, the feeling is different. He has belonged to the world, lived and worked in many places, but, of all journeys, this one is into the unknown as never before. There has always been a reason for his destinations, but he is uncomfortable with not having the usual drive to experience new things. Worse still, he does not know why.

Eventually, he knows he is in Dorset, and that is a blessing. The long, rising hills and swooping vales are unmistakeable, and he smiles at their undeniable beauty, knowing he will soon be at Clouds Hill.

He is sore in the saddle. Why would he not be, after such a long time in it? His body is tired, more so than he expected. He does not fear the onset of middle age but does not want it to be a best friend. There is not a damned thing I can do about it, he tells himself. If it must live with me at Clouds Hill, I shall not speak to or feed it. It must live up the hill or beyond. It will not be allowed upstairs or in my reading room. No doubt, I shall hear it complain, from time to time, but I shall not respond, or encourage it, for, once it has its feet under the table, it will be a most disagreeable lodger!

There are times on such a journey when one is numb to the beauty of one's surroundings. All that matters, at such moments, is to maintain a forward momentum, and so it is almost by stealth that his very own Dorset embraces him. Hills no longer seem too steep. Indeed, he begins to attack them, causing onlookers to stare at him in amazement. Sometimes, he takes his hands off the handlebars, and free-wheels, but does not stop, knowing that Clouds Hill is but two miles away.

The first sign that there is an unexpected welcome party is a line of vehicles in the vicinity. There are fox and stag hunts, in these parts, he knows, but these vehicles have no dog cages, and lack the mud-splattered motif of the usual beaters and guns. Lawrence is without panniers, and does not cut the figure of a national hero, but he dons a wide-brimmed hat, and tilts it over his face, so that he is unrecognisable. Nothing he wears suggests he is – has been – an aircraftsman, and no one at Bovington Camp or Wareham knows that cycling is his preferred mode of transport.

He passes Clouds Hill as quickly as possible when he sees the crowd of pressmen loitering near it. It is hard for him to ignore those who have strayed inside his boundary, and are fiddling with their cameras.

Someone has tipped them off in Bridlington, he figures. Damn them! But I will not give them the satisfaction of snapping a tired man, a hollow replica of whom they are seeking.

So he moves on and out of sight. A few look at him, and he turns away.

"Lawrence is not a big chap," one says to the man next to him, "and we're not looking for an everyday cyclist. I expect nothing less than him, garbed as an Arab, atop a camel!"

The others laugh because there is little else to ease the boredom. They have been camped there for hours, staff and freelance. Sometimes, one puts them on alert, causing all to rouse themselves from their lethargy, and that sets in train more false alarms.

Lawrence gradually pulls away, resentful that they are occupying his property, his country, as he sees it. Knowing what they want – headlines, a juicy scrap – the easiest course of action for him would be to give them what they want, but haven't I given them enough? he argues. They will dine off me for ever if I let them.

The perception is that he is encouraging this game of cat and mouse, that he loves the aura of mystery that is burnished by every tale of his daring and cunning.

And there had been a time, in his younger days, when it had been hard to deny he found the gossip enjoyable. How he had privately laughed at the scandalised Arabs who had denounced him for having Dahoum live under the same roof! He had met Selim Ahmed, Dahoum's real name, in an archaeological dig in southern Turkey. They moved in together, and Dahoum became his helper. How Dahoum laughed and cried when he saw that Lawrence had mounted his nude carving of him on top of their house! Even in England, where Dahoum had marvelled at all the great advancements of London, he had gone to no great trouble to hide his protégé. Instead, they had gone everywhere together. Each had taught the other something of which he was proud.

Those camped outside Clouds Hill trudge to their cars, some to sleep with one eye open, others to find lodgings in Dorchester or Wareham, with the intention to be back by first light.

One, Henry Stephenson, says to another, "He's out there, I know, playing with us. We're easy, he thinks. He's taken on so many enemies, and won so many battles, that this is a mere game to him. This is a trap, and we're being made to look chumps."

"You're tired, old chap. You may be right, but he can't stay away for ever. This is all he's got now," replies the other.

"That's what we suppose, but he's gone to ground is my belief. He's dodged bullets and bayonets, and we ought to acknowledge his survival against the odds. But we'll have our story."

"What makes you say that?"

"Because he needs us as much as we need him."

"Think so?"

"Bloody well know so. You just watch."

Stephenson's eyes twinkle, as if he has a plan to make sure he gets his copy, and Lawrence gets his come-uppance for his annoying delaying of the inevitable.

Lawrence decides he will not return and reward them for their patience. He has one or two friends on whom he can call, but he refuses to be a refugee in his own country, his own backyard. There are sacrifices one makes, but Clouds Hill will not be one. To fight another day is his aim. Survival is everything, even if it means a little inconvenience.

Stephenson has done his homework and visited Lawrence's neighbours. Bovington Camp sent him packing, even detained him for a few hours on a trumped-up suspicion of espionage, and he enjoyed it, for he is a journalistic mercenary, and there will be someone, somewhere, who will buy his account of false imprisonment. Long ago, he realised that, by specialising in all things Lawrentian, he could make a healthy living. Sometimes, he sails close to the wind, invites searching questions from editors about rumours of pederasty.

"You could finish this newspaper if he sues," warns one big shot. "He's a bloody hero, has the ear of Churchill, they say. This business over the Arab boy better be correct."

Stephenson shrugs arrogantly, a prelude to a take-it-or-leave-it offer.

"Let me know by mid-day. If I don't hear by twelve, I'll sell to someone else."

The editor thinks Stephenson a sort of spiv, is reminded of someone who exploited the desperate during the Great War. Hair slicked back with olive oil, wearing his only tie, a dark green one with a grease stain, he is cock-sure that he can get the fee he wants.

"And who are your sources?"

Stephenson sneers, tuts. "You surely don't expect me to reveal them, do you? You pay such and such for a column, but it takes me months to build up my network of trust. You're not just paying for words; my career is at stake, too."

"If this back-fires ..." says the editor, clearly tempted.

"Shake now?"

The editor looks at the outstretched hand, and before he knows what he is doing, he is holding it. The hands remain together for a second, perhaps two, then separate. The deal is done. They do not have to like each other to do it. After all, it is only sordid business.

When Lawrence finally gains access to his cottage, it is with the assistance of a horse and cart, a tarpaulin, and two neighbours who have described to him what has been happening during his absence. He knows and trusts them, and they are only too pleased to help. They, too, hate the press and the disturbance of a peaceful Dorset road. The plan is simple. One man arrives at Clouds Hill with the horse and cart, ostensibly bringing provisions for the arrival, the next day, of Master Lawrence. He tugs his forelocks, and begs the reporters stand aside so that the horse can pass.

Stephenson senses a ruse, and questions him.

"He comes tomorrow, you say? How do you know?"

"Why, by letter. Here it be, if you are doubting of the truth."

The other pressmen gather round. Stephenson recognises the handwriting as Lawrence's. In the past, Stephenson has had two examples shown to him by editors threatened with legal action for libel.

The ruse becomes a rat, which Stephenson smells. He knows Lawrence is self-sufficient, frugal, unlikely to need the help of two locals to make his return comfortable. This is the last thing he would do. Then Stephenson eyes the tarpaulin. He must be under there! he thinks. That's where he is. That would be typical of him.

"Keep them all there for just a minute longer," whispers Lawrence as he skips down the hill behind the cottage. He knows every rock, every tree and stump, even in the dark. In his hand is a key, which he uses to let himself in, and when he has locked the door from the inside, he chuckles.

And that, my fine friends, is another battle won, but I do not want a war. Truly, I do not, he asserts.

Then, without warning, Stephenson lifts up the tarpaulin to discover the accomplice, who rises dramatically from the dead, a wide grin on his face.

"We've been had, men," says Stephenson. "He's taking the piss. It's all a game to him. I said I felt he was out there, watching us."

The first cart man says, "Why don't you all go home? He won't be saying anything to you today. Did you really think he was in the cart? Why, Master Lawrence baint stupid, and if I baint mistaken, he be putting a nice record on his gramophone, this very moment. Let him alone now, gentleman, and go and have a cup of tea."

Stephenson says, "Damn! He's sneaked in while we were being distracted here, but there's more than one way of skinning a cat."

The two men in the cart turn round and leave. Stephenson is sure he hears one of them say, "There's more than one way of skinning a cat!"

"He's already in the cottage?" asks one of the pressmen.

"Of course," says Stephenson, "but we can wait. He has to come out, some time or other. Leave him to me, men. I'll flush him out. We'll have our interview yet. We have our headline already: LAWRENCE SNEAKS IN THE BACK DOOR. That'll hurt him."

When the pleasure of nipping into his cottage undetected subsides, Lawrence slips into bed, and falls asleep. So tired is he that, contrary to expectation, he fails to dream. Usually, the combination of prolonged exercise and pure air plunges him into a vivid, alternative reality that is both exciting and disturbing. But not tonight, not even though he is aware that one or two reporters are likely to sleep rough, perhaps in the grounds.

In the morning, he stretches, and goes upstairs. There is only tea for breakfast. The water has not run freely for ages, and appears a little brown, but he knows the agony of going without it, so boils it for longer. They will see the smoke, and know I am here, he guesses, but that is what I want: to remind them I have outwitted them.

Stephenson is leaning against his car, smoking a cigarette. He coughs violently, then settles to calm thought. Going to war with Lawrence, if he does not get the interview that guarantees his best pay day yet, needs to come a long way down the line. Lawrence, he knows from the letter Lawrence sent to the editor, and which was published, is piqued. There is a huge difference between Lawrence telling the world of his bruises, physical and mental, at the hands of vindictive, vicious thugs, and Stephenson doing it for him.

The advantage Stephenson thinks he has over Lawrence is that Lawrence does not know what he looks like, but Stephenson is mistaken. Lawrence uses one of his contacts in Whitehall to make a few enquiries, procure a likeness, and the match between what he thinks Stephenson looks like and the photograph he is sent is almost perfect.

So when Lawrence strolls out with a tray of mugs of tea for the reporters huddled at the entrance, he spots Stephenson. Now which have I laced with arsenic? he asks himself, restraining a smile.

Surprised, they approach him – nervously.

"Morning, gentlemen. I trust you have slept well. There is no sugar. You see, I've only just come back, and shopping is top of today's to do list," he says in, for him, a jolly way.

This gesture wins them over, gives them hope of a few newsworthy titbits. They sip and smile. One or two are even in awe of him, and regret their parasitic conduct. There is something in his face that transcends the cunning tactics Stephenson attributes to him.

Lawrence fields questions, and, teacups placed tidily back on the tray, the reporters scribble their hearts away. The early questions relate to his journey on his bicycle, and he tries to varnish his answers with humour. They appreciate this, and want more, as much as he can give them.

The day is cold, and Lawrence begins to shiver, having deliberately gone out to them without a coat, so that he can excuse himself when the low temperature becomes unbearable.

Stephenson notices that Lawrence is preparing to withdraw, and decides that, on this occasion, he ought to toss in a big question, one that will elicit a response that will sell thousands more copies on the news stands of Britain. In an ideal world, he would prefer a one-to-one with him, and sees that the others will use the same material, get the credit which should be rightly his. But the question hits the sweet spot, and Lawrence is momentarily thrown.

"And what brings you back to Clouds Hill?"

The others watch. There is the truth, and there is a public response. The latter is slow coming, but when it does, it sets them scribbling. Stephenson does not show his disappointment when Lawrence says, "To take stock, embark upon a few literary projects. I had in mind a translation or two, if I can find a publisher."

So there are supplementary questions.

"What challenges have you in mind on the world stage? There is, of course, what is fomenting in Germany. Has Mr. Churchill a role for you?"

Lawrence now sees the trap, and fends him off with, "That is a question you must put to Mr. Churchill."

"But you have been a great asset to him," says Stephenson.

"One does what one believes in. But, gentlemen, I must go inside. It's too cold to stand out here, and I shan't invite you in. The cottage is not adequately aired, and there is a dreadful, fusty smell."

All but Stephenson are grateful for these crumbs, and they believe they have enough to file a report of some description, which is better than what they thought they would have.

An hour later, Lawrence checks his property, and all have gone, but he ought to go up his hill, to make sure no one is hiding. There is always more money for a snap of an unguarded moment. So he picks up his rifle, checks it is loaded, and begins the ascent.

Then he sees the man.

"You still here?" Lawrence asks him. "Well, well, well." The man does not reply but stares back unflinchingly. "You going, or do I have to put a bullet between your eyes?"

The man's silence dares him to pull the trigger. Lawrence takes aim. Stephenson is different from the others, needs dealing with, as all dangerous men do. One shot is all it will take, and he can dispose of the body by leaving it to the buzzards high up at Maiden Castle. Lawrence sees Stephenson is determined to stand his ground, and fires.

Lawrence strides towards the dead reporter, sees that he has missed the chosen spot, and has shot him through the eye. He knows that the bullet has destroyed Stephenson's brain, but examines the dead man by poking his forefinger into the eye socket.

He then returns to his cottage, feeling much better, leaving the bullet-ridden scarecrow, attired in old clothes of his, with just one eye, tied to the tree. It is both therapy and target practice, and, on this occasion, more the former than latter.

"Time for tea," he declares. "Karachi special, I think. Perfect."

CHAPTER TWO

A moth, careful not to burn itself, flaps noisily against one of the two candelabras. In the thinning light, Lawrence moves to the edge of his settee, and the leather creaks. He rubs his tired, blue eyes with the knuckles of both forefingers, and though he has only a few pages of Tess of the d'Urbervilles left to read, he lets the book rest, upside down, on the floor. The ending he knows well, having read it several times before, but he likes to save momentous events for another time, to lift his spirits, or move him to tears. Indeed, he thinks of himself as a sort of literary squirrel.

On one of his visits to Clouds Hill, Hardy had expressed dismay at the public outrage that had greeted his novel, and Lawrence had said, "Don't let such opinions depress you."

But Hardy had replied, "I have invited it, you see. It's the curse of publication, as you yourself must know only too well."

Nodding to Hardy, Lawrence had then taken another sip of his tea. There was no point denying this truth. Of all men, he valued Hardy the most, even though they would never converse again.

Standing up and stretching, Lawrence notices that it is almost time to use the last of the natural light, so he leaves his cottage, and strides purposefully up the hill, at the top of which he urinates. He varies the spot daily, when the urge becomes too great to ignore, and sees the landscape in different ways. Sometimes, he is tempted to shout out loud, simply because, among the trees, his friendly neighbours, he is a king, God, even. This solitude confers upon him a special status, wraps him in a serenity he finds, these days, nowhere else. An owl screeches, and Lawrence descends carefully. The slope is steep, and more than once have his feet slipped on mud or shale.

He cannot be bothered to undress, and slides into his sleeping bag embroidered with *Meum*. There is no need tonight for *Tuum*. Before he extinguishes his candle, he looks at all the upright books he has read.

"At ease," he says to them.

Then phut. The acrid smoke from the wick lingers a short while. An intense blackness is Lawrence's bed-fellow.

Sometimes, he dreams. Thousands of times, he has been back in the dangerous desert, even to Oxford. Once, in a long sequence of images, Churchill sent for him, and Lawrence woke up, thinking, "He has riches of all kinds, but though I write, I am poorer than ever."

But sleep he does.

In the morning, when he senses it is time to rise, he is grateful to have awoken. His books are still there. And I have read them all, he marvels. Every single one of them.

He discovers the day is fine. The early morning dew makes him more careful as he climbs, with his spade and strips of newspaper, up the hill behind his cottage.

There in his garage below is his Brough motorcycle, and he smiles at the prospect of an afternoon's heady ride to Lulworth Cove. Once, Bernard Shaw had asked him whether a camel felt more powerful underneath him than his Brough.

"A motorcycle would be completely useless in the desert," Lawrence had answered, "and a camel would be too slow in the winding lanes of Dorset."

"Ah, but on a camel, you would have the time to stare, really look at the landscape, appreciate its beauty."

"That is not the point of having a motorcycle. Neither is getting from one place to another, though that is a useful function. It's the danger, the speed, that fine judgement when steering round a tight bend. There's nothing like it," Lawrence had explained.

"Be careful. Just because no bullet has claimed you in some hot and foreign country doesn't mean you are invincible."

"It is our common lot. I don't fear death," had said Lawrence.

"Then you should do, dear boy. You jolly well should do."

"Besides," had laughed Lawrence, "my garage is too small to house a camel as well!"

He is tempted to steal an early look at his precious Brough, but is hungry and thirsty, so returns to his cottage. Only his thirst can be satisfied, as he keeps little fresh food in, perhaps a chunk of cheese and some bread, which he stores under his bell jars. There are, of course, the tins for guests: corned beef, beans, prunes. Visitors, envious that their lifestyle does not release them to the same extent, help themselves, and are quite happy to eat that way, looking up at him as he picks at his food on the shelf above the fire. There is no kitchen in the cottage, and the informality of tins means more time spent together, talking. And there is tea, always tea, or water.

It is too early for music on his gramophone, but, mug in hand, he goes upstairs. Torn between the sheets of paper left untidily next to his typewriter, and the half-finished letter to Lady Astor, he takes a moment to think straight, and stands by the dead fireplace, leaning on the shelf he had fixed at a strategic height. From here, he recalls, have I looked down and conversed with so many people of whom I am in awe. How I am embarrassed, in comparison, by my meagre literary accomplishments! I wonder these men of letters come at all. That they do really lifts me when all life seems pointless.

He passes his hand over his stubble. Finish the letter, then shave, he decides.

So strong is his wish to make *personal* contact in his letters that he will not resort to the cold metal of his typewriter. Instead, he sits and, without hesitation, confesses his dismay at the pressmen who openly and invisibly invade his privacy. Lady Astor will, one day, cease to indulge me, he predicts.

He fetches his cut-throat razor, and begins to pass it rhythmically over his whetstone. Is there not a man who has not done what he now does: lets the lethal blade hover over a jugular vein? It could be over quickly, he calculates, and then those who hide behind bushes, or brazenly knock at my door, would get their sensational headlines, once again, on the back of my well documented valour, my willingness to execute not only one of our own but even myself.

So when the letter is finished, and he has resisted the temptation to remove himself from the ever-thickening feeling of purposelessness by slitting his own throat, he shaves and puts on clean clothes. He sniffs the ones he has removed, and makes a mental note to wash them.

Outside, he is cautious, and scans the hillside, a habit acquired years ago when emerging, at sunrise, from his tent. The threat posed by snipers is one he can never forget, and though he does not expect to be shot on his own property, there are dangers of a different kind. Years ago, he learned that where there is a brow of a hill, there is the unknown on the other side, and this caution is what wakes him up, stiffens his resolve to survive, at all costs.

Clouds Hill and Bridlington are, however, a far cry from Turkish-held enclaves, and his instinct tells him it is safe to go about his daily business.

Letter in his pocket, he opens his garage, and pushes his motorcycle into the space in front of it. Once astride his camel of the road, he kick-starts it, and moves it slowly onto the road. He does not forget to lock his cottage but impulsively leaves it open. He has an instinct that it is a curiosity into which few, including the pressmen, would let themselves for nefarious reasons. He feels confident that his books and personal life are safe. After all, Clouds Hill is not conspicuous from the road.

On his way to the Post Office, he passes a military vehicle or two, and is reminded of when he had another name, a fresh start, a plan to reinvent and unburden himself. He feels the wind on his face, that he is speeding away from rumours that enshroud him like a Dorset fog, and he accelerates. It is all or nothing with him, these days, and he has not yet given in to inactivity or self-doubt, which he suspects await him somewhere along the line.

"Morning, Mr. Shaw," greets the postmaster, quietly enough to keep his customer's true identity a secret. In the queue, there are two women the postmaster knows are inquisitive to the point where they can be thought of as nothing but local gossips. He knows that people write to Lawrence using different names, and that Lawrence encourages this for reasons more to do with how and when they have come to know him than a desire to be elusive or mysterious.

"Morning. Fine day," says Lawrence, handing over his two letters, the addresses turned downwards, so that the names of the intended recipients cannot be read.

"Indeed, it is."

The postmaster, knowing that Lawrence is one of his best customers, smiles as he picks up the coins passed over the counter separating them. Lawrence recognises the smile as a reassurance that his privacy is safeguarded in that particular neck of the woods.

The two women have seen him before, remember his piercing, blue eyes, and look into his face for a sign that he is willing to engage them in conversation, but he side-steps them briskly, and merely nods politely, before rejoining his motorcycle.

"And who, may I ask, is the gentleman who has just left?" asks the taller of the two women, the one in a green coat with a dead fox wrapped round her collar.

"He's much too short for you," jokes her friend.

"But he has a name?" persists the first.

"And what can I do for you?" asks the postmaster, his face devoid of any suggestion that he might fracture the confidence Lawrence has in him.

There is no need, Lawrence decides, to return to Clouds Hill. The day and the lanes stretch out before him invitingly. He knows every imperfection in the road, and is confident that he can avoid those he does not with some tail-sliding here, some swerving there. It is all in the challenge, you see. He and engines are blood-brothers. There is mutual trust between them. Together, they conspire to be invincible, and their criss-crossing England has added a veritable strength to that conviction.

Lulworth Cove is their destination, and the Brough, one of many he has owned, with its throttle fully opened, delivers him unscathed, barely breathless.

Oh, near-perfect circle! he cries within, at first sight of the water. These dips and bends and hollows and holes will never stop me coming here to worship you!

He crunches to the furthest point from the slipway to the sea, and, down to his vest, and shorts he dons behind a rock, wades into the water. With an ecstatic gasp, he glides on his front from the beach. Turning to look for his clothes, his point of reference, he floats on his back, and though the water is cold, he relaxes, and stares up into the limitless heavens. I could be anywhere, he muses. Anywhere.

Being deep, the water in Lulworth Cove is cold. England has too few days of strong sunshine to warm it, but he grew to bear cold water in training camp. It was, over time, a question of mind over matter.

On his back, he sees an object in the sky, hears a faint sound in the distance. Is it a buzzard or plane? he wonders. Using his hands to rotate himself so that he can follow its flight, he eventually identifies it as a plane making its way along the coast. Soon he can hear clearly its engine spluttering and coughing, then droning. Lawrence thinks it would be good to race his Brough against it. No, to pit *himself* against it. But he considers the idea too foolish, even if exciting. Judgement in these things is all-important. He feels his ribs, and moves his shoulder blade, reminders that everything, even life, can be snatched from you when you least expect it. How did I survive that plane crash? he asks himself. Who, what invisible power, chose me to live and them to die?

The longer he stays in the water, the freer he feels, less concerned that he has not written anything for several days. The output does not always match the desire, with him, even if ideas buzz in his head like frustrated flies crashing into his bell jars. He knows that, Seven Pillars of Wisdom and The Mint aside, he has produced pitifully little of worth, and often castigates himself for this.

He glances back at the beach when the plane ceases to hold his gaze. A man is standing near his clothes, looking at him. Lawrence observes. There is little money in his bag, enough for a bite to eat, to keep hunger at bay till he is back at Clouds Hill. He does not wish to be the victim of petty theft, so, slowly, he breast-strokes towards the land, but the man, older than himself, certainly, stands his ground, and watches.

As Lawrence pulls himself into an upright position, the soles of his feet hurting from the crippling stones, the man calls, "Cold?"

Lawrence notices that the man has a moustache, is smartly but comfortably dressed, is standing at ease, giving the impression that he is confident, sociable.

"Very," replies Lawrence.

There is no towel so his hands wipe off as much water as possible.

"Invigorating?" asks the man.

"Very," repeats Lawrence.

"You are the only one to brave it," informs his interlocutor.

Lawrence turns, and sees that, indeed, there is no one else in the water.

"So I am."

Lawrence becomes increasingly nervous that the man, who appears to be smiling but might be squinting as the sun dazzles him, has singled him out. The fact that the stranger shows no intention of allowing him to dry and dress himself in peace prompts Lawrence to bring the encounter to some sort of conclusion.

"Must get on."

"It *is* you. I thought it was, back there. I was going to ask as you were striding down the slipway."

"Well, it's definitely me," laughs Lawrence.

He is not irritated by the man's persistence, but does not want to encourage him. Such chance meetings have happened, from time to time, but Lawrence has always denied, to those swearing they recognise him from somewhere, that he is the man who led the Arab Revolt against the Turks.

"I knew it was. Just came to satisfy my curiosity, I suppose."

"I'd shake your hand but I'm wet."

"It's all right. I'll leave you alone, then."

The man makes to leave, and Lawrence suddenly feels ashamed that he has been so laconic. There is also something in the man's bearing that suggests he might have had a distinguished career of some sort: that perfect mixture of confidence and humility, of purposefulness and measured pace of speech and action.

"No, don't go on account of my being wet through. Who are you?"

The man stops, turns, and squints.

"Dry yourself, or you'll catch a chill," he says, before walking away.

Lawrence stretches out on the stones, wonders whether his already short body is shrinking, shuts his eyes, and thinks about the man. He has definitely studied my face somewhere, and was determined to verify his suspicion. He drew me from the water, yet I do not recognise him. There is a whiff of the military about him, and though it is faint, it is unmistakeable. I should be more careful about these matters in public, where my privacy invites target practice.

He wrings out his shorts behind a rock, and dresses himself quickly. Hunger gnaws at his stomach, but with years of controlling appetites of all kinds behind him, he decides to walk to Durdle Door, then go back to Clouds Hill, where he can eat frugally, and read, or listen to music.

The annoyance he feels at having to side-step tourists on the cliff-top dissolves the moment he sees the sun splashing on the waves passing through the door and scampering up the beach. Nimbly, he goes down the steep, makeshift steps onto the shingle. He resists the temptation to swim again, and sits and marvels at the door. So far removed from the exotic locations of the Middle East is he, that he – at least for the time being – suspends thoughts of further far-flung adventures. This shushing of the waves on pebbles soothes him. *If I had company, at this very minute, the beauty of this spot would be diminished. Talk would distract, is more at home at Clouds Hill.*

When the charm begins to wane, he returns to his Brough, and heads home. There, he makes tea, puts on a record, and eats corned beef. The best things in life, he knows, cost little. Privacy and solitude are priceless.

From his pocket he takes out a handkerchief, and onto the floor falls a piece of paper. He picks it up and reads: **John Hume Ross, February 1922-1923**. The words had been printed, presumably, to disguise the author's true hand. *I thought as much*, he nods. *But why? Who* matters not, but *why* does, so he sits at his typewriter, and goes to bed only when his hypotheses, about why the name he had assumed as an Aircraftsman at Uxbridge is on the piece of paper, are fully formed. In the morning, he will look at them again, and, dispassionately, draw conclusions enough to help him fill the day devising survival strategies as cunning as any he has adopted in his life.

CHAPTER THREE

Clouds Hill is small, but perfect for Lawrence, who bought it for the privacy he thinks he needs. Its rooms bulge with people he knows. He sees them come and go, ghosts and the living: soldiers, artists, writers. It is the intimacy of the spaces that draws them all, yet it is only the dead who never leave.

First light, he reviews what he wrote, the previous night, and measures the risk to himself, assesses where he is vulnerable. Outside, between his cottage and garage, as he breathes in the fresh air, he feels he might have exaggerated the threat, but knows full well the way it works in the security services: a smile is a mask; alliances are flimsy, built on shifting sands. His training has honed his intelligence. There are, he suspects, those who would repay his leadership among the Arabs with a bullet or two. That is how it works: trust has five letters but sometimes no substance.

There is no one with whom he can share his suspicions, as no one he knows and trusts has that nose for danger. His has been heightened so much that Clouds Hill begins to feel more like a colonial outpost than the rural idyll he had once felt it to be. With years of careful calculation behind him, he is convinced that not even his detractors would risk the scandal of an assassination. Too obvious. Subtlety, in England's green and pleasant land, is more their style.

In the afternoon, he writes letters in which he does not reveal his fears. To do so would change everything. And writing letters is all he can do to keep contact with the people he finds interesting. There is something in the act of speaking to them, in an epistolary way, that keeps him in touch with life as he would like to lead it. He makes arrangements, keeps his friends, people he admires and respects, close. His pen is his wand. Any other way, none of this would work. He does not try to be affable, but is so, and he entices people, via his pen, into the here and now, with the promise of tea, and talk as fine as a china cup and saucer.

Later, upstairs, the autumnal light still falls through the windows, and there is a strong sense that it is browning as it reflects off the wooden panels. He estimates that the candles should see him through the evening, and places a cushion on the arm of his settee, so that he can stretch out, rest his head without hurting his neck, close his eyes, and nap.

He feels that the beams of wood above him are much closer than usual, oppressive, even. So much time has he spent in this room, assembling words to produce Seven Pillars of Wisdom, that he knows claustrophobia when he feels it. It has a dull patina to it, he always thinks.

"Into this room I have crammed Syria," he once said to a small gathering of privates from Bovington. "And, in doing so, I have transported myself back to those days which, though illuminated in ink, now have a thin film blunting their sharpness. It is as if I have made up those battles, imagined the trust I inspired among my Arab friends. And now that I have betrayed them by selling my Arabian dagger, I sense that I will have to pay a price."

His guests noted his sombre tone, the foreboding of doom, and there settled a silence, till Knowles – or it might have been Palmer – said, "Buck up, old chap. Let's have some music. Nothing too sad, mind. Can you remember the weekend dances we had?"

A half-smile played briefly across Lawrence's face at the memory of men dancing with each other, while they waited for a grander occasion, when local women were drafted into draughty village halls trimmed with wilting bunting.

Now, when Lawrence's instinct seems to confirm that, the last page of Seven Pillars of Wisdom written, there would be a consequence, a personal one, for the part he had played against the Turks, he lights the candles. He has already double-checked that the door downstairs has been locked, and now sees that his rifle, which he had left on the window-seat, is loaded.

"And will I use you, one more time, in anger?" he addresses it affectionately. "Will you come to my rescue, and not fail me? Tonight you are my companion, as the day has made me wobble. See me through the night, in Dorset, not plagued by scorpions but venomous, stinging thoughts, nevertheless."

Little escapes Lawrence – the increasing loss of yellow and brown leaves, the gradual, seasonal creeping of darkness – but even he cannot be ever-present in the banking and twisting lanes of Dorset. Therefore, he often misses the black car progressing at a speed respectful of the humps and hollows lying in wait.

The driver sometimes stops in a safe place, and watches the road for other vehicles. He has even seen Lawrence on his motorcycle, has admired the way he opens up the throttle and hurtles forward as if on an urgent mission. The car driver always wears a trilby, and his collar up. As his face is heavily covered, no one can see, at a glance, that he sports a black moustache. He has fine leather gloves, and even when he is stationary, and the engine is off, he grips the steering wheel, as if ready to move at a moment's notice.

He takes the same route, at different times of the day, familiarises himself with the light, the autumnal mists which drape then vanish from the landscape. There is also a pattern to the traffic, and he has a good idea of who passes when.

Lawrence always varies the times he goes out – a habit formed to keep the enemy guessing – and the man sometimes taps the steering wheel in frustration if he misses the roar of the flying Brough.

One day, a military vehicle pulls up in front of him. The uniformed driver jumps out, and gestures for the other driver to wind down his window.

"Everything all right, sir? Broken down? Got a rope in the wagon should pull you to Bovington Camp."

The other man makes eye contact, but his face remains largely averted, as if not wanting to be fully seen. The soldier scans the car, from which he gets a whiff of freshly polished leather seats and a walnut dashboard.

"Yes, fine, Corporal. Just admiring the view, taking my journey at a leisurely pace."

The soldier sees that the smile is artificial, not one he sees in the Mess, where most of the men are expansive in all that they do.

"A military background yourself, sir?"

"What makes you say that?"

"The stripes, the fact you recognise my rank."

The car driver shrugs and says, "A lucky guess."

The soldier nods and returns to his vehicle, in which another soldier says, "All right?"

"Cold bugger. Said he'd stopped to admire the view, but the hawthorn is tall and sprouting. Warm out there, but he's wearing a hat and a thick coat with his collar up."

"So?"

"Odd bugger."

"Takes all sorts."

In the mirror, the driver says, "Nice car. Not one from round here."

"What makes you say that?"

"What are you? Do I have to explain my every word to you?"

"No. Just wondering."

"Well, stop fucking wondering. Take it from me, there's something fishy about him."

"What makes you -"

But the Corporal's cupped left hand stops him from finishing his sentence.

One time, when the man in the black car is in the vicinity again, he asks a labourer to confirm that the road he is on leads to Clouds Hill.

"I'm hoping to catch a glimpse of your Lawrence of Arabia. A bit out of the way for a man of his fame," he observes good-humouredly.

The labourer, pitch-fork in hand – he had been spreading a bale of straw for some pigs – scratches his head. Used to strangers asking the same question, he has sometimes sent them completely the wrong way, on purpose. On the day he is approached by what he assumes is yet another nosy tourist, he sees that a penny might be made out of the encounter, and summons a ridiculous facial expression he hopes might suggest an acute loss of memory.

"Now let me see. Lawrence of Arabia, you say? Not heard of him, though that don't mean he baint living, these parts. 'Tis on account of me being buried in pig shit – begging your pardon, sir, for my plain speaking – that I don't get to know folk beyond this lane, which suits me, if I be honest."

"Will you take something for your memory?" says the driver, keen to end his interaction with the malodorous pig-herd.

Leaning on the handle of his pitchfork, the farm-worker suppresses his excitement at the silver coin the driver is proferring.

"Well, they say he lives tucked away off the main road, a mile or two from here."

"And you see him often? Have you ever spoken to him?"

The labourer contemplates pushing his luck by holding out for an extra payment, but is not yet in receipt of the silver coin, so says, "Not spoken, but I wave to him, when he acknowledges me. Always gives a little salute to say hello. A gentleman, 'tis certain, though one who rides like the wind. A man who drives that fast be on a mission to heaven or hell, be my thinking."

It is always best, thinks the driver, not to meet the subjects of his assignments, and it has been particularly hard to ignore all that he has heard about Lawrence's personal qualities. Therefore the struggle to distance himself from him has been challenging, to say the least. One brief encounter with him, to make sure he knows how Lawrence looks now and not on posters or in films, is all he wants.

"You have been helpful."

The labourer gratefully accepts his reward, and, as he watches the car disappear, he says, "Now if you'd a-asked me, I'd have told you that it baint no good trying for him today, as he hab already gone Dorchester way, two hours since!"

At Clouds Hill, the driver parks his car out of sight, and walks to the front door of the cottage. In his coat pocket, his right hand bulges over an object he has learned to use expertly. In his left is a pencil and notebook. What difference does one more reporter make? There is no answer to his knocking, and to deviate from the plan by waiting behind a tree for Lawrence's return might invite failure. Too many things to go wrong: Lawrence returns accompanied, has a gun himself, sees the black car and becomes suspicious. No, it cannot be today, the man decides. There is an earthy smell of fungi, of rotting leaves, which disgusts him, so he drives off, unaware that he has given Lawrence clear evidence that he has had a visitor. Not for nothing has he spent time with brave Arab soldiers skilled in setting traps, and tracking the enemy.

So when he returns, he carefully avoids the area in front of his cottage, and stands his motorcycle next to his garage. He has a number of ways of knowing if someone has been to his door, and he chooses according to his wishes and circumstances. If he plans ahead and makes the time, he loves to arrange pebbles in a certain pattern, so that a visitor would disturb them on the worn path to his door.

But on the day in question, he resorts to merely pouring a couple of buckets of water on the soil in front of his door, so that anyone approaching it to knock or try to intrude would leave footprints. He himself smoothes the wet area with a piece of wood, after he locks the door. In the past, he has tested this method, and has discovered the prints of foxes and birds. It works.

He feels a delicious anticipation as he goes to check for evidence of visitors. It is a game he relishes. And there they are: footprints close to the door. He places his right foot next to the clearest of the prints. A man's, certainly, he concludes. I wonder who has been, he muses; I expected no one today.

There are clever, intelligent people, he knows, who would spot such a trap as a mud patch, but this particular visitor did not.

Some autumn leaves have blown onto the prepared soil, making it appear no different from the rest of the ground, and have stuck in the mud.

"So, someone has been," he says aloud, "and if they are intent on seeing me, they will return. There is no note, which means either their business can wait, or they do not wish me to know they have been."

Occasionally, a soldier, or a way-farer seeking a drink of water, has turned up, but that has become increasingly rare.

Then he spots something impressive, and his heart races. It is not easy to spot, this deliberate attempt at communicating, but he sees it, and identifies it as the sort with which he has become familiar, and which is a part of a game intelligence agents cannot resist. It is a sort of signature.

"Clever bugger," acknowledges Lawrence. "Wouldn't surprise me at all if he had left footprints on purpose. But here is the message: my initials."

Lawrence crouches to look at the letters engraved with a pointed stick. They are not big and obvious, or small and indecipherable. But they, he is certain, were written by someone with a connection to his past, as the letters are **TES**. Shaw, his other name: a shield, an identity. And though he has been in other, dangerous situations, those three letters carry a meaning as important as any scratched inscriptions he has found on stone monuments come across on his archaeological travels, years ago.

He examines the area more closely, in case there are clues he has not yet noticed. Then he hears a gunshot, which makes him lose his balance. Rooks scream and flap noisily out of the trees up the hill. Have I been shot? is his first thought, wobbling on his haunches. It is a sound he has heard thousands of times before, but this time is different, no ordinary pop at a pheasant or two.

From behind, he hears the crunch of footsteps on pebbles, and he skips nimbly behind his garage until the person comes into view. I should carry a hand-gun from now on, he decides. But when he sees who it is, he slumps against the wall, nearly cries.

There stands Selim Ahmed.

"Dahoum?" says Lawrence.

Dahoum smiles and stretches out his hand, as if inviting Lawrence to follow him. Lawrence takes a first step, and jumps when another gunshot rips through the air. In the blink of an eye, Dahoum vanishes.

"Gone so soon?" whispers Lawrence. "To leave me twice is doubly cruel."

CHAPTER FOUR

Before he becomes concerned about his security at Clouds Hill, he has to face another rupture in his working life. Lawrence contemplates retirement from the RAF, and is preoccupied with his future lack of funds. He knows that a writer is driven more by poverty than wealth – indeed, the established wisdom is that a poet *should* be poor – and his anxiety becomes a vein running through the letters he sends. For example, somehow the long distance between himself and Robert Graves permits him to express himself freely on penury to his fellow author. You see, it's those blessed interest rates that have done for me, he curses – and my incompetence with money.

The sense of an ending does not overwhelm him, but he suspects that, perhaps, the money he has spent on making Clouds Hill more comfortable might soon be needed to feed himself. There will be enough for meagre meals and, of course, books, but the loss of some of the latter during the installation of his bath and boiler dispirits him. He acknowledges that books are worth nothing if not read, and they are what he has come to value the most, even above the thrill of testing high-speed boats.

So he counts the pennies, puts aside enough to host his coterie of writers and other regulars upstairs, where music, debate, and candles always light up the room. For some time, he has been looking forward to what he thinks are more favourable conditions for writing than at Bridlington, and Pat Knowles detects an air of unexpected *fin de siècle* in his brief note warning of his intention to take some leave owing. Ever-reliable Pat, spanner and wrench never far away, installs this, paints that, and secures the other. All that he does is his loving gift to Lawrence, who looks to him to make his permanent home-coming as comfortable as possible.

When he arrives, legs and hips locked from the long journey on his Brough, he has, at first, surprisingly few words for Pat, who has prepared a plate of cold meat and potatoes, but then expresses gratitude and a promise to repay this kindness.

As always, Pat notices, Lawrence draws the most appropriate phrases from his bottomless well even when tired, and is upbeat when Pat comments on his weight loss.

"You are mistaken. Bridlington feeds well. Fish a-plenty! Staple diet. That's one thing not in short supply."

"You look after yourself, nevertheless. Welcome home."

Pat fixes Lawrence's blood-shot eyes, sees a vacancy that troubles him, and believes that Lawrence's permanent return from Bridlington cannot come soon enough. For a man who has worked in Plymouth and Karachi, and whose fame has spread around the world, Lawrence's ride back to his beloved Clouds Hill has no emotional impact on him.

In the days following Lawrence's long ride home, Pat visits regularly, and enquires if there is anything he needs.

"Time," answers Lawrence quickly. "Just time."

It is as if that concern had been festering just under the skin, and had now been lanced.

"Then take it, in your own time."

"I shall write a few letters, and then …"

Lawrence stops short of shrugging, but there is an expression of fear in his face about what the future might hold for one who helped shape the course of the war.

"Get straight, then. Dorset will be your best friend, if you let it," reassures Pat.

But what Lawrence dares not admit is that he is finding it hard to come to terms with a life that undulates as dramatically as the Dorset landscape. It is not possible for him to adjust as Pat advises.

"I will be retiring from the RAF, not life."

His attempt to laugh falls short of authenticity, and Pat receives it as a sort of weak sneer at what Lawrence feels is unwarranted molly-coddling.

"Nevertheless," Pat persists, "it will be different for you."

"But I have been a regular visitor here. I have fashioned this house for my own purposes. It is no stranger to me."

"It's you who are a stranger," finishes Pat, leaving him to work things out for himself.

"Thanks, Pat. I appreciate your help," calls Lawrence, and Pat acknowledges with a raised hand, but does not turn.

Lawrence sighs. I have survived this far, he thinks. Death claims us all, and I have led a charmed life. Why I do not know. But it is time for tea.

When he thinks back to his first occupation of a semi-derelict Clouds Hill, he does not recognise it as a first step to the cessation of a nomadic life. He has lived in so many places that Clouds Hill, in a state the outside would think suitable for only temporary occupation, seems a natural base for his go-anywhere-at-anytime lifestyle.

At various times on its journey to acceptable improvement, Lawrence has invited a range of people, with whom he feels he has an affinity, to sample its unique ambiance.

"My dear boy," his mother once said to him, when she came to stay. "It is everything I imagined it, though a little small."

"It is perfectly adequate," he replied. "Sassoon found it soothing, and its dimensions have not deterred Forster or Shaw."

"But they are like you, are they not? For all your gallivanting in the Middle East, you are one of *them*, and I am glad of it. It is unhealthy, I believe, no matter how patriotic one is, to spend so long sweating inside a uniform. We are what we think and feel, after all."

"Make yourself at home. You know me well. Sometimes, I sleep with a book by my side, and when I look at Seven Pillars of Wisdom, feel it in my hands, I am more proud of what I have written than the part I played in the actual events."

"You are an incurable romantic, and always will be, and I suppose a book is better than no sleeping partner."

Lawrence sniffed, knew what she was implying. It was a topic of conversation he thought they had lain to rest, years ago, but it was out of her mouth before she could stop it.

"Quite."

No matter what the attraction of the house's location, Sarah Lawrence never really appreciated it as much as its owner, and so went to China with her son Robert.

"Goodbye, dear," she said. "China is a long way."

"But England will be only a thought away."

"I never thought of it that way."

"Then you should. You really should."

It is slightly disconcerting for Lawrence to note that disagreements he has had, over the years, return, and not only in bed, at night. They jump out at him without warning. Even the more trivial ones stun him momentarily, and he is stricken with guilt beyond reason. His mastery of words he has used like a cut-throat razor, or an Arab sabre. It has impressed some officers above him, carved a pathway to advancement, but others, the bullish, even aggressive ones, have resented the humiliation he has inflicted upon them.

One day, after a night when the other men in his dormitory had been in particularly high spirits – a ribald song provokes uncontrollable laughter in such cramped conditions – Lawrence awakes to the rattling of a stick against the leg of his bed. This is often the early morning salutation, but, this particular day, there is no accompanying quip, no mildly affectionate word of encouragement. Today it's, "One minute to dress, then get your arses outside for inspection. And you," he whispers to Lawrence, "will be cleaning out the boiler, later."

That is RAF training: lots of physical exercise and mind-numbing tasks to hone submission, and ensure obedience.

Outside, there is fog so dense that the men can see the individual particles. The roll is called, and the men stand to attention, awaiting dismissal, but it does not come. Instead, the officer, who has berated their appearance during the inspection, waits and waits. Without moving their heads, the men watch their unblinking superior. Lawrence thinks they are awaiting the arrival of a big wig, but eventually the officer says, "At ease."

After a further minute, he begins his message.

"Your training is nearly over, and, on Monday, you leave."

"Where to?" asks a voice from the middle row.

"Wherever we fucking send you!" bawls the short, square-browed man in front of them, his chest puffed out. Lawrence thinks he looks like an over-fed pigeon, and a smile flickers around his mouth.

"What you find so fucking funny?"

And that plays straight into Lawrence's hands.

"The absurdity of the human condition, which renders us compassless as any ship which slipped away to war in ancient Greece," answers Lawrence, staring straight ahead as if fixed on some faraway Aegean destination, and not making eye contact.

The officer convulses into taking a step forward, but a suitable riposte eludes him. Lawrence's education at Oxford is not known among the ranks, but there is a grudging admiration for his general knowledge. This time, Lawrence thinks he might be too obvious, but the words are out before he can check them. What Lawrence is sure of, however, is that his fellow trainees are glad that a man who has ripped them untimely from their beds, seemingly without a reason – surely, the news of their imminent departure could have been delivered at a more sensible time – is being well and truly put in his place.

"The human condition?" asks the officer quietly. "And what, may I bleeding ask, is the human condition? You see, I aint had an education. I was dragged up."

Lawrence is now wary, hopes that what he thinks is a smart put-down is sufficient to explain the incipient smirk the officer had detected. To further humiliate his interrogator Lawrence thinks will expose his true intention. Being put on a charge, at this stage of his training, might blight his future.

"All I meant to say, sir, is that, one day we are here, and the next we're gone, and that it's always been that way since the dawn of time."

Gradually, the officer himself smiles.

"Then why didn't you fucking well say so? Don't let words get in the way of meaning. It might land you on jankers, or something worse, even at this stage!"

The others laugh spontaneously at his light humour, prompting him to caution them.

"Easy does it, men. No one gave you permission to laugh at my wit and repartee."

He then goes on to explain the arrangements for their departure, and Lawrence begins to feel that, though he is glad there is a fresh challenge ahead, he has learned that there are different ways of handling people, and that he needs to be more circumspect and less hasty when dealing with his military superiors. England is not Syria, after all.

Difficult moments such as this he deals with, though their cumulative effect is a loss of confidence, a feeling that he ought to reappraise what he can and cannot do.

"It is no use me pretending that my life will be blessed by the conventions of normal marriage and family life," he says at Max Gate.

"What is normal?" asks Hardy, when his second wife, Florence, is out of the room, making tea, and cutting a generous slice of fruit cake.

"You ever regret having no children?" asks Lawrence. Hardy looks down at his glass of whisky, which he rotates in his hands, but before he thinks of an answer, Lawrence realises his gaffe, and is horrified by his careless insensitivity. "I'm so sorry. I wasn't thinking. It is, of course, a private matter. Forgive me."

"It just never happened, and that's all there is to say. One adjusts."

"True," says Lawrence, acutely embarrassed.

Florence returns and asks, "So what have I missed?"

Hardy replies, "The fickle hand of fate. Do you agree?"

Lawrence nods and says, "I do. Exactly that."

Florence looks from one to the other, and pours the tea, without a word.

On the day of Hardy's funerals, in London and Stinsford, the day the nation had its wish, and Florence kept his heart, Lawrence was in Karachi. There was no possibility of him returning in time, and he was conspicuous by his absence.

But now that he can, he visits Stinsford, shuts off the Brough's engine, out of respect, before its noise disturbs the people living nearby, and wheels it down to the churchyard gate.

The first time he sees the tombstone bearing Hardy's name, he gasps at the engraving, which reveals Hardy has been buried in the same grave as Emma, his first wife.

"And does it not cause you immense pain to see their names, and know they are buried together?" he asks, when he next sees Florence.

"It is Stinsford which has him – his heart, that is. But a skeleton and a still heart? I would be foolish to be jealous, and when I join them, as I intend, it won't matter a bit. What harm can we do each other? What kisses beg or take, when the worms dine on our putrefied flesh?"

Lawrence kneels, touches the pale stone, pictures a serene Hardy, eyes still retaining a glint, hears his soft, Dorset tones, and knows now that the price of fame is too high.

Already there are marks on the tombstone. Above, the yew tree offers a degree of protection from wind and rain, but it contributes to the grime that has begun to appear. The engraved names, dates, and places of birth are still legible.

"Tom, I miss you," whispers Lawrence. "It was a privilege to have known you."

The urge to embrace the stone is almost irresistible, and he kneels but does not pray. There is no connection with God.

The churchyard is bathed in clean, lemon light. In this place, he thinks, there is eternal peace, but it would be presumptuous of me to squeeze myself into this corner, when I am gone. His family is here, and family I am not. Yet I am comforted by the possibility. But if I am buried here, I should hear Tom's and Emma's dwindling conversation, and profound silences, perhaps an interjection or two from Florence, when we are all worms' meat. Or maybe we could rise as spectres, and stroll together, tell again what we are, and think. But that is too fanciful, too optimistic, too vain. I should know better.

Lawrence is about to rise. Almost overwhelmed by the loss of Tom Hardy, he covers his face with both hands. Hot tears run onto his palms.

Then he feels a hand on his shoulder, and draws breath sharply. His heart panics; he has not heard anyone approaching. For a split second, he thinks it is Tom responding to him, but the voice is deeper, different.

"You knew him?" asks the vicar.

Lawrence rises, and waits for the vicar to recognise him, but he does not. At least, there is no sign that he does.

"I did. I was abroad when he – his heart, I should say – was buried here, and I will always regret that."

"He would not have been bothered, not been surprised. It was just the way he was. At least, that's how people spoke – speak – of him. He was not such a regular visitor in his old age as when he was growing up, I believe."

"I hope I have not disturbed or alarmed you by my presence here."

"Not at all. I was on my way to the rectory after prayers."

The vicar looks over his shoulder at the small church behind them.

"Are you an admirer of his writing?"

The vicar shakes his head, and says, "I have read one or two of his works, but have little time in the parish for my own leisure pursuits. What is your name? I don't think I have seen you in the congregation."

"No, that is so."

"Well, maybe we will be able to tempt you, one day. It has been interesting to have met you. For future reference, in case our paths meet again, please tell me your name. Your face has a certain familiarity, and yet I cannot put a name to it."

"Henchard," comes back Lawrence quickly. "Michael Henchard, corn factor in Dorchester."

The vicar nods, leaving Lawrence to push his Brough to a place where he can start the engine without waking the dead.

The vicar relates the story of his encounter to his sexton, the following day, as they prepare for a funeral in the bottom corner of the churchyard.

"And he said his name was Michael Henchard," finishes the vicar.

"Then 'tis as they say," remarks the sexton, his face draining of colour.

"And what do they say?"

"Why, that fiction be stranger than truth."

"Don't you mean the other way round?"

"No, and if you reads The Mayor of Casterbridge, you'll take my meaning. Now, pardon me, vicar, but I've a grave to dig, and then to fill, later, so I must make a start."

With that, the vicar retires to the rectory.

* * *

Lawrence returns after his week's leave, knowing that the next time he is there, it will be for what he believes is ever.

"Till the next time," says Pat.

Lawrence says nothing, and roars away more quickly then ever before.

He drives like a madman, thinks Pat, but try stopping him!
Try telling him anything!

CHAPTER FIVE

Chartwell soothes Churchill as no other place. Paintbrush in hand, he longs for the day when his studio is finished, so that he can hang his paintings there. Skilled with the pen, too, he inhabits an artistic life about which few others know, and into which fewer still are invited. Lawrence is one of the lucky ones, as Churchill is aware of his love of the arts and places they have been together.

Lawrence is no trained eye but is fascinated by the power paintings wield.

"You would say, wouldn't you, if you find my work grotesque. I wouldn't mind that, coming from you, who have an instinct for these things. I've known you a long time," says Churchill, unconsciously holding the brush as he would a cigar.

Lawrence is nothing if not loyal, but delivering the truth as he sees it is what sets him aside from other men, and his assessment of what is before his eyes is frank.

"The landscapes are charming enough but lack a narrative focus," he says. "Here, for example, The View of Jerusalem. You have captured the glory of a brooding Heaven, but the city is coy, almost without identity. But the sky is magnificent. And in Near the Pyramids, you have the geometric lines of the pyramids and their shadows, but they are the only shapes in a barren desert. The painting is saved, however, by the movement in the blue sky, and the hint of sunlight to the right."

Churchill peers intently, then steps back, taking his time to evaluate Lawrence's assessment.

"You should know better," chides Churchill. "Deserts are rarely barren."

"True, but your desert here is."

Churchill examines again his painting, and says, "You may be right. What do you suggest? The odd snake or scorpion?"

They both laugh heartily, then Churchill shrugs.

"But," modifies Lawrence, "there are many paintings to admire in your collection. You will exhibit them, at some time?"

"Exhibit? Hang is nearer the mark. Oh, I know what you might be thinking: they will be one of my many memorials, and they *will* be, in a way. But they are not vanity, Lawrence. That is the last thing my paintings are."

Lawrence hears a stiff tone of certainty in this denial. He wants to say that the act of painting is worthy, but knows, from personal experience, there is always a whiff of vanity in the showing, the publication, or the selling. It is only natural, he wishes to add, but does not.

"When a work of art is handed over to the public, it becomes no longer the artist's. It recedes from the composer, till it is but a distant memory."

Churchill smiles, recognises the strength of his friend's argument.

"Indeed. Indeed."

"But do not let my view of these things disappoint you."

"Come," says Churchill snappily. "If you were a drinking man, I'd pour you a large whisky or brandy, but as you are not, you must be satisfied with a pot of tea! Perhaps, a scone, too?"

Churchill leaves the room, and orders the refreshments, and Lawrence thinks about his visit to Chartwell. Impulsively, he has just turned up. Such he thinks his relationship with Churchill to be: a mutual acceptance of what each has become to the other through a realisation of what they have become to the nation. Then why, wonders Lawrence, do I detect a strain in his demeanour that cannot be fully explained by my critique of his paintings?

Churchill looks thoughtfully out of his window, onto his estate. From that very spot, he has taken many important decisions. Being surrounded by such space ensures a clarity of thinking. There has sometimes been a struggle between his head and his heart, but he trusts his head only when he has listened to his heart. Always in that order. Then, as if the chilling clarity is now decisive, he makes a mental note to contact the appropriate person.

"Fetch Mr. Lawrence," he orders his man. "The view is better from here, one of the finest in England."

When Lawrence arrives, Churchill is gently stirring the tea in the pot. In a pensive mood, Churchill notes that it should not have taken Lawrence so long to join him, even allowing a minute or two for a polite exchange with his man. Lawrence would say a kind word or two, it is certain, but knows his way to where tea is usually taken. Perhaps, he has been to wash his hands. He would not have lost his way, he who has committed more maps to memory than anyone else with whom Churchill has worked.

"Ah, there you are! I thought something might have happened to you."

"It did," replies Lawrence. "I suddenly realised what those paintings mean to you, and it set me thinking."

There is a conspicuous pause while Churchill pours the tea through the strainer.

"Still, you're here now," says Churchill, smiling. "Milk?"

Lawrence nods affirmatively.

"I like a lot of them. That's why I've dragged my feet: I was looking at your other paintings."

Churchill then attacks what he has been putting off, knowing that he risks offending.

"It needn't be like this. You know, at Clouds Hill. It is, of course, a sign of your damned … your damned goodness that you don't need anything more grand. It is admirable – truly. We are all pale imitations, by comparison. But the money …"

41

Lawrence does not flinch at all this praise. Often he reads about himself, and some articles are along Churchill's lines. Clouds Hill is not Chartwell, and it is because of that that he cannot accept Churchill's genuine offer of financial assistance. All that he has done for Churchill and the country has value but no price.

"I am more than comfortable," says Lawrence, then sips.

"Maybe, but nevertheless …"

"It is kind, but I could not."

"I wish you would."

"Well, I cannot, not even for all that has happened."

Churchill chortles.

"There is not money enough for all that has happened. Still, don't stand on ceremony. If there is anything …"

Lawrence shakes his head, and thinks Churchill a little taut.

"And Chartwell goes well?"

"It is my sanctuary. The world is in peril. There is no rest, as you must know. Men like us …"

"Like you, you mean. I have retired from the RAF."

Churchill frowns.

"No, you haven't. Not really. Men like us go on for ever. We never retire."

There is no arguing with Churchill on this. Churchill has no escape. Lawrence has Clouds Hill.

They let the matter of money drop, and discuss a range of other topics, even through a second cup, after which Lawrence insists he must go. Their conversation has lacked its usual passion, has stumbled from place to place without finding one on solid enough ground to rest.

"Good to see you, Lawrence. Don't leave it so long, next time," says Churchill.

They walk, without speaking, to Lawrence's bicycle, which is standing exactly where he left it, the front wheel at the same angle. Old habits die hard. Why should Lawrence trust a man he suspects had a hand in the murder of his own mother? Rumours that Churchill was angry that she, Jennie Spencer-Churchill, deceived him about the nature of his father's will continue to enshroud him like the thickest of Dorset fogs. Any man who thinks he is wrongly deprived of his rightful inheritance would be angry.

The final handshake is more business-like than friendly, as if Churchill were still angry about the chapter Lawrence had written on the Paris Peace Conference. Damn your honesty, your scintillating integrity! snorts Churchill.

Then, decisively, Churchill makes a telephone call to a number he has memorised, and which is changed at irregular intervals. The conversation is brief, and afterwards he pours himself a stiff drink.

"So," says the man to himself, at the other end, "we are all part of the same hypocrisy. He who pays the piper calls the tune."

There are letters Lawrence could write, a mixture of obligation and routine, but he postpones. Instead, he writes a list of names he believes still work in the Intelligence Service. There is no easy way of knowing, but all of them are aware that Lawrence has done his bit for King and country. The list is long, and against some names he puts a question mark, a cross against others. Then he writes a list of those who are left. Some he met in the Middle East Department, one or two in Karachi, where it was supposed that his work in the RAF was a smokescreen for his espionage.

"You here for commies?" he is once asked by a colleague.

"You know as well as I do that I could be shot if I respond to that," replies Lawrence. "That's classified information."

"Why else would you be here?"

"It's my job. I go where I'm posted."

"But this is a dreadful place. You requested to be here? You see, we know who – what – you are, and something does not quite fit."

"It is true that it's not Arabia, but I have to earn a living, somehow. Besides, there's a lot of free time here."

"And what do you do?"

Lawrence smiles, taps his nose, and says, "Classified information!"

They both laugh. The interrogator respects Lawrence's privacy, has noticed that he is not stand-offish, and likes to make notes he hides in various places. Only when he is writing does he feel that he is making good use of his time. But he knows that not just the intended recipients read his letters. The monitors look for patterns, hidden messages, to make sure that he is batting just for England. There are those in power who believe that the further away he is from Britain, the better. It is hard, his critics say, to work for Britain while despising the way the Arabs were left with nothing. Look, there he is, all attired as an Arab, in Paris. Proof! And Churchill is left in no doubt, by others in the British delegation, that Lawrence wears his heart on his sleeve standing next to Faisal.

Seeing that Churchill is part of the duplicity makes Lawrence glad to retreat to Clouds Hill, removed from the rest of the world. Always, between them, what is not said maintains the balance of respect and suspicion. Knowing that Churchill is ruthless keeps Lawrence's wits about him.

As it is winter, Lawrence feeds his fires well, upstairs and down. When the flames are drawn up the chimney, he puts on his coat, and goes outside with his lamp. He feels the icy air on his cheeks and scalp. The moon is bright and white, and lights up everywhere, so he can see where he is placing his feet on his way up the hill. At the top, he turns and looks down on his cottage.

No place for a woman, Clouds Hill, he thinks. I can lick my wounds, stretch my money. How could a wife live here now, when it has been fashioned as I want it? It is too late for all that. Far too late. The stars wobble. None of this he would share with a woman. He is as close to the Milky Way as he is likely to get in England, and the stars swarm as he focuses on them. All that far away, he marvels, and yet seen in other, distant lands, too.

He breathes in the sharp air. Let things go, he tells himself. Do not hold on to the pain of a Turkish beating or worse, or the memory of Dahoum, or I shall take my eyes off the here and now. Otherwise, what has made me may destroy me. But being positive ebbs and flows like the sea on Weymouth beach, and only sleep helps.

Down on the road, a truck's headlights cut through the darkness. Knowing that the fires will now be roaring, he carefully goes back down the hill.

Upstairs, he does not care for music, but writes a letter full of his usual courtesy and geniality, but when he has finished, he stretches out on his settee, and says aloud, "What is the point of all this? I shall never be clean of it, I know. They will never let me be. It is my worst enemy. If I could write as well as Hardy, I would not mind, but, as it is, I would swap this place for his grave to be free of this oppression."

He falls asleep. The fire has settled, and there is something defiant about not caring whether you sleep in a bed or on a settee.

In the morning, the fire is all ashes, and Lawrence notices the drop in temperature. Unusually, at this time of day, he is alert, and remembers there is nothing like the feeling of imminent death to focus the mind. So he sits and specifies that, in keeping with his preference for a private rather than public life, his funeral should be simple, that no mention of his exploits should be made on his tombstone. He dates and signs his wishes, knows that what he has done has somehow helped to bring their execution nearer.

Meanwhile, in an unremarkable office in an anonymous building in London, four men are sitting round a table. The man who took the call from Churchill tells the other three that Operation Sandstorm can now take place. This is not the first time the subject has been discussed. Each man knows the name of the others, but they are not their real names, just the latest they have assumed. After all, the first rule of secret operations is to maintain a high level of secrecy. Trust is as fragile as a moth.

"So, Smith, you will deal with the hours immediately after the sandstorm. Talk to the appropriate people, and make arrangements. Tell them what must be done but not why, and do not deviate from the plan. It must seem that this is a matter for the military only. We don't want any questions asked. That is what we do: deal with things quietly. Understand?" says Michael Alexander, his blue eyes fixing each man, one after the other.

Smith wriggles in his chair. This job has made things awkward for him. He is valued for his efficiency, but he questions everything, which can be a strength as well as a potential weakness in intelligence work.

"And do you really think he can mobilise a peace movement? It would cause the Boss not a little embarrassment, I admit, but -"

"He's not on his own. He knows Oswald Mosley," explains Mills. "You can't take chances."

"Besides, these are orders. That's what we do – in the national interest," reminds Alexander. "Follow orders. That is, after all, how we built the British Empire."

Smith nods because that is what Alexander wants to see.

"Mills, the funeral. The Boss intends to be there. Security is everything. Manage the cameras. Allow them access, but check their passes. It must seem a fitting farewell. There will be a crowd. Expect that. It is good for public confidence in the state. Oh, and it will be in the afternoon, straight after the morning's inquest."

The man who sits in his coat, collar up, and still wears his trilby, strokes his moustache, and listens carefully to what is being said. The others know that, in his pocket, his hand rests on a gun, his best friend. Records show that he was the best shot in the British Army, and often worked behind enemy lines, equally proficient with a knife and leather ligature. Aloof in the barracks, he specialised in the art of assassination, and now he accepts whatever brief he is given.

Alexander will see him after the others have gone. There have already been preliminary ideas mentioned about the where, when and how, but Trilby – the name he goes by – is deliberately vague. Failure only occurs, he believes, when details are carelessly shared. Does not his work, in the past, prove his methods effective?

Alexander is worried about Smith. Lawrence knew him in a past life. They have pored over maps and strategic plans together. Admittedly, that was years ago, but there has been trust between them. Mills, too, is uneasy, as although Smith will have no direct involvement in the key part of Operation Sandstorm, the management of the aftermath is important for its long-term success.

"Sit this one out?" says Mills to Smith.

"How can I?"

"You can," clarifies Alexander.

"I can't. I know too much."

Trilby stops stroking, and looks at him.

Alexander does not contradict Smith, and stays calm. They all know there is a no-release clause, once a job has been assigned.

"You can sit it out, but there are consequences for every decision, every action."

Smith is looking forward to his pension, has been good at his work, has never let the department down, and he thinks, "Fuck. Of all the fucking assignments!" But he maintains an inscrutability that earned him his job, in the first place.

"A job's a job. Always has been, always will be."

"Good," says Alexander. "Then I am a happy bunny."

Lawrence looks at his lists, and settles on the names that are ticked. As he goes through them, he gives them a mark out of ten, ten being potentially the most use to him, one denoting a confirmed back-stabber. No one is awarded maximum marks, but two tie on nine. Both are reliable, excellent in all they do. More importantly, one – Carrington – owes him a favour. Once, Lawrence had spoken up for him, and had secured a promotion. Now Lawrence will call in the debt, without being too obvious. Such men as Carrington need no reminding where they have come from.

So, it is Carrington, decides Lawrence. A letter proposing a meeting, for old time's sake, is his preferred mode of contact. He addresses the envelope and prints CONFIDENTIAL on it, and laughs at his joke: that he knows nothing reaches the person for whom it is intended without it being read by a designated agent.

But Lawrence does not know that Carrington no longer has that name. Now he is Smith, or Mills, or Trilby, or Alexander, and Lawrence has no idea that he is walking into the eye of the sandstorm.

CHAPTER SIX

Lawrence is buoyant, one minute, deflated, the next. Some days, he writes promising poems, makes notes towards a great work of fiction he knows he might never begin, let alone finish. Mixing with great writers only enhances the feeling of hopelessness that sometimes engulfs him. Seven Pillars of Wisdom attracts much praise, but it is not, in Lawrence's opinion, up there with the best works of those who have visited Clouds Hill for long discussions and strong tea.

This period of adjustment everyone told him he would experience, and which he played down, is causing him to question how he is spending his time. The excursions on his Brough become an excuse for avoiding focused work that might lead to publication and an improvement in his financial position. They become more frequent, in line with the persistence of the reporters begging for stories, and so he takes to staying away, as far north as the Midlands, to discourage them.

But this tactic does not really work. The reporters are, on the whole, the front line for editors and newspaper proprietors. It is a thankless task, though there is some prestige attached to the subject, and Lawrence is always polite. That is, until one day, when Stephenson blocks his way. Lawrence kills his engine, but remains astride the Brough, as if giving notice that this will be a short-lived conversation.

"Good morning," he begins. "I need to pass, please."

"Good morning," replies Stephenson. "I'm sorry about all this."

"All this what?" says Lawrence.

"This … circus."

"Of which you've made yourself a part. I know you need copy, but there is nothing more I can tell you that is not already in the public realm. Really, there is not. So may I pass?"

Stephenson stands aside, but says, "It's the bits that *aren't* in the public realm that interest me. Sometimes, great men need more than their tremendous feats of daring to perpetuate their myths. I and my kind make and break reputations." Lawrence remains calm; his motorcycle does not wobble an inch. "I just want to rule something out, that's all, and I need your help."

"You mean, you want *me* to rule it out," says Lawrence. "If I answer this, will you go and never return?"

Lawrence already knows the answer, but it is worth a try.

"For ever is a long time."

Lawrence gets off his motorcycle, and heaves it back onto its stand with the handlebars. Stephenson is not expecting this, and is uncertain how he will phrase his question.

"The clock begins ticking as soon as I hear the first word of your question."

Lawrence lays his leather gloves on his seat. Only a yard away from his interlocutor, he waits, is prepared for the question to be along the salacious lines of past ones.

"What I was wondering," begins Stephenson. But he cannot construct the sentence so that he does not offend. There is no easy way to ask about Lawrence's alleged homosexuality. His heroism has been well documented. Nothing Stephenson can write will win Lawrence more plaudits. Regurgitating old stories will put Stephenson down the journalistic pecking order, and there's no money in that.

"What were you wondering?" prompts Lawrence, now close enough to smell cigarette smoke on Stephenson's breath. "The clock ticks rather quickly at Clouds Hill."

"I was wondering whether it is true that the absence of a woman in your life reflects your ... sexuality. I mean ... well, people say that ... you know, you might be queer."

"Queer? Do you mean odd?"

"No, not queer in that sense. I mean queer as in homosexual."

"What do *you* think?"

"I was hoping you'd want to set the record straight."

"I have no comment to make."

"None whatsoever?"

"None."

Stephenson shakes his head, sneers exaggeratedly, as if to say, now come on, old chap. You don't surely expect me to accept that at face value.

Lawrence, however, is anxious to get away, and no one else is there to witness what happens next. Stephenson, he remembers, has always been a lone wolf. So Lawrence looks over Stephenson's shoulder, and Stephenson turns to see what he is looking at. It is then that Lawrence drives his fist into the side of Stephenson's face.

Crumbling to the floor, Stephenson spits out two teeth, and moans. His jaw is broken, and he cannot even curse, so awful is the pain. He is dizzy, and tries to hold onto the cold floor, but passes out.

Calmly, Lawrence examines his hand, which now hurts. I must have caught him just right, he thinks, before disdainfully leaving his persecutor for dead, and riding off. Dorchester is his first thought, perhaps Max Gate, but he cannot put himself in such a hallowed place after he has just assaulted someone. He does not regret the devastating punch, but knows that Mrs. Hardy will see the memory of it in his eyes, and he could never lie to her. It is a risk he does not take, for the dead's sake as well as the living.

So he rides to West Bay, where, on the beach, he is happy to be distracted by the threat of crumbling cliffs and crashing waves. Feeling alive again, he does not totally forget Stephenson, but puts him out of mind enough to think clearly how to end his persecution at Clouds Hill. It has become almost more than he can bear.

The solution comes in a bitterly cold wind that brings the first flecks of snow of the year. It is obvious now he comes to think about it. It is the editors who must be stopped. The reporters who swarm around Clouds Hill like wasps from a nest are only there because newspaper owners and editors are prepared to pay them. Stop the demand for a story, and there you have it.

But who has the power to compel the big boys? There is only one man: Winston. It is worth a try. Lawrence has called in none of the debts he is owed. Yet, the last time they met, there were so many unspoken words, significant gaps and silences, that Lawrence is wary of seeing him face to face. A letter would be better, would give Winston space to think how to handle it, and Lawrence is confident Winston will do just that, despite the recent tension between them.

The day goes well for Lawrence. Only occasionally does the image of Stephenson, unconscious and on the floor, return to sicken him. In Bucky Doo, Lawrence sits and watches people browsing the market stalls. Before they pack away their wares, he even buys a big saw, which looks just the job for felling some of the smaller trees.

Then it is back to Clouds Hill, but not before his Brough has attracted admiring glances from men, who inspect it at quarters close enough to draw Lawrence back to it, to protect it, and answer questions.

"How fast can it go?" asks one man. "My cart baint as quick, I wager."

"And you would win! I go as fast as I can. They'll bring in speed limits in places like this, one day, if accidents happen, so I make hay while the sun shines."

"It's a beauty," says another. "Is it easy to ride?"

"No more so than a horse, from which you can fall and break your neck!" answers Lawrence.

"I never thought of it that way," says the first. "Don't I know you from somewhere?"

Lawrence has been here many times, and has, up his sleeve, stock replies to fend off genuine but unwanted interest.

"I expect you do. I play the fiddle at fairs and weddings. You'll have seen me anywhere along the coast."

He says it with such conviction that the man feels that is where he must have seen him before. But Lawrence senses danger. If he is recognised, and others nearby hear who he is, his privacy will disappear. It is this celebrity he loathes but cannot live without.

"Must be getting on, then," he says decisively, and that disperses the Brough's admirers.

When he has gone, one of the men says, "He baint a fiddler. I'd know him anywhere. Can't fool me, he can't. Why, he be Lawrence of Arabia, who lib Wareham way, they say."

"And so it be!" exclaims his friend. "Short bugger for a soldier."

They both laugh, having now a tale to recount in all the inns of Bridport, in the years to come.

As Lawrence approaches Clouds Hill, he recalls the blow he delivered to Stephenson's jaw. It had not been a spur of the moment decision, more a he-had-it-coming-to-him one. It had been just a question of when.

Stephenson is no longer there. Good, thinks Lawrence. Let's hope he's learnt a lesson. In the dark, Lawrence locks his Brough in the garage, and goes inside his cottage, but he has not been there two minutes when there is a knock at the door.

"Who is it?" he calls.

"Police."

Shit, thinks Lawrence. He's made a complaint.

Lawrence has done worse, and believes his action justified.

"What do you want?"

"To talk about what happened earlier to a Mr. Stephenson, who says you assaulted him. May we come in? Get your version of events?"

Lawrence lets them in. There are two of them. The one doing the talking is a Sergeant with a handlebar moustache; the other is a regular officer, standing a pace behind, and is either learning his trade or providing unconvincing back-up.

"Can't be too careful, this time of night."

"I understand. This morning, we had a visit from a rather distraught member of the public, alleging you struck him a blow that looks like it's broken his jaw. I asked him to describe what led up to the assault – *alleged* assault, I should say – and he said that he had come to interview you. After what he says was, with hindsight, a rather too sensitive question, he says you hit him. I told him that it was a serious allegation he was making, against one of this country's finest men, and that it does not sound like the kind of thing you normally do. The complainant was in such pain that he was unable to repeat what had happened, so I told him I would investigate. Is his version accurate?"

"Pretty much," admits Lawrence, "though he did not say what it was that provoked me so much."

The Sergeant turns to his backup, and says, "I told you that Mr. Lawrence would not do anything like that without a good reason."

"He questioned my sexuality," adds Lawrence matter-of-factly. "He's had this coming. He writes such tales about me that I wonder I have not broken his jaw before now."

The Sergeant frowns and shakes his head, before saying, "Indeed, it seems that our Mr. Stephenson has been sailing close to the wind for some time. He has no right to say such things."

Lawrence does not push his luck but lets his case rest. Prepared to be arrested, he awaits the handcuffs, but they do not appear.

"My home has been swamped with reporters since I returned," he explains. "There is a limit to what a man can bear."

The back-up nods, having taken in everything bar the reason for Lawrence's disgust.

"Indeed, I shall put in my report that ..."

The right words escape him, so Lawrence helps him out.

"He tried to steal my good reputation."

This time, both officers nod simultaneously.

"Which is worse than breaking and entering a property! Therefore, I shall close the case, and if the scoundrel persists with his ridiculous allegation, I shall charge him with attempted theft, and wasting police time!"

Lawrence wants to laugh, but resists the temptation. He has not engineered what feels like a collaboration, and wants Stephenson to understand that, this time, he has bitten off more than he can chew.

"Thank you," says Lawrence. "I'm glad you've been able to see it from my point of view."

"We will pay him a visit, and threaten him with a cold cell if he continues to harass you," says the Sergeant.

"All I ask for is privacy."

"And you shall have it. A man like you who has given so much to this country …"

Lawrence does not want to listen to all that, having heard it a thousand times before. Besides, he wishes to write a letter he hopes will put a stop to all these unwarranted visits by the pressmen.

"You are too kind. Now, let me not detain any longer the forces of law and order. You have much more pressing cases than mine to deal with. I would offer you a drink, but you are on duty."

"Indeed, we are, Mr. Lawrence. Indeed, we are. But would you do me the honour of shaking my hand? It would mean a lot to me."

Lawrence does so, and shakes the other officer's hand, too, and that is the end of the police's involvement.

When the officers have gone, Lawrence is not remotely bothered that his reputation has successfully deflected Stephenson's pursuit of justice. However, he must now write to Winston. If anyone can twist the arms of those that pay the reporters, it is him. He knows people in high places, and Winston himself is on the highest rung of the ladder.

* * *

With the knife he acquired on his travels, Churchill opens the envelope. The writing on it is familiar. And what has he to say to me, so soon after his visit to Chartwell? he wonders. Churchill reads what is not a long letter. Somehow its brevity conveys the urgency of Lawrence's request: that Churchill puts an end to the siege of Clouds Hill. Only Churchill has that level of influence.

"Damn him!" he says, tossing the letter onto his desk. "They will throw their arms in the air, and lecture me on the importance of freedom of the press. I know them, but if I do not help, Lawrence will say I have betrayed him again. His pen is as eloquent as mine." Churchill thinks deeply about the dilemma. "The nation will not forgive me if they discover I have been disloyal to him. I must intervene – but not directly. There must be no paper trail back to me. Yet the words I choose will be a smokescreen. I curse this entanglement, which is of my own making as well as his. It is the price of fame, which is only a shade lighter than infamy."

Nothing is committed to paper. He calls in his private secretary, and tells him what to say, and to whom. He is the soul of discretion, and has previously spoken to all but one of the people named by Churchill.

It happens quickly. Few refuse to take a call on behalf of Churchill. One by one, the Hunt Masters agree to call off their hounds, and Lawrence notices almost immediately. So pleased is he that he feels it safe to entertain again.

He buys a bottle of sherry, but stops at that. The money, you see. Or lack of it. But it is nice to have in for guests, even though he does not drink himself.

He cleans the house, irons a shirt, bathes, nervously chooses the records he will play. The mood is all-important. There is no sound of a car's engine, just three raps at the agreed hour.

Breathing deeply, he opens the door to a woman with dark hair and red lipstick. Her coat collar is a fox fur. It has been so long, Lawrence thinks. In her eyes flicker stars.

"You look beautiful," he says.

"And so do you," his guest replies.

They laugh, and he shuts the door.

"I didn't think you'd -"

But the sentence is smothered by her lips.

When the kiss ends, she says, "You haven't changed."

Yes, I have, he wants to say, but she will discover that soon enough.

CHAPTER SEVEN

Lawrence is slow to take the woman's black coat. In black, one melts easily into the darkness. She unbuttons it, and invites Lawrence to relieve her of it. He has watched many officers do it debonairly, but forgets it is easiest from behind, and she laughs at his clumsiness.

"Here, let me do it," she says.

"It's been a long time," Lawrence explains.

"Too long. But there. Hang it up nicely, won't you? I don't want it creased when I put it back on, in the morning."

There at the outset she lets him know she will stay the night. Did he not invite her? Not on impulse, but with a genuine motive?

"I wondered whether you'd got my letter."

"You said not to reply, that your letters are opened. I assumed you'd know I'd come."

"Of course," he says awkwardly.

He is more at ease with letters than speech, and forgets the order of things he needs to say.

"Don't worry. I've destroyed the letter, just as you asked."

"Thank you. It all must sound melodramatic, but if it finds its way into the hands of some people ..."

"I understand. After all, that is why I've never heard from you in months, isn't it?"

Lawrence feels a sharp edge to her voice but sees the smile that says his rules will not spoil their evening. Goodness knows, she has waited long enough for it. It would not work, he had told her, if she came to Bridlington. It would have been all over the newspapers, and that is not what he wanted. His life, so far, has been void of traditional domesticity, but that does not mean he does not like her, or care for her in a way she can accept.

"The money arrives? It is not as much as I'd like, but I have less, these days."

"Yes, and I am truly grateful, but are we going to stand here all evening?"

"You found it all right? Were you seen?"

"I had the dynamo working on Dad's bike, or I should not have been able to find my way."

Lawrence laughs. How fate hinges on such things! Their clandestine tryst depended on her borrowing her father's bicycle!

"Would you like a brief tour of the castle, or shall I take you straight upstairs?"

The woman pouts, but he does not understand her innuendo, having been in the world of men too long to pick up such subtleties. She takes his hand, in role, looks seductively over her shoulder, and, step by step, leads him upstairs to what she wrongly assumes is his bedroom.

"Follow me," she whispers.

All these months of separation have not robbed her of what he likes best about her: her acceptance of him as Thomas, a man she chooses because he is handsome and has impeccable manners, and not because he is famous.

"Watch the steps. They're rather steep."

The woman feels the warmth from the fire as she nears the top. Lawrence still has her coat over his left arm. There is nowhere he can hang it; he will just have to lay it on the settee.

In the room, she makes for the fire, removes her gloves, and holds her hands to the heat. Lawrence watches her face turn orange. It is fuller, and her body is more voluptuous than he remembers it.

The main thing for Lawrence, at that moment, is that her money has been arriving. He promised her he would send it, and he likes to be a man of his word.

"It is cold out," he remarks.

"Feel," she commands, placing her hands on his cheeks.

"You need RAF gloves," he tells her.

She leaves her hands there, locking his head in place, so that she can examine his soul in his eyes. This is a man who has travelled widely, and she needs to know whether he has returned for good, or if he is merely on leave. What she sees satisfies her, for the moment, but there is a faraway look, too. She puts it down to being a long time apart, a natural consequence of them living in different places, she in Dorset, he in Bridlington. But he has kept his word. It is with her he wants to be.

In the corner of the room are his RAF gloves, and he fetches them, and insists she puts them on. They are, of course, far too big, and she laughs as she flaps them.

"They don't match my dress!" she points out.

"They are warm."

"If you insist."

Lawrence calculates, and thinks he has made a mistake, that someone will wonder how she has acquired RAF gloves, but it is a mistake he does not try to rectify, not wanting to alarm her.

She keeps them on, loiters by the fire. It is the fact that he has never missed a week's payment since he last saw her that gives her the confidence to make small talk: what has been happening locally, her father's arthritis, her job in the kitchens at Bovington Camp. Lawrence listens, next to her, trying not to laugh at her hands in the gloves. She notices in him a few differences. Has he not lost weight? Did he really have crow's feet?

"The ride from Bridlington. Lost pounds. It's a long story!"

Her you-can't-fool-me regard from under her knitted brow catches him out, and he tells her he was putting on too much weight anyway.

They look for common ground. She has waited for him, has turned down several proposals, and her father thinks she should not hang around for a man with such wanderlust. There are times when she has to go along with his logic, but not every woman waits for a man with such a romantic aura. Who wants a man who has never been beyond Weymouth? she puts to her father, and he nods and agrees that he can see why other men cannot hold a candle to him.

When the first significant silence settles, Lawrence offers the settee, and moves her coat to the table.

"Sherry?" he asks, but she is more interested in the gramophone.

He sees her peering into its large speaker, and remembers that she has never seen Clouds Hill in its current state, the one he has striven to create. She feels at home, is intrigued to get to know the man she has come to consider her very own.

"Does this work?" she asks.

"Yes, it does. It's not the best sherry in the world. You like sherry, I recall."

"I do, but put on a record. Do you have any we can dance to?"

"I don't really dance," he said.

"Then let me teach you."

"You don't like sherry, do you?"

"Not as much as dancing. Do humour me, Thomas."

Thomas. Who last called him Thomas in such seductive tones? His hand shakes as he tries to judge the exact place to gently place the needle. Unsure that one can dance to his choice of music, he stands, and waits for the first few notes. There is a crackling, and then music. Lawrence cannot name the piece, but the music draws them together: she puts her head on his chest, and arms round his waist, and he has his hand on her shoulders. He can feel her warm breath through his cotton shirt, and he knows where he stands with her. When she looks up with her dark brown eyes, he knows she gives herself to him, and that he must accept her, on this night for which he is responsible.

Is this what I have been looking for? This woman has waited for me, he reflects, as she guides him around the small dance-floor, but she knows little, nothing, of what I have been through. Had she known about the collusion of … others, she would go, leave me here, ashamed that I am so steeped in secrecy that she can never really know me. But she is last in a line of people I must protect, for all our sakes.

The music ends, and the crackling returns, and Lawrence strokes the back of her head gently, and kisses her forehead.

"Another record?" he asks.

"Let's sit down. A sherry would be nice. I haven't eaten, so it will probably make my head spin."

Lawrence's heart sinks. Being so self-absorbed, it never occurred to him that they might eat together. There is little in but sherry.

"I'm sorry, but there are only a couple of tins in. I hadn't thought."

She shakes her head playfully when she sees his embarrassment, and says. "This will never do. You need a housekeeper, a sweetheart to take care of you."

Lawrence does not know how to respond. The house fits him, but him only. As women he has known go, this one understands where he is at, seems to accept him for whom or what he is.

He pours her a sherry in a whisky glass.

"Sorry about the glass," he says. "You do like sherry, don't you?"

She sips, and nods approvingly.

"You don't have one."

"I don't drink."

"This is strong," she coughs. "I hope you're not trying to get me drunk!"

She leans into him, and he likes the warmth radiating from her. There is no turning back now, and when she intertwines her fingers with his, he knows she has him for the night.

"I'm back to stay," he whispers.

"Good," she replies, squeezing his hand. "I've told Dad I'll be back in the morning."

He says nothing, and closes his eyes till it is time to go to bed, downstairs.

Both are nervous, he not sure that this is what he intended, she certain it was, and somehow, after clumsily and hastily removing their clothes in the strange glow of the fire, she draws him to her, and there is no going back.

Soon, she falls asleep, his arm around her. Is this the one? he asks.

He sleeps fitfully, conscious she is next to him, as others have been. This time it is different, no meeting of souls. He has experienced that, and it no longer warms his bed.

Did I put out a chamber pot for her? he wonders. I cannot ask her to climb the hill. There are too many questions holding him back in semi-consciousness. The woman beside him is unemcumbered with such considerations. He could learn a lot from her, but lets go of her, and goes where dreams invade his peace.

* * *

Carchemish: fallen pillars, rocks, maps, sketches. Archaeology requires a precision when recording finds, but also water, as the sun bakes everything. Snakes take refuge in fissures at the hottest time of day, and Lawrence has long since learnt that failure to drink water throughout the day can have dire consequences. So Dahoum fetches it, replenishes the water containers as soon as they are empty. Lawrence notices his smile as much as his willingness to learn.

Soon Lawrence finds that Dahoum feeds him Arabic phrases sweet as dates, and when Lawrence has mastered them, Dahoum follows with others, till Lawrence has a working proficiency with the language. Yet he has nothing – in a material sense – to give Dahoum for his devotion to him, so he reciprocates by teaching him English. It starts amusingly with caricatures: How jolly well are you? I say, old chap. But when he hears and sees how seriously Dahoum takes his lessons, he is ashamed of himself, and takes time to teach him more useful phrases, which Dahoum instantly consumes.

Seeing a desire to learn, Lawrence teaches him mathematics, and soon Dahoum is given the responsibility for the archaeological site. Other Arabs note the friendship that blooms like a desert orchid, but when Dahoum goes to live in Lawrence's house, they frown, talk hurriedly among themselves, and this only serves to make Lawrence more determined to encourage him.

Lawrence takes him to England, where they deliberately wear their Arab dress to provoke stares from passers-by. Dahoum loves to switch taps on and off, can hardly believe he can control the flow and temperature. But there is nothing patronising or imperial about Lawrence's adoption of him as a friend. After all, Dahoum has taught him much more than vice versa.

It is Dahoum's obscenely premature death that now stalks Lawrence's dream. The night the woman dreams nothing, Lawrence is sitting on the carpet outside of the bedouin tent, wearing Arab attire. The sun is not yet fully up, but the cold of night has gone. Still on his tongue is the taste of spiced lamb.

"Dahoum," he calls over his shoulder. "Come and join me."

Lawrence waits and assumes Dahoum is still asleep, as young men are wont. The blue-grey sky begins to pulse, and still there is no sign of his right hand man.

Why should he join me? he asks himself. If I had stayed, not left him to the clutches of typhus and famine, he would show me his smile, his devotion. I was not even here to mourn him, so swiftly was he buried. Did he call for me, at the end?

Lawrence returns to the tent, and vows that, one day, he will immortalise Dahoum, set free his people.

"Take me, too, Supreme Will," he cries, lying down, hoping never to wake again. "Embalm me in all the scented oils of Arabia, for you have taken the font of my contentment, and left me, grief-stricken, for eternity."

* * *

When he awakes, Lawrence is in a sweat, and the woman who feels the abnormal heat radiating from him puts her hand on his forehead. She has Dahoum's dark eyes, he notes.

"Whatever it was is over," she says soothingly. "It's in the past, my darling."

But Lawrence knows it is in the eternal present. Of all nights, he comes again to let me know he has not forgotten me. This time, however, I am not on my own.

Her face hovers above him while he comes to, and then he is guarded, as her silence invites him to describe what he has been through, and he cannot, will not, share that.

"Nightmare," he explains glibly.

"Is that the effect I have on you?" she jokes.

He recalls her beneath him, and their urgent love-making, and then, wordlessly reaching across her to extinguish the lamp. In the blackness, he feels safe. There is no need for further talk.

"No, something in the war, a beating."

"You were beaten?"

"Yes. It happens in war. Turks. Too many of them."

"My poor Thomas. You were badly hurt?"

She decides to heal him by touching him intimately, but he recoils, and she apologises, and he says, "I'm not really awake yet."

"Shall I make some tea, then?"

"No, I'll do it. You have a lie-in, if you want."

Hastily, he puts on the clothes left in a pile by the bed. It is a relief to boil the kettle, return to his routine.

She follows him, and he explains that he must go up the hill while the tea brews in the pot.

"Why?" she asks.

"To pee," he says.

"Oh, I see. Well, don't let me keep you."

He goes beyond his usual spot, not wanting to be seen. What is the etiquette in these circumstances? When does he politely let her know that she must return to her father, and tend to *his* needs? Flattered that she has lost none of her feelings for him, and yet not wanting things to be splashed all over the newspapers, he needs to let her down gently. He is not sure where he wants this to go. This considering another person who will demand attention will be a strain, he is sure, yet total honesty will hurt her, and that is not what he wants.

He goes for a little walk, to rehearse what he will say, and notices that the bicycle which had been leaning against a wall of the cottage has gone.

As soon as he enters, he knows she has disappeared, too. She has left half of her tea. The bed is straightened. Perhaps, she is upstairs. He looks, but she is not. There is, however, a note on the shelf above the fire.

"Thank you for looking after me. It was good to see you again."

No matter how many times he reads it, he cannot decipher its meaning. He suddenly feels her absence keenly. She has slept at Clouds Hill for one night, and, if Lawrence is not mistaken, knows that others he has loved still reside there, in some other way. As soon as he had gone up the hill, she knew that she could not share him in a conventional way, and had underestimated how much he belonged to a wide world of which she had no experience.

Ah well! he thinks. I must not be complacent. No man wants to leave behind a grieving widow.

CHAPTER EIGHT

Her father waits for her in his chair, its arms threadbare. The antimacassar needs washing, having absorbed the brilliantine he rubs daily into his white hair to keep it in place. He knows where and with whom she has been, and has, on many occasions, told her she is playing with fire, that men like Lawrence are shooting stars: they score the firmament so that people can track their trajectory, but fade and disappear. But his warning is pointless. It is a personal choice, she always reminds him.

"Take care your joints don't seize up, sitting here without a fire," she scolds when she sees him by an empty, funereal grate.

He does not respond. She thinks he is snoozing; his pose is typical of him when he is in that chair. But there is no snoring, no sound of any kind coming from him. His mouth is open, and then she notices his awful colour.

She rushes to him, and shudders at his stiffness and cold fingers. He is dead, but she talks to him as if there is a chance he might be saved if only he does what she tells him.

"Now don't you go giving up on me, Dad. Just you wake up, and stir yourself. You know the doctor said you've got to stop those joints from locking."

When he does not answer, she begins to whisper urgently to him, tells him not to scare her so, till she has to admit that he is definitely dead. The horror of this compels her to clasp him to her, and she recoils at the strange, stiff feel of him.

Then his silence scares her. Rarely has she left him on his own, but, last night, she abandoned him for the bed of a man she is convinced loves her as she him. She might have saved her father, fetched help, if she had not been so selfish.

"Oh, Dad, I'm sorry. Forgive me."

She has to pull herself together, and will have to call a doctor to certify his death, and he will ask her to explain the circumstances leading up to it. Never a good liar, her face will betray her. Though it is her right to go with whom she pleases, she knows that if it gets out at the camp, she will be ostracised, vilified. Why, she has taken the moral high ground herself, in the past, when one of the girls was found to be making ends meet by selling herself cheaply in Weymouth. How she poured scorn on the woman who peeled and boiled potatoes during the day, and gave relief to tourists and errant husbands, at the weekend!

She thinks of Lawrence, then realises she must not involve him. He could advise her what to say. But what am I thinking of? she cries within. This is the last thing with which I should burden him.

Only she and Lawrence know where she was. I know, she thinks, I could say I went to bed, and fell asleep before Dad came up, and I came down to find he had passed in the night. It is only eight o'clock, and I am not due in the kitchens till nine.

She takes off her best dress and puts on apparel anyone might snatch if they are in a hurry to fetch help. The nearest neighbour is a hundred yards down the lane, and she must rouse him.

"What the devil be the matter, girl? You nearly knocked the door off its hinges!" shouts Peter.

"It's Dad," she gasps. "He's gone."

"Gone?"

"Dead."

Peter grabs his coat, and follows her. She has no alternative but to take him through her planned alibi, and he does not question it.

"Stay with him, and I'll go to the camp, and fetch someone," instructs Peter.

She knows she has no choice but to wait, but there is no saving Dad, she wants to say. All the life has fled from him. Why, already he looks different.

Until someone from the camp returns, she tries to come to terms with the possible implications of having been with Lawrence when her father was breathing his last. Is this how it must be with Thomas? she wonders. Since they first met, she has pretended she has never heard of Lawrence of Arabia, but has known life would be different. Anything else would be wishful thinking.

She starts to fret about how he will react. This is the last thing he will want. On no account must she tell anyone that she stayed the night at Clouds Hill. She suspects, when all is out, he might drop her, deny everything, and that would be disastrous. Better to have him on a part-time basis than not at all. He has not been back long enough, become used to life in Dorset again, to be able to handle such a crisis, as she sees it.

Peter has to walk to the camp, having turned down the offer of the deceased's bicycle.

"Never ridden one, never will," is all he has to say on the matter.

The guard at the entrance listens to his story, and phones someone, who takes ages to arrive in a truck.

"You sure he's dead?" asks Private Poole, the driver.

"Would I come here if he wasn't?"

Private Poole's long exhalation keeps his anger in check, and no more words are exchanged. The other soldier sits in the back, and says nothing.

"Found him just like this," says the woman.

The man sitting in the back, Private Catchpole, feels for a pulse, and, not finding one, says, "I'll fetch the stretcher."

Peter looks on, then says, "Can I go? I expect my breakfast will be cold now."

"Thanks, Peter. I really appreciate it," says the dead man's daughter.

The body is carried into the truck, and Private Poole says to her, "Can you get in, too, please? You'll need to speak to someone, and fill in the paperwork. Standard stuff."

"Of course."

At the camp, she pops her head into the kitchens to explain. The others are wondering what has happened. It's not like her to have time off. Naturally, they are all sorry to hear her news, and Cook says she should take the rest of the day off, to which she agrees. The sooner Lawrence knows, the better. He will know what to say, and make her feel better. She is sure that, in his line of work, he has had to deliver bad news of this kind to lots of people.

She is lucky. He is just about to go to Dorchester on his Brough, feeling that the press may resume their onslaught at any moment. His heart does not sink when he finds her at the door, and he can tell by her face that something awful has happened.

"What is it?" he asks, forgetting to invite her inside.

"It's Dad. He's dead. I got back earlier, and there he was, in his chair, eyes rolled back, and stiff as a board."

Without invitation, she rushes to him, and clings to him tightly. It is his natural instinct to comfort her. For a fleeting moment, he recalls their physical intimacy, only a few hours earlier, and suppresses his incipient arousal.

"Come in, and I'll make you some tea."

"Sherry? To steady the nerves?"

He pours her a generous measure, and she tells him in detail what has happened since she left Clouds Hill.

"Who did you see at the camp?" he asks.

"I didn't ask. Should I have?"

Lawrence sees rising panic, and reassures her.

"No. Just wondered."

She holds his hand, and he does not flinch. He is too busy wondering if she has mentioned that she had been at Clouds Hill, and she guesses what he is thinking.

"I said I had gone to bed, that, though I hadn't heard him come up the stairs, I had been so tired that I went out like a light, and that I wouldn't have heard him anyway."

"Did they ask what time you discovered him?"

"No. At least, I don't think so. Why?"

"They will contact the police, who may interview your neighbour. It's important your times are roughly similar."

"Why?" she cries, gripping his hand more tightly.

"In case one of you is not telling the truth."

* * *

No one makes a call to the police. A doctor at the camp makes a cursory examination of the body, and pronounces that the cause of death is heart failure. He needs to complete a death certificate, and runs his finger down a list of names and telephone numbers till he stops at an undertaker's in Wareham.

"Has the next of kin been informed?" asks the doctor.

Lance Corporal Cole says, "She knows. We responded when a neighbour came to tell us about him. No phone in his house, you see, so our boys brought him here. The daughter came in our truck with him."

"Do we have a contact address for her? I have no name for the deceased."

"Not that I know of. Can't live far away. Need to see one of the boys that went to collect him. They know where she lives."

"See to it. I'm a fucking doctor, not a search party. This place gets worse by the day."

Lance Corporal Cole stands by the corpse in the near-empty room, as the doctor flounces out in professional indignation.

"Now what am I supposed to do?" Lance Corporal Cole asks himself. Then he says to the corpse, "I know you didn't mean to die but it's damned inconvenient!"

Eventually, after several enquiries made to various superior officers, who do not want to take responsibility for the body, he finds one of the two men who brought the body back to camp.

"First cottage on the left, towards Dorchester," Private Catchpole explains. "Dark eyes. Pretty."

"We need her name and address. Go now and take them straight to the doctor. He needs to sign the death certificate."

"She works in the kitchens, she told us. Can I just go there?"

"Just fucking well find out her name, will you? I don't give a damn how. Just do it."

So Private Catchpole goes off. The kitchen assistant about whom he enquires is not there, and Cook will not reveal her details. Nor do the kitchen assistants come to Cook's aid. Instead, they peel and chop potatoes, set pans to boil them in, and do not look at their visitor.

When it looks as if Private Catchpole will not go easily without the information he requires, Cook draws him to one side, and says, "Look, I doubt she'll be coming back at all."

"How do you know?"

"Been told, that's all."

"Who told you?"

Cook sighs, having more than enough to do in the kitchen.

"Someone of a much higher rank than you. Now, I must get on," she says curtly.

"Fuck you, then!" spits Private Catchpole.

"Tetchy!"

Lance Corporal Cole has gone. The corpse, too, has disappeared.

"What the fuck's going on?" says Private Catchpole.

When he finds Lance Corporal Cole, the latter is so puzzled by the news that he jogs to the doctor's consulting rooms.

The doctor makes him wait outside. Lance Corporal Cole can hear a conversation but cannot distinguish the words. Having worked in the camp since the mid-'20s, the doctor is used to unusual events, and listens to what the Major is saying.

Eventually, the door opens, and the doctor invites Lance Corporal Cole to take the place of the Major, who stares straight ahead as he marches back to his own office.

"You look as if you've seen a ghost," remarks the doctor, looking more wan than earlier.

"I'm not surprised. That body. You asked me to find out the name of the daughter from the kitchens."

"I did, indeed, and you've come to tell me she's no longer working here."

"That's the first thing."

"And the second?" sighs the doctor.

"The body's gone."

"Lazarus," quips the doctor, but the visitor frowns. This is no time for humour.

"How do you know she's no longer working in the kitchens?" asks Lance Corporal Cole, not knowing the story of Lazarus.

"That's not for you to know. Look, this is the end of it as far as you are concerned. Done with. Finito. Understood?"

Lance Corporal Cole nods, knows that, though there is more to this than meets the eye, he should not pry into matters that do not concern him.

The undertaker comes and takes the body away from the chapel of rest, to which it has been taken. On the tag on his wrist, someone has written Bovington Camp and the date, and name to be confirmed. On the duplicate death certificate the cause of death is said to be heart failure. The doctor then resumes his usual consultations with malingerers and genuinely sick soldiers, glad to have extricated himself from a situation in which a Major has taken a special interest.

Later, that day, Peter is paid a visit by Captain James, a promising officer whom those above him consider to be reliable and confidential. Peter goes over the sequence of events, as he recalls them. Yes, she had come round to his cottage to give him the sad news of her father's death. Yes, he had seen her, the day before. What had she been doing? Why, riding her father's bicycle up the lane. He had been fetching some wood for the fire, and had seen the beam of light generated by the dynamo. "Evening, Peter," she had innocently called. Yes, it was dark. Early evening, he guessed. No, she had not told him where she was going. Yes, she had momentarily stopped to say hello when she had seen his lamp.

Well, thinks the Major, she went out, so why did she say that she had been in all night?

"Will that be all?" asks Captain James.

"For the time being. Oh, and Captain James."

"Yes, sir?"

"Well done."

"Thank you, sir."

They salute each other, more as a sign of mutual congratulation than regulation.

The woman goes over the same ground, time and time again, and Lawrence is patient, despite his desire to do chores that have piled up. She clings to him, and he comforts her.

"Thank goodness you're back at Clouds Hill," she says, drying her eyes on her handkerchief.

"Did they say what was going to happen to your father?"

"No. I'll go in later about him. They've given me the rest of today off."

"That's good of them."

"Yes, it is."

There is more sherry for her if she wants, but she declines, pulls herself together to the point where she feels she can go home, and sort through her father's possessions.

"Here," says Lawrence. "Take this, till you know what you're doing."

She feels his hand covering hers, bending her fingers round the coins he can spare for her.

"Thank you," she says, fighting back tears.

Private Catchpole is waiting for her when she arrives home.

"We've come to take you to the undertaker's to see your father," he says.

Private Poole says nothing. Content to simply follow orders, he opens the door of his truck.

"The Major says the funeral is paid for, but, firstly, I'm to take you back to camp to sign a few papers."

"Of course," she says, leaning her father's bicycle against the wall. "But who has paid for it?"

"*We* have. The British Army. At least, I imagine it's us."

"But why?"

"You'll need to ask someone higher up than me."

At the camp, the woman is ushered to the Major's office, where he is waiting for her.

"Now, then," he begins, "I'll get straight to the point. Why would a woman who works in Bovington Camp kitchens spend the night at Clouds Hill?"

"Isn't that a matter for me alone?"

Then the Major takes out a pair of gloves from his drawer. RAF issue, the leather embossed with Bridlington. She realises they have been in her house while she was out.

Confused, she knows it is none of his business, but cannot construct a defence of any kind, not knowing how he acquired the gloves.

"I don't understand. What is all this about? Why am I here? I was told there are papers to sign."

"What do you tell him about the camp?"

"Nothing. I work in the kitchen, then go home."

The Major shakes his head, and says, "Not any more you don't."

"What do you mean?"

"You wouldn't expect me to go into too much detail. Not if you know what's good for you, and do exactly as I ask. There will be money, as a sort of compensation for lost earnings, but for total compliance, too."

They won't get anything out of me, she resolves. I won't betray him.

"What has he done?" she asks.

"He?" When she says nothing, he adds, "We all need a little help, from time to time. Do you think you could help us?"

"How?" she asks exasperatedly.

Slowly, the Major spells out what he wants from her, in a more gentle tone. After all, he wants her to go along with the official line. She never takes her eyes off him, and he recognises what Lawrence himself was attracted to, even has to remind himself not to flirt with her. He expects her to interrupt, ask for clarification on this and that matter, but she does not. Something inside tells her not to let him know what she is thinking. Having watched and listened to a master of the art of inscrutability, she is able to elicit more from the Major than he intended, until he realises the trap, and draws the conversation to a conclusion.

"And what if I don't?" she asks, emboldened by his generally conciliatory attitude.

"Oh, you will. That is one thing I am absolutely certain of: that you will."

He stands. The interview is over.

"And the papers for my father?" she asks.

But he does not answer, merely leaves her alone, and she feels, at that moment, the loneliest person in the world.

CHAPTER NINE

Lawrence turns up his coat collar, and dons a wide-brimmed hat he bought specifically to cover his face when there is a need. There is snow, and he knows this is the ideal moment to make the short trip to Pat Knowles, the friend who has done so much to take care of Clouds Hill. The air is silent, windless, and the flakes rock and fall to the ground like weightless, white oyster shells.

He is sure he cannot be identified, as the snow obscures Pat's house, and he watches his step. There is much about which he wants to talk, and Pat must be wondering why he has not yet called. Pat knows better than to intrude. Over the years, he has gleaned enough about Lawrence and his work to know that it is best if Lawrence makes the running. How can I count all the luminaries that pass through his front door? wonders Pat. I am a friend he trusts, though I would be hard pressed to name another. It is enough that he flits in and out of Clouds Hill; I ask no more.

Lawrence is lucky. Pat would have missed him had his instinct not told him that the conditions would make it difficult to travel to Wareham. Imagine his joy, therefore, when he opens the door to see Lawrence the snowman. Pat recognises him instantly by his size, though he cannot see his face.

"Stand aside, Pat, or I shall perish!" exclaims Lawrence.

"I wondered when you would come. I've been expecting you."

Lawrence pushes past him but does not want to create a mess in the heart of the cottage. Pat takes his hat from him, and helps him out of his coat.

"Thank you, Pat. It's good to see you again."

Pat thinks to shake hands but cannot till he has draped the coat over a chair he then places near the guard of a snoozing fire.

"I'll put another log on," says Pat.

The handshake is firm, enthusiastic, has been too long coming. Into it, Lawrence presses friendship, gratitude, need.

Pat chooses the biggest log from the basket, knowing that Lawrence will stay a while. There must be something important to say. After all, Pat has witnessed the comings and goings of all the reporters for weeks, and there have been times when he has wanted to take matters into his own hands, but has known that would be futile. Lawrence would not have thanked him for such an intervention. Pat knows that, perversely, Lawrence relishes the cut and thrust of the chase and evasion.

"Will it last?" asks Lawrence.

Pat knits his brow. The siege? The snow?

"Not my call," replies Pat. "Tea? Chocolate? Coffee?"

"Chocolate," decides Lawrence. "Yes, chocolate. More comforting."

"Sit down," invites Pat. "Don't stand on ceremony."

Nothing is said while Pat pours milk into a pan, and puts it on a hot-plate. Carefully, he stirs cocoa powder into a milky paste, then adds hot milk, when it is ready, stirring thoroughly.

Lawrence sips, closes his eyes. Bliss.

"I'd forgotten your cocoa was so good."

Pat smiles. It is up to Lawrence now.

"How are you?" Pat nudges.

Lawrence sighs. Where to begin?

"How long were they here before my return?"

"Days, maybe a week or two."

"Did you speak to them?"

"Told them I was a sort of caretaker." Lawrence guffaws. You're so much more! he thinks. But anything to stall or bamboozle them. "Well, I am – sort of."

"And what did they say to that?"

"They asked if I could let them in to take a look. They even wafted notes under my nose."

"And what did you say?"

"I said it was more than my job was worth, that you'd slit the throat of any bastard that stepped over the threshold. Said you'd killed Turks like that, that it was your preferred method, that you liked to see terror in their eyes when they realised you'd ended their life."

Lawrence said, "Pat, I appreciate your help, but your threats didn't exactly send them running!"

"Just one severed jugular is all it would take." Pat draws his finger from ear to ear, and makes the sound of gurgling blood. "It made them think. By God, it did!"

Lawrence does not want to be too critical as Pat has helped to make Clouds Hill what it is, while Lawrence has been elsewhere. Besides, Pat is only being protective, and is on Lawrence's side, and Lawrence needs as many as possible like that.

"Well done, Pat. I cannot be too harsh after what I've done to one of them. I expect to be arrested any day."

"I heard," says Pat.

"Who told you?"

Pat shrugs, not wanting to dispirit Lawrence. Reporters have been talking to as many locals as possible. Has Lawrence been violent before? Are you sure? The press has persisted, waving a ten shillings note under noses as an incentive. And the word is out that Lawrence has broken a reporter's jaw. Soon, Pat hears of it. In fact, almost everyone with whom he is acquainted is telling him.

"You can't stop people from talking," says Pat.

"Things are building up, though there is a lull, at the moment, but it will start again, and the sharks will gather when they taste blood in the water."

Pat is anxious to change tack; this is not how he wants it to be between them. So he perks up, and asks, "Is the water brown? I've been running it. It clears, in time."

"It's fine."

Pat smiles, knows that Lawrence has no idea about plumbing. It is the last thing he would notice, being preoccupied with more urgent matters.

"Let me know if it goes brown."

Lawrence licks the chocolate from his lips. Pat will take him seriously, so he says, "Things are coming to a head," but he cannot tell him what happened to the woman. Pat knows her, but if he has any inkling of her relationship with Lawrence, then he does not show it. So Lawrence steers clear of that line, and concentrates on the possibility of him being arrested.

Concerned, Pat says, "Things have been worse. This is your country. You have rights: to privacy, a bit of peace and quiet. Can't … someone high up help?"

Lawrence does not tell him that Churchill is responsible for the current respite. Pat must know nothing of it. That is what makes Pat's company special: he is untainted by globe-trotting, unsuccessful attempts at nation-creation, and a life of restlessness.

"This is what I want you to do," says Lawrence, suddenly sitting up straight. It is a considered plan of action. "If I am taken, or disappear, I want you to post this letter. Do not entrust it to anyone else."

"Why not?"

"Because if it does not reach the person to whom it is addressed, I am a dead man."

"How will I know if you have been taken or have simply gone away? You come and go at your own will."

Lawrence is momentarily caught out by the flaw in his plan, but his whole life has required him to solve problems, think on his feet, and soon he has a solution.

"If I am going away for two nights or more, I will tell you."

"And if you forget?"

"I won't," says Lawrence. "You have never forgotten me, and I won't forget you."

Pat looks at the name and address on the envelope, and considers the power he now has. It occurs to him that others will see the details, and might be tempted to open the envelope.

"And have all your letters arrived at the good and mighty?" he asks.

"Yes, and I have expected them to. Oh, Intelligence has probably read every one of them, but they will have been hugely disappointed at the mundanity of the content. And I know they have tampered with those sent to me."

Pat does not like to probe, but finds Lawrence's life so fascinating that he asks, "How do you know?"

Lawrence warms to Pat's curiosity, likes nothing better than pitting his wits against others, especially those whom he is sure even Churchill instructs, for that is the secret of survival, he has learned, having once worked in military intelligence: keep your friends close, and enemies even closer.

"What would you do?" teases Lawrence, not really wanting to give away any tricks of his trade, for though Pat has always been a loyal friend, the golden rule is: never let your tongue loose, as it can be your undoing.

"I've no idea," says Pat, and he genuinely has not.

"Well, you set a trap."

"A trap?"

"One that cannot fail to reveal if someone has read your letter."

"But what do you do?"

Pat deserves better, decides Lawrence.

"Well, on one occasion, I asked a certain woman to place two short strands of her hair between the two sheets of her letter. When I carefully opened the envelope, the hairs had gone."

He remembers how ashamed he had felt asking Florence Hardy to test his theory. She, of all people, the widow of the man he revered the most, had seen his request as a form of amusement. "I cannot promise they will be my hairs," she had said, "as mine have turned as grey as ashes, but I will not disappoint you. In your letter to me, write about matters so inconsequential that, in years to come, I cannot be judged ill by historian or critic. I would hate my loyalty to be called into question."

Lawrence had flushed at this, not having imagined that her reputation might be impugned.

"Of course. I hope I do not make you uncomfortable. I will understand perfectly if you wish to change your mind."

"Not at all!" had protested Florence. "It will liven up the hours, which pass slowly since Tom breathed his last."

"Then my letter will be the epitome of trivia."

"Not too trivial!" had laughed Florence. "There has to be some phrase or line to provoke a reply."

"I shall see what I can come up with."

"Then do, Thomas. I'll look forward to it."

Pat looks momentarily impressed, but has too much on his mind to enter fully a world against whose window he can only press his nose. The death of his mother still weighs heavily upon him, and the arrangements for his forthcoming wedding are not yet finalised. Lawrence is spared all this entrapment by social convention. For his part, Pat has none of his friend's lust for vagrancy, despite all the glitter that Lawrence sprinkles on it. Pat is a practical man who knows that, though the views from the stars are magnificent, there is a danger that, so high up, one does not see things on Earth as they truly are.

"But I am forgetting myself. I have not asked how you are. Your mother's death must still hurt," says Lawrence.

Pat shrugs, so used to Lawrence's comings and goings that he knows there are matters Lawrence neglects more out of dealing with the pressures of his identity than thoughtlessness.

"I have taken over the cottage's lease," Pat tells Lawrence.

There is no mention of his mother. What can Pat say but life goes on?

"There is security in that," observes Lawrence.

"Clouds Hill is yours, but …"

"I take your point. I mean, it's a roof over your head."

Pat looks up at the ceiling, then says, "So, I am in charge of this letter, and your life hangs by a thread if I do not post it at the correct time. Bloody marvellous!"

"Are you sure you can deal with it?"

Lawrence is serious, but Pat is tickled by the absurdity of this responsibility. He is more a man for tinkering with water tanks than sending for the cavalry. But he is secretly proud that he is entrusted to help.

"Look at me, will you? Where have I been? What have I done? This is the closest I'll come to excitement, to a lesser glory. This envelope" – Pat waves it for dramatic effect – "is my Saturday night pass-out. No more Bovington blues. This makes me somebody."

"Don't tell anyone else," warns Lawrence, "or I shall slit your throat."

"Wouldn't dream of it. Another cup of chocolate?"

"Yes, why not?" says Lawrence.

"Yes, live dangerously," encourages Pat.

"I do," says Lawrence. "I bloody well do."

Lawrence changes tack, and makes further enquiries about local matters. Never usually one for complaining, Pat bemoans one or two occasional shortages of certain vegetables, and returns to the army as a focus. His observations about increased vehicular activity in the lanes strike a chord with Lawrence, who asserts that the world is still a dangerous place.

Pat says, "They say we are preparing for war."

Lawrence knows Pat is fishing for inside information, and it is hard for Lawrence to explain the complexity of possibilities for Europe. How can he tell him that Henry Williamson beseeches him to meet Hitler? There are ways of maintaining peace, and a more than passing acquaintance with National Socialism might offer hope. There have been animated conversations and correspondence between Lawrence and Williamson, and Lawrence has been careful what he has said, knowing that Churchill is keeping a close eye on him. "The people like you,"

Churchill once told him, but did not add that this is what makes him a threat. How can I prepare for war, Churchill asks himself, if a national hero is working for appeasement with this nation's biggest enemy?

"An army is useless if it is not always ready to defend the nation. What you see and hear reflects heightened tension. No one wants war, but we must accept that the German people are increasingly attracted to Hitler."

"Bovington is definitely fidgety," says Pat in a tone suggesting that he knows something is afoot, that this is not just a dry run for potential hostilities.

Lawrence deftly links Pat's observation with damage to Clouds Hill.

"You any good with ladders? I've one or two broken tiles that need replacing. Boulders are the culprit: revenge for my not liking reporters swarming all over the place. That's the problem with the press: they hear a wild story about me, and, the next minute, they want a confirmation or denial."

"Have you ever wondered who sets these hares running?"

"I *know* who does, but let's leave it at that. I can't pay you much for the roof work, but it's urgent now, what with this weather. Need to make it watertight."

"Leave it to me."

"Thanks, Pat."

After a pause, Pat asks, "How's the writing?"

"Don't ask. Any more of that chocolate? And a biscuit or two?"

"Don't you know things are tight?"

Lawrence laughs.

"There is always food. You just have to know where to look for it. I've eaten snakes and lizards in the desert."

"No biscuits, but I can stretch to a slice of toast and beef dripping!"

"Perfect," says Lawrence, absolutely sincerely. In his world, where few things are perfect, toast and dripping fit the bill.

Pat crouches to the fire, and stokes it. There is just enough heat coming from it to toast the two slices of bread left from the loaf. When the first is brown, he spreads the dripping onto it, and Lawrence takes a big bite. The salt and warmth are comforting, and he chews more slowly the second slice, hoping to make it last, to distract himself from sinister thoughts.

"You must come round and let me make toast for you," offers Lawrence, licking his fingers.

"And will there be beans?"

"If you want."

"I do. Remember last time?"

Lawrence does. In his head is a montage of such gatherings: his RAF pal, Jock Chambers, Privates Russell and Palmer, and, of course Corporal Dixon – great friends, all of them.

You can't go back, knows Lawrence. It is always tempting to think that you can, but it is a vain hope.

Their conversation is, one minute, like a blast of heat from the fire when a new log is fed to it, another, like its dying embers. This is partly due to Pat watching what ignites Lawrence, and what does not. Pat judges Lawrence's fine fluctuations in mood, and Lawrence appreciates his sensitivity.

The clock on the mantelpiece strikes ten, and the two men await the last stroke. Both know it is time for bed and Lawrence's departure.

"Is it still snowing?" says Pat, going to the window.

"It looked set for the night."

"You're wrong. It's stopped."

Lawrence puts on his coat and hat. Though Pat would not throw him out, Lawrence does not want to outstay his welcome.

They face each other by the door, for last words.

"Promise me one thing, Pat."

"It depends what you want. I've said I'll post the letter. What else?"

There is a twinkle in Pat's eye, and no edge to the question.

"Look after Clouds Hill for me."

"Do it yourself!"

But Lawrence does not smile.

"I mean, when I die. It'll be all that's left."

"Seven Pillars? The Mint? The Odyssey of Homer?"

These achievements soften Lawrence's expression – but briefly.

"No, Pat, listen. This time, next year, I won't be here."

"Off on your motorbike again?"

"No. No more tours planned, but I fear I shall take the open road to oblivion, one way or another."

Pat pretends he does not understand, but he does. And for the first time, he believes his friend, and knows that there is not a damned thing he can do to save him. Somehow, Lawrence has already written his will in the stars – in indelible ink.

CHAPTER TEN

The problem with finding a base for the Secret Intelligence Service is that those who would like to infiltrate it have a good idea of the type of building for which Intelligence is looking. Enemies of the state know that drab buildings are preferred, that often there is a sign that tries to mislead snoopers. However, clever spies can see, with a bit of diligence and patience, whether a taxi firm, a typical front, is genuine or not. The most effective spies choose inconspicuous places to meet, but Intelligence needs total secrecy where a base is concerned, and has a more difficult task. Can there ever be such a thing as a secret in their line of work?

Picture a grey building six or seven storeys high, with a creaking lift to the top floor, in London. Not even the management company suspects that it is anything other than the office of a taxi firm. The newly installed telephones paid for by cash are ostensibly to cope with the alleged increased demand for taxis. That is the official line. Several regular gratuities buy the key personnel in the building. "Taxis is what they do," they always reply to enquiries. "Good rates, too. The best around." Of course, they have their suspicions, never having seen one of their taxis, but the back-handers, and a fear that they might have got themselves into something from which they cannot extricate themselves, are sufficient to buy the silence Intelligence requires.

No one works regular hours on that floor. Some days, the doorman – he is new, an appointment suggested by the taxi firm – never sees a soul, but he has been trained to nod, and speak only when spoken to. It is easy money, but there are days when he wants to probe, suspecting that there might be something unusual about the visitor, something he cannot quite put his finger on.

Men with a military bearing, in hats and long, dark coats, come and go irregularly, but are never seen together. Sometimes the doorman looks across the road at the man next to the lamppost, and is sure that he is watching the building, but the observer always moves away when he thinks the doorman is focusing on him, or turns to look elsewhere. Why next to the lamppost? wonders the doorman, to whom it does not occur that the subject *wants* to be noticed, for an unknown reason. Without this diversion, the day passes slowly. Why do they employ me? he asks himself. It is money for old rope.

On the top floor, behind a desk on which are three telephones, sits a well groomed man with a pained facial expression. He has the air of someone with too much to think about. Believing that he has his priorities right, he is more than a little irked by what he has been tasked to oversee. There is a bigger issue he should be addressing, and he knows that he ignores his instructions at his peril. He is confident he has a grip on Bolshevism, and feels that Socialism, too, is a threat in Britain. Strong leadership is what he admires, wherever it is found.

When the knock comes on his door, he calls, after checking the agreed salutation for that meeting, "The day is cold, for this time of year." There is a pause of ten seconds before the response, "Yes, but soon spring will be here," is made. Anything other than those exact words would be a breach of security, and there would follow a procedure the man wishing to be admitted would soon know is in train.

S, for that is the man already in the room, puts the gun back into the drawer whence he took it. He presses a button on the wall, and there is a clicking sound in the door's lock. The door opens automatically, and S smiles. It is, indeed, the man he has been expecting. Good. Mistakes can be costly.

"Do come in, Trilby. I'm glad you're here first. Sit down, won't you?"

There are only two chairs in the room, and Alexander, as Smith, Mills, and Trilby know him, is occupying one. Trilby quickly looks round the room, even under Alexander's chair, before sitting down. In Trilby's profession, caution is key. One mistake and the pitiful pension he will, one day, receive will not be drawn and enjoyed. He keeps his right hand in his pocket, the content of which is his best friend. One cannot be too careful.

"Who else is coming?"

Trilby is a little tense, wonders whether he is in for a surprise.

"Oh, you know: Mills and Smith."

Trilby looks at the clock on the wall; he himself is on time. Is he about to be told something Alexander does not want the others to hear? But this is par for the course. Many a mission has been scuppered by a failure to proceed on a need-to-know basis.

"Is this about what the Boss wants us to do? If it is, Smith is not his man."

"Really?" says Alexander.

"Really."

"I see," says Alexander, neutrally.

"Do you?"

"It'll be in May," states Alexander, after a lengthy pause in which he calculates that it is best not to discuss matters he had not planned to. Such lack of focus is dangerous at sea, he remembers, from his naval days, but also on land.

"Why May?"

Alexander shrugs.

"Ours is not to reason why."

"Ours is but to do and die," says Trilby, "so I ask again. Why May?"

Alexander leans forward confidentially.

"Because, old chap, they are orders."

Orders are what lead to a payday, so Trilby does not overplay the righteous indignation card. Yes, there is always a risk that things might go awfully wrong, but he knows too much now to change the course of the assignment. He really ought to stop it, this fishing for an acknowledgement that he is pivotal to the plan's execution, this preening of the ego, which goes hand in hand with eliminating someone.

"So, is there a date? Yes," continues Alexander.

"May I know it?"

"In time. You know how it goes. What's important is that all the other bits are in place. The bigger challenge is ... but that doesn't concern you. For King and country – all of us. This organisation is vital for the nation's security."

"And my being here today?"

"To report on how your preparations are going. As ever, I don't have to tell you what to do. The only stipulation is that there must be no shots to the head. Nothing messy, you understand. And I don't even want to know what country you will go to afterwards, but you will lie low for a couple of months. Naturally, we will meet your living expenses, during your absence. They say Spain is hot, so one more hothead won't make any difference."

Trilby ignores the side-swipe; there is nothing to be gained from retaliation to a cheap insult.

Smith is next to arrive, and finally Mills. The doorman suspects nothing, and it might have something to do with the tip they slip into his hand.

Today Smith is more positive. Having everything in hand helps, and Mills, too, is alert. There has to be a perfect understanding of how each plays a part in the Boss' plan, how each protects himself from what will eventually trigger massive news media attention.

Trilby is still rather twitchy about Smith, but when Alexander calls each to detail progress against responsibility, Trilby nods, if not quite appreciatively, at least in a way suggesting satisfaction at what he has heard.

There are only two chairs, so Smith and Mills have to stand. This is no social gathering, and there is nothing like standing to focus the mind.

Alexander can see that Trilby is uneasy with Mills on one side and Smith on the other. Trilby has never liked being hemmed in, and stands up and offers his chair, which both decline. Trilby does not sit down again, prompting Alexander to make a start.

"During May, you go nowhere. By the first day of the month, you will have been prepared for at least two weeks. On the morning of the day, you will each receive a call. Stay by the telephone. Make sure the receiver is in place. The person at the other end will say, 'There is a sandstorm in the offing.' Then you say, 'But it will soon be over.' Do you want me to repeat that?" The other three shake their head. "Don't write anything down. Any questions so far?"

Trilby is itching to leave and, being only the catalyst, does not care what happens afterwards. That is for others to deal with.

"Can I go now?" he says.

Mills then says, "And what if the Boss cancels the operation, on the day?"

Alexander pulls a face at Mills, and says to Trilby, "You can go in a minute." Then, to Mills: "He won't cancel. This is what must happen, for the country. There is no reason to deviate from the plan."

"Fine," says Mills. "Just so we're clear about it."

"Actually, you can go now," says Alexander to Trilby, who pulls down the brim of his hat. The doorman will not see his face, nor will Trilby acknowledge the inevitable valediction.

Trilby is two steps from the door when Smith calls, "Passchendaele. Were you there?" Trilby stops but does not turn. Instinctively, he knows Smith is addressing him. "Nineteen-seventeen. Late October." Still Trilby does not react. "You rescued two Canadians, took out a vipers' nest. Bloody hero. VC if I remember correctly. Always were a good shot. Bloody good shot."

Trilby leaves. Alexander starts to go over the arrangements with the other two, where there is a necessity for operational cohesion, as their roles are entwined. If one of them slips up, the whole operation could fail. Trilby will, of course, be the ultimate cause of the death of Lawrence, but the time of day will be fixed, so that the whole network necessary to manage the aftermath is in a heightened state of alert. Therefore, Alexander has no problem with Smith and Mills agreeing how they must synchronise their actions.

Yes, Lawrence always leaves Clouds Hill on his Brough at some time, most days. It has been observed that a frequent destination is the Post Office. Being an inveterate writer of letters, he has a need to go on a daily basis.

Yes, Trilby is clear where Lawrence will meet his end, and it will be arranged for someone to observe what happens so that the alarm can be raised at Bovington Camp. Alexander listens intently, then says, "They will, of course, have a plausible reason for being present? You see, what concerns me is that whoever sees what happens must have no idea that they are witnessing anything sinister. They are not to be part of the plan. They are there to report to the Camp. The person chosen must be someone of unimpeachable character, and, of course, have some initiative. It would not do to have someone who is easily spooked. I don't want to know their name, but you need to satisfy me that they are single. They will need to take an extended holiday afterwards."

Mills starts to speak, but Alexander holds up his hand.

Smith says, "I've been over this with Mills a thousand times. The press release has already been written. The particular time of day will be added, and, of course, the mode of extermination. We do not yet know what Trilby has in mind."

Alexander is restless, as he always is when putting together a plan. The Boss trusts him. This is not the first time an operation of such complexity has been devised, but this is different. This is Lawrence, and Alexander knows that Lawrence knows the key principles of secret intelligence work, and is, therefore, a survivor. Of all men! he privately laments. Of all men!

"Who are your key contacts?" Alexander asks each. They tell him, and he shakes his head. "Not their names. I want to know their status. Do they have the authority to do what you're asking them?" They nod. "And they know nothing yet? That's right, isn't it?" Again they nod. "How do you know you can trust them? I mean, it must seem a part of their normal duties. At least, most of the time. You see, it's the hospital that needs to be quick off the mark. Whatever their record for holding an inquest, they're going to have to break it. No civil policeman should get beyond the Camp gate. And the press will try everything: disguises, cutting through the perimeter fence, outrageous names. Bovington Camp needs to be as tight as a camel's arse in a sandstorm."

Smith smirks at this expression, but Alexander pulls him up. There is no room for humour or complacency; that is disrespect for the nation's hero.

As they progress through the plans, the lines of communication and key actions, Alexander asks questions. Occasionally, there is no answer, but that is not his cue to demand they go back to the drawing-board. Over the years, he has learned that circumstances can change quickly. The absence of an answer just means that a reliable answer is not yet available, and Alexander opts for reliable – always.

At the end of their session, Alexander is in danger of feeling mildly confident, always a dangerous moment, he had once been told, but the status of Operation Sandstorm is so high that he cannot make an objective assessment of progress without a certain degree of optimism. His job is not for the faint-hearted, Churchill once reminded him. Faint hearts never win a battle, let alone a war.

"Good," Alexander concludes. "Good."

Neither Smith nor Mills has ever heard him repeat himself in that way. There they all are, three men imbued with a growing smugness, but none dares reveal a sign of it. Unprofessional. Definitely.

Alexander stands up. It is time for Mills and Smith to leave. Mills goes first, then Smith, ten minutes later. In that time, Alexander does not speak to Smith but wonders what has made him more up-beat about his part in the operation.

Unusually, Alexander offers his hand. Smith examines him intently, as if searching for something, some knowledge or a speech he had wanted to deliver but had not because of the others. Their eyes stay locked more tightly than their hands, and it is Alexander who blinks first.

"Smith," calls Alexander, as he presses the button to unlock the door. Smith looks at him with that inviting expression. "Well done. That's all."

"Thank you, sir," Smith replies, then goes.

When he is alone again, Alexander runs through what he has heard. His training has taught him that spot-checks undermine morale, despite their necessity. Besides, he might as well do all the work himself if he is going to spend too much time checking. Nevertheless, complacency can be fatal. So, Trilby – tick. Witness – tick. Arrangements for lock-down – tick. Security of the corpse – tick. Management of the news media – tick. What could go wrong?

Enough, Alexander chides himself. You'll drive yourself into an early grave. He takes out his hip-flask, pops two pills into his mouth, and takes a long swig of brandy. One drink, he claims, makes him think clearly. What is the weak point in all this? If I'm honest, he thinks, it's the Major, who stands to gain or lose everything. Great rewards will come his way if he manages to get Lawrence into his grave without suspicion. But Alexander has already checked him out. And that's just it: a man who has never yet made a mistake will, one day, show that he is a mere mortal. It's just a matter of timing, and the timing of a mistake can never be known until it is too late.

There is always something Alexander can be doing, and the realisation that Operation Sandstorm is on course prompts a feeling of self-worth. The pills take effect quickly, and S decides that he will go to Soho, which he occasionally visits at night.

The club is in an unprepossessing building in one of the less remarkable streets in that district. There is nothing on the building's exterior to suggest that it is anything but a dwelling similar to those nearby.

But people, mostly men, come and go, stay for an hour or several. Police are never called to eject members, who realise that the club – for that is what it is – offers services to all types of people, and its closure would be a detriment to all.

S rings the bell. Behind the door, the burly doorman recognises a regular visitor.

"Early today, sir," he remarks, allowing S to step inside, before closing the door.

S is immediately swathed in warmth and cigar smoke, familiar signs that he is among friends.

"Indeed, I am. Change is as good as a rest, eh?" answers S, smiling.

"That is what they say, sir. May I take your coat?"

S unbuttons his long, navy coat, and hands it over. Just then, a woman in a long, sequinned dress, the colours of a peacock's fan, appears.

"We don't usually see you at this time of day, do we?" she remarks.

Her smile is genuine, her tone friendly. People pay a lot for them. She takes his arm, and leads him through a door into a big room, in which there are settees, armchairs and chaises longues. Only one or two people look up, and that is what S likes about this place: it is a sanctuary to all who need one.

"Can I get you a drink?" asks the woman, now near enough for her expensive perfume to be discerned in the heady tobacco smoke.

"I think not, at the moment."

"Will you see Maria? I think she is around somewhere."

S deliberates, then decides.

"No. Roman, I think."

"He's free, I believe. Let me take you to him."

He allows Pearl, for that is the name S calls her, on account of the expensive pearls without which she is never seen, to lead him to another room, on the first floor.

Pearl does not knock but takes S into a room of bohemian character. Roman, a muscular, squat man of Eastern European appearance, looks up from his book.

"Our resident scholar," quips Pearl.

S nods a little nervously to Roman, glances at the marble-topped table on which sit jars of oils and creams. He has visited Roman, who is better, in some respects, than Maria, twice before. Roman does not make a noise by clattering the tools of his trade, unlike Maria, who sometimes thinks she is the centre of attraction, and not her visitors, as Pearl likes to call her guests.

Pearl slips away.

"So," says Roman, taking a step forward.

S, too, takes a step, then the ritual begins.

Two hours later, the treatment is over. S slides money under his favourite jar, and Roman bows gratefully. Pearl will accept her fee more formally in her reception, as is the club's rule.

As S descends the staircase, contemplating his exceptional revivification, he stops to allow a man and a woman to pass.

Only fleeting eye-contact confirms recognition. It is enough, though, to set S's heart racing. The other man says nothing, but glances over his shoulder. Yes, it is him, he confirms. Well, well, well. Would you believe it? Still, that is the life we lead, he acknowledges. A flitting into and out of shadows, an adoption of different names and masks. Neither of us should be surprised. We are both part of the same hypocrisy, which sets us apart from others, yet binds us so tightly that we stumble upon each other when we least expect or want to.

"Is everything all right?" asks the woman.

Distracted, the man replies, "Yes, I think so," but he cannot be sure, and it is only when he is an hour into his treatment that he does not give a damn one way or the other.

But before their therapy upstairs with Julian takes effect, the woman is not convinced. The stranger comes from way back, somewhere, but not in a police station. His questions were political. How long have you worked for George Lansbury and the Labour Party? Has Lansbury expressed support for violent methods of protest? Are you aware of any links Lansbury has to the Communist Party?

"How do you know him?" asks the woman.

"He interviewed me."

"Did you get the job?"

"Let's just say I withdrew from the running. But it was him, definitely him."

"How do you know?"

"Well, when he asked me a question, he seemed almost affable, but when he pointed the gun at my head, he seemed to change completely."

"Did you tell the police?"

"No."

"Why not?"

"Because I thought he *was* the police."

"And he wasn't?"

"No."

"Then who was he?"

The man hesitates, is not allowed to say, "One of us," but lies instead with, "An associate. That's all. A man in too much of a hurry, under too much pressure. Leave it now. Relax. Here comes Julian."

CHAPTER ELEVEN

Clouds Hill is more a place to come home to than stay in, day after day. Lawrence does not like to set out too late, wherever he is going, and the later he returns from a trip, the more he relishes turning his key in the lock, lighting the candles, and listening to the music of one or more great composers. Some days, he rides a mile or two before he decides his destination. The sense of freedom this gives him lifts his spirits, and he is ready, once again, to connect with people, ideas, places.

Some trips, however, have to be planned, especially if he is going to see people, and that means writing a letter. For some time, he has been itching to visit Max Gate again. Florence Hardy is always kind to him, and was never resentful of her dead husband's affinity with him. Yes, there were moments of jealousy, but was that not what attracted her to Hardy: that mystery surrounding someone who spends so much of his time in an imaginary world that one yearns to go there, too?

He edits extensively his letter requesting her approval of a visit from him. Usually, he has no problem expressing himself, but the letter he hopes will secure him permission to visit Max Gate is so full of stops and starts that he has to do some work on it. However, the final copy is just right.

Dear Mrs. Hardy,

Please accept this letter requesting a visit to see you at Max Gate, on Wednesday week, as confirmation that I can never pass a day without an acute sense of gratitude for the friendship you and your husband show me. I say show in the present as I sense Hardy still inhabits the lanes and heathland of our part of Dorset. Too many words have passed between us for him to be merely a ghost. I shall, of course, understand if you are already committed, but a visit to see you at Max Gate would be an enormous comfort to me.

Yours,

T. E. Shaw

Florence is not sure how she will occupy herself, the day the letter arrives. The light is good, and she promises herself a walk, when she is feeling stronger. There are days when she tires of visitors, who mean well but fail to see that she still, after several years, needs space to come to terms with her loss, in her own way. There are days when she feels Tom's absence keenly. She anticipates his entrances at set times. Oh, he is here, I have no doubt, she tells herself, and he would gladly receive Lawrence, who always seemed to unlock him in a way I never could.

So she writes a brief reply to confirm that she would be glad to see him on the date in question. Max Gate is clean and tidy. She does not bother to move books she has been reading. Lawrence would never regard them as clutter but signs that the intellectual life of the house is still there.

On the day of Lawrence's visit, she makes herself presentable. She has always found him so agreeable that she would hate to discourage him from visiting in the future by appearing untidy. But she knows that he is not coming to inspect her carpets or to find cobwebs draped from ceilings, and sits down and waits.

She hears him before she sees him, and her heart skips a beat. There on the lawn they have stood and listened to her husband enquire after Lawrence's health, literary ambitions, and meetings with fellow luminaries. How was Bernard Shaw when you saw him? He said that? Did he really? Ah well. And has Forster anything he is working up?

When Lawrence arrives, she opens the door to him. There is no one like him to light up the day, set her pulse racing.

There is a blazing fire. Lawrence sits close to it, in a chair she knows he finds comfortable. Tea is brought. Lawrence smiles, and the woman who does for Florence blushes, even curtseys, and Florence giggles.

"You've made quite an impression," says Florence.

Lawrence smiles; it would be unnatural not to. They watch the teapot, skirting round the subject of Hardy himself. Florence is under no illusion, and plays the game. At least she knows that Lawrence will not pry, that his friendship with Hardy mattered.

"I hope my calling has not disrupted your routine," begins Lawrence.

"Not at all. My days of routine are over. Days drag, and in winter it is especially gloomy when night falls early."

"Indeed, though I draw inspiration from its special atmosphere," enthuses Lawrence.

"That is because you're a writer. You're *supposed* to be sensitive to such changes. Tom locked himself away for hours when the urge took him."

By mentioning him, the door opens. Tom is present again. Lawrence thinks that he can smell him, though years have passed since he was physically in that room. That is it: Tom had just nipped to Dorchester on his bicycle, or walked to the church at Stinsford. As Lawrence surveys the room, he is sure that nothing has changed. Mirrors, clocks, paintings and photographs are all in the same places as when Hardy was alive.

"I *was* a writer, but the muse has deserted me, I'm afraid," admits Lawrence.

Lawrence momentarily bows his head, as if ashamed of his barren spell, then sits up sharply. Is this not why he has come: to feel alive again in a place where so much has been achieved by a man he considers to be the greatest writer?

"There were times when a poem would not come to Tom. Then he would get up and do something. It is quite normal for inspiration to elude one. It has escaped me all my life!"

Florence laughs. Lawrence remembers Hardy once fleetingly commenting disparagingly upon her literary aspirations, and decides to be encouraging. She knows she chose, in marriage, the role of support at the expense of her own efforts with the pen.

"Every day is a new start – for all of us," Lawrence says.

"Dear Thomas, you are so positive, but I'm under no illusions. I am quite content, these days, to look after Tom's legacy. But you have years ahead of you, and I expect great things of you. Perhaps, you could try a different theme from Seven Pillars of Wisdom."

"And I would like to, I truly would, but I fear that the life I have led has not equipped me for the vast canvas that Tom filled. What do I know of human nature?"

Florence pours him tea, and he reminds her that he takes it just as she serves it. No need to say when. She cuts him a generous slice of apple cake, and he does not protest. He has sampled it at Max Gate before, and knows it to be excellent.

"Does a writer need to murder someone before he can have a murder in his story?"

"I suppose not."

"Then get on with it, Thomas. I offer myself as your editor. You must start a great novel immediately, and I shall guide you through it."

"You would find me too dull, I'm afraid, but you give me hope. Coming here, I now know what my life should be. That has been my frustration for years: one foot in the military, the other in the study, dealing with the truth – that my days of soldiering are over."

"And you know it now?"

"I do. Being here at Max Gate with you and Tom again confirms it."

"Then I am glad, though it is lonely here, and I feel now that Tom only looks in on me, now and again. He has not totally deserted me, I know, but I will always be a subsidiary character in his drama. He belongs to too many others for it to be any different."

And do I belong to too many others? wonders Lawrence. Is it too late for me to know real intimacy?

Florence sees pain in his eyes, and she does not intend to be sad any more, so she changes the subject, and Lawrence is, as ever, polite, and enquires after her health.

"It must take its toll, having people turn up here," he says.

"Yes, it does. Sometimes they climb and peep over the wall, and it scares me, but Tom was so private. I have not been in the best of health recently, and I am sure that I shall not live as long as him. Somehow he seems to have lived two lives: one in our world, another in the fictional worlds he created."

Yes, thinks Lawrence, and that is what I want. It is the ultimate adventure, far more exciting than the ones I have had abroad. And it is not too late, he tells himself. Not in terms of the years I have left. I hope to have plenty, but I doubt it. Where shall I begin, though? Can I write with all these comings and goings at Clouds Hill? But it is there or nowhere. Nowhere else will do.

"The little table you gave me is very useful," remarks Lawrence, when conversation begins to wane.

"Good."

"It is something I shall always treasure."

Florence smiles. What would life be like with such a man? There would be few arguments, for sure. At least Tom was there for me, and I knew the person he was. Lawrence needs a lot of attention, too much, perhaps.

"So, has it all died down at Clouds Hill?" she asks.

"Cat and mouse," answers Lawrence.

"I read all about it. The man whose jaw you're supposed to have broken was most critical of you."

Lawrence can see a curl of amusement around the corners of her mouth.

"I imagine he was."

"So you really did break his jaw."

"I did, though not intentionally. The punch was supposed to warn him off."

"I remember what it was like when Tom died. The reporters were like starving pigeons gathering at my feet for crumbs for their editors. Despicable behaviour."

Florence shudders at her recollection of their intrusion into her mourning.

"It was ever thus," consoles Lawrence.

"Broke his jaw!" laughs Florence.

"What is so funny about a broken jaw?" asks Lawrence, truly bemused by her amusement.

"Nothing – if it's *your* jaw that's broken. But you: T. E. Lawrence. I've always associated you more with quickness of pen than fist. And when do you appear in court?"

"I won't. The police cite acute provocation on my own property."

"And what exactly did he do or say to provoke you?"

"He asked if I was queer."

Florence thinks she has misheard.

"Queer?"

"Homosexual."

"Oh, I see."

Florence looks this way and that. Tom had never said anything. Why should he have? Lawrence is so handsome that he can have the pick of the county!

"Do you?" teases Lawrence. Then, to alleviate her embarrassment, he says, "Such impertinence deserved a punch. My timing was perfect!"

Florence tops up Lawrence's cup, and offers him more cake, but Lawrence declines.

"Then you can take a piece for your evening meal," says Florence.

"That would be nice," says Lawrence. "Did *you* make it?"

"Me? Goodness, no."

"Then my compliments to the cook."

"I shall pass them on."

They talk about inconsequential matters, and Lawrence studies her. Her face shows her continued grieving for Tom, and there is a pallor Lawrence guesses is a sign of incipient ill health. He has seen it before, particularly in women. Florence is no tragic figure – yet. But Lawrence wonders how she really feels about Hardy's heart being buried in Emma's grave. Florence followed his wish, but does she ever care about what the world makes of it?

"And do you manage to get up to London much?" asks Lawrence.

"Occasionally. Dorchester is less exciting, but Max Gate is where I belong – at least, for the time being."

"I have been to far-flung places, but I'm glad to be at Clouds Hill, where I shall end my days."

Florence looks at him, frowns at this morbid talk.

"You are preparing for it? There is much you will do before then," she chides.

Lawrence wants to tell her that no one knows when the end will come, and that he senses that his own feels close.

"Of course," he says, smiling, but the parts of his face do not fit together as they usually do, and she is not convinced.

After a silence, Lawrence asks, "Did Tom ever say anything to you about me?"

"Just that he was fond of you."

"He said that?"

"He didn't have to. It was obvious."

"And did he say anything about my writing?"

Florence cannot remember but says, "He thought you a fine writer."

"Really?"

"Fine was the exact word he used."

Lawrence flops back into his seat. Relief has never felt sweeter.

"Then I shall write again, something worthy that Tom would think fine."

"Do it for yourself," says Florence.

"I will," says Lawrence, "but my words limp across the page, these days. If I think Tom is reading them, they will stand upright, and march, at the double."

Florence gives in. There are days when she misses Tom till her bones ache, but there are others when she wishes that he could let her get on with life.

"As you wish."

Lawrence does not wish to outstay his welcome, but does not want to be rude by leaving prematurely. Eventually, the woman who does for Florence knocks for the tea tray, and this gives Florence the chance to steer the visit to a natural conclusion.

"I feel I must let you get on," says Lawrence.

"Not before you have sorted through a few of Tom's books I have put aside. They are dusty, and not ones I believe he ever read."

"If you are sure."

Lawrence chooses two from a pile of ten, and Florence presses another one on him. Regretfully, he cannot take the rest. Clouds Hill is small, and he has many books already.

When Lawrence offers his hand to shake, Florence takes it in both of hers, and kisses him on the cheek. He can smell lavender, and almost shudders at the coldness of her lips.

"Don't leave it so long, next time," she says.

"I won't. Soon, spring will be here."

She closes the door when he has gone, and Lawrence does not look back.

Lawrence places the three books on his settee, and dozes off for half an hour. When he comes to, he picks up one of them, and a piece of paper falls into his lap. Is it a bookmark? He unfolds it. The letter, for that is what it is, begins, *My dear Em*. As he reads it – and it is on one side only – his hand shakes.

He has read, even signed, documents that have changed the lives of men, but what he now reads throws him into turmoil. What should he do with it? It is almost certain that Florence knows nothing about it, or she would not have allowed it to remain in the book.

It is definitely Hardy's hand, and gives the impression that it was hastily written. But why had it not been delivered to the intended recipient? If Hardy had changed his mind about giving it to Emma, why had he not destroyed it?

Part of Lawrence says that he should give it back to Florence, but she might be upset by its contents. The letter is undated, and, therefore, could have been written while Emma had been alive.

Though a letter, Hardy had incorporated a poem, but not one for the public gaze. In it, Hardy is young again, and Emma is full of life, and not a worm-riddled corpse in a coffin:

> *You come to me, <u>my</u> Emma, all a-blush*
> *against the sky's wide, drowsy, roseate flush,*
> *your hair dyed scarlet by the <u>bleeding</u> light,*
> *and beckon me to follow in the twilight's hush.*
>
> *Above your head the sunset's incandescent <u>halo</u>,*
> *your Cornish face suffused and all a-glow,*
> *and though across the landscape slides the night,*
> *with pounding heart your steps I'll <u>gladly</u> follow.*

Several words, however, are underlined, as if he were not satisfied with them. The underlining lacks sureness of stroke, and it occurs to Lawrence that it might have been Emma who had done it.

Therefore, she had read the poem, and known it was a tribute to her. Had *she* hidden it, denied Tom its possession, for some reason?

Lawrence wrestles with his dilemma. The poem belongs to the nation, is one way of looking at it, but what would it do to Florence to hear him speak again? This poem resurrects him. She has read all his other poems, and some have been daggers in her heart, but she has survived. Lawrence looks at the fire. Such important words: they are Hardy's. So, for the moment, he places the sheet back in the book, until he comes to a wise decision.

Back at Max Gate, Florence is smiling, knowing that her gift, hidden in the third book she insisted was worth taking, too, might prompt Lawrence to write again. They are only words, she says to herself, and to me they mean nothing. Nothing at all.

CHAPTER TWELVE

It is a matter of some concern that the Boss insists there should be a burial in Moreton. A cremation, of course, would have been more practical – no risk of exhumation, no rallying point for perceived enemies of the state – but Mills has a major problem: the wishes of Lawrence's family, particularly his mother. It is certain she will want her say, and, despite Mills' responsibility in Operation Sandstorm, there is little he can do until he knows if Lawrence has left specific instructions about his funeral in his will. Then, of course, there is the inscription on the headstone. It should be simple, uncontroversial, Alexander tells Mills, but that is easier said than done.

"There is money if there is any embarrassment. The Boss says Lawrence has, on his own admission, next to nothing saved. My guess is that the Frampton estate will offer to pay, but check – quietly. Handle this one sensitively. We don't want his mother becoming prickly about money. On the other hand, we all know who he was, what he did, and how people will flock to Moreton," says Alexander. "A pauper's burial would just not do."

"I understand," says Mills.

"And we don't want our Arab friends turning the burial into a propaganda coup. It has to be in the best possible taste."

"There will be road checks into and out of Moreton. The Boss will bring his own security, I imagine."

"Naturally. The nation will need him in the coming years. There are things you can do: search the Frampton estate, the church, the Moreton cemetery. There are always madmen who want to make a name by attaching themselves to a national hero."

"Of course. He was more than a Colonel. *Is* more than a Colonel. He has become an icon, and we must use that to help us. Any attempt to suppress his fame will arouse suspicion. But simplicity will be important. By all accounts, he is a man who values that. The service will be at St. Nicholas' church, in Moreton. Cameras will be everywhere, including for newsreel. The Boss must be seen close to the coffin. The cameras will want to capture that. And if it is the wish of his family that he be buried in Moreton cemetery, then the walk is not far. Only the important players must be at the graveside. No fuss. And there must be guards for a day or two. In the twentieth century, Dorset is not known for its body-snatchers, but you never know."

"The Boss won't want to hang about. His wife will be with him," points out Alexander.

"I imagine."

Alexander does not mean to sound critical, but looks at Mills sharply.

"He will need to get back to work. There is much for him to do."

"I know. Oh, and one more thing: I will reserve plenty of spaces for the cars."

Alexander frowns, and says, "You've drawn the short straw, Mills. There are many imponderables. Liaison with Lawrence's family will be a challenge. He is a national figure, and we can't hand the funeral over totally to the family. A bit like when the big guns pulled rank over Thomas Hardy's body." Mills looks blankly at him, and so Alexander continues. "I see a union flag draped over the bier. That should not be a problem. It will promote our values. Reports of all kinds will go round the world. The union flag is a potent symbol. The Boss will be keen to see that."

Mills nods. Used to short straws, he is not one to worry before it is time. He has all the information required to put together a plan, including a map of Moreton he has personally drawn.

On it are marked important places, and the distances between them. The cemetery in which Lawrence is likely to be buried is unremarkable, just as Lawrence would like it. In his early assignments, Mills questioned the morality of what he did, but he now sees it as merely following orders. I am an intelligence officer, he admits to himself, and, one day, I will pay the price.

Mills knows that the best place for the grave is at the far end of the cemetery, which is not very big. There is just enough room for family and important visitors, and the gate can be easily marshalled. All that remains now is to review his checklist, from time to time. The pressure will be on when the deed is done. At Bovington Camp, he has had talks with the Major, who only looks at him on arrival and departure. The Major has identified the soldiers who will monitor the roads into and out of Moreton.

"You need not worry on that score," he says. "They are the pick of the Camp."

"Good," says Mills.

There is tension between them, as there is when soldiers are asked to do politicians' dirty work, but the Major is professional. There are always orders to follow, and that is what he infallibly does.

When Mills goes, the Major takes a document from his desk drawer, runs his finger down a list of names, and puts an asterisk against three. There is nothing to choose between them, but it is Catchpole he underlines. With one stroke of the pen, he engraves into history a Corporal, who will do guard duty.

* * *

Meanwhile, Trilby thinks that his plan is close to being flawless. He studies the Brough, even visits the factory in Nottingham where he can get expert advice. The motorcycle is big and heavy, not designed for swerving, which is helpful. The man to whom Trilby addresses his questions thinks that the company is about to secure an order. Trilby pays particular attention to the steering and handlebars, and they take two motorcycles onto the road, for a test ride. Trilby follows, and it is soon clear that, though the motorcycle is wonderfully powerful going in a straight line, it is less agile when turning corners. All he wants to know is whether it is engineered to react quickly. Just as the representative thinks he is about to close the deal, Trilby postpones a decision, and says he will be in touch.

Now Trilby has a further decision to make: how to verify that Lawrence is dead. There will be little time to hang around. Another pair of eyes is necessary – for his own peace of mind, and in case additional measures need to be taken.

Trilby has worked with two others on several jobs, and both have been proficient, but, for Operation Sandstorm, only Peters will do, being the calmer of the two. If necessary, he can drop Trilby off somewhere, then take the car elsewhere, laying a false scent. No harm done. And Peters agrees to the proposal, though Trilby does not tell him the name of the intended target. However, somehow, despite the high level of secrecy in the SIS, Peters has heard something big is in the offing, and suspects that this is it.

"You just confirm death at the scene," says Trilby.

"Do you really need me?"

"No bullets, no mess."

"So, he's well known, then."

"It's just an accident, that's all."

"Come on, old chap. Hush hush is a giveaway."

"There is a plan. I'd like you there, but if you'd prefer -"

"Just you and me?"

"At the scene. There's nothing else you need to know."

Peters is intrigued. Dorset is not where he normally works. Trilby shows him a map, and explains where and the approximate when.

"So, not too far from Bovington Camp. A military job. Am I warm?"

Trilby nods. There is no use denying it. Peters is an intelligence officer of the highest calibre.

"Who else is involved?"

"You know that's confidential, but once you've torched the car, you're done."

"And that's the last I'll hear of it?"

"You'll read about it."

Peters has learned that, with hindsight, there is always an irresistible logic behind intelligence operations, whatever the degree of danger inherent in them. Sometimes, to ask too many questions about the wider context of a job – he has come to view operations as such – is to invite doubt and insecurity, both corrosive, so he is content to disappear quietly after torching Trilby's car. Peters has lost count of the number of vehicles he has burnt. It is his speciality.

* * *

"You had me worried," says Lawrence.

The woman declines a sherry, needs to keep a clear head. The Major's offer to her is one he insists she cannot refuse. Lawrence listens to her as she recounts what he wants her to do, and how she will benefit if she agrees. There is something not quite right, and Lawrence does not tell her what he is really thinking.

"And that is where I have been," she says, feeling pleased that she has told him everything.

Lawrence, however, is cautious, gives nothing away. It is possible – as he has been one himself – that she is now a double agent. All the descriptors are there: a full confession to gain your confidence, the possibility of gleaning further valuable information, and money enough to turn one's head.

"And did he say why he wanted you to do all that?" asks Lawrence.

"No, but you must be careful. I've told him nothing so far."

"You've turned him down? Don't do that."

Lawrence stops short of saying that she would be useful to himself, too. Things are becoming clearer. This is coming from someone higher than the Major, and has the hallmark of the SIS, and, therefore, maybe Churchill. Lawrence has long since predicted that all this would happen.

"I'll do whatever you want," the woman says, genuine fear in her eyes. But this is not the first time Lawrence has been tempted to let down his guard, so he stays alert.

"Tell him everything I do and say."

"But that is spying on you. I won't do that."

She shudders, so Lawrence tries to make her feel more secure. The death of her father has wrung all her energy from her, and she is not sure she can carry off what Lawrence is asking her to do.

Unless he has misjudged her, Lawrence is absolutely sure she can be of use to him. As long as she comes over to the Major as a *reluctant* informant, she will be safe. Lawrence guesses that the Major, being primarily a military man, will see this as a distraction from proper soldiering. Over the years, Lawrence has seen it, first hand. When lines blur, high-ranking officers curse and become tetchy.

"Take the money, and tell him the truth. Keep it mundane: where I go, what I'm reading."

"He said he'd know if I got up to tricks."

"He's not that clever, but it is true that liars are eventually caught out."

"He also said that you'd try to use me, too, and that I was doing my bit for the country."

Lawrence blinked, and she saw it.

"I won't, but if all this gets uncomfortable for either of us …"

"What?" she asks, genuinely not understanding.

"It's happening sooner than I thought. I don't really want you implicated."

"But I am," she retorts, "and I never asked to be."

"I know," says Lawrence, "and I'll understand if it gets too much for you."

"You don't want me any more?" she asks, tears welling up in her eyes.

He puts an arm around her and draws her to him. Somehow the touch of another human being makes him feel odd.

"It is me they're after, but they'll use anyone to get what they want, and you never signed up for all this."

"Did *you*?" she asks.

His silence is eloquent.

* * *

Occasionally, Lawrence goes back to the book in which he found and keeps the poem he believes Hardy wrote about his dead first wife Emma. It is as if he imagines its existence, or believes someone might have come into Clouds Hill, and stolen it. But it is there, every time he looks.

Then he has an idea: he will copy the poem, and the underlining, in case the original is ever lost. This he does – for future generations, he believes.

As he sits and drinks a cup of tea, he suddenly feels that maybe this is some kind of test, that Florence is playing a game, and will, if he does not return it, upbraid him. He recalls that the book in which he found the poem was the additional one she had added with a strong recommendation. This, he thinks, is her way of conveying to him the burden she must carry – Hardy's spoilt yet enduring love for his first wife. By passing it to Lawrence, Florence preserves the poem but not at Max Gate, and it does not remind her of a time when Tom and Emma were young.

Lawrence resolves to do nothing – for the time being. If challenged, he can deny all knowledge of it, say he had not opened the third book. After all, it was not of his choosing.

* * *

Next on his to do list is the letter to Carrington. In Syria, Lawrence had saved his life. Carrington had volunteered to ascertain if it were safe to go over a ridge, but had not spotted the sniper. Fortunately, Lawrence had.

"Thanks," had said Carrington. "I owe you."

"And one day I'll ask you to repay the debt."

"Anything," had said Carrington.

Now Lawrence intends to remind Carrington of his promise.

The letter is vague, mentions a bit of a reunion in a pub in Wareham. Lawrence has no address for Carrington, and does not want to ring any alarm bells. When Lawrence reads the letter, he rips it up.

Neither does he have a telephone number for him. This frustrates Lawrence. He is out of touch with others in the military, and is not sure whom he can trust. But he rings one or two people, and circumspectly tries to discover who is in touch with whom.

"And what about Carrington?" asks Lawrence.

"Not heard of him in ages," replies an ex-colleague.

"Then he is either dead, or has gone to work in the SIS."

There is a brief silence before the contact says, "One or the other, but no idea which."

That is all Lawrence asks.

A few days later, Lawrence receives a letter from his contact. Apparently, Carrington caught a deadly disease out in India, and died.

Lawrence smiles. A good try, he thinks, but this means Carrington is off limits, not because he is dead, but because someone wants me to think he is. Then I am in a worse position than I thought, he concludes.

When Smith is told that Lawrence has made specific enquiries about him, he is momentarily thrown. He knows, is his first thought, but what draws him to me?

An equally big question he now has to answer is should he tell Alexander? Smith can never forget Lawrence has worked in the desert with him. Yes, thinks Smith, he wants me to know he knows, and now we are all so steeped in plotting that there is no easy way out for any of us.

But the golden rule is: do not panic.

* * *

Lawrence smiles. Do they not know who I am, that I once walked on water as well as sand, and took thousands of Arabs with me? I am invincible. I have executed men before, and will do so again if necessary.

And, Carrington, they may say you are dead, and you may even long for a Clouds Hill of your own, but there is no such thing as an *ex*-SIS agent, and I shall personally supervise your resurrection from the grave. The debt still stands and must be paid in full.

CHAPTER THIRTEEN

L awrence has met Henry Williamson only twice, but there is a strong affinity between them. Of course, Lawrence never tires of hearing or reading about the famous truce, at Ypres, in the First World War, which Williamson experienced so keenly that it shaped his vision of a permanently peaceful Europe.

They exchange letters in which Lawrence learns that Williamson sees Hitler and National Socialism as benign influences in Germany.

"Just think," says Williamson to anyone who will listen. "What can *we* become once we are rooted again in Nature? The prospect of another war in Europe is chilling. I shall go to Germany and ask for peace."

To Lawrence, in particular, he pleads for support: "They will listen to you. You have seen so much butchery in the name of the British Empire that your golden tongue will persuade the powers to find another way. Young Germans are fit and strong, whereas ours are pale and weak-limbed. Sue for peace with me, Lawrence, and we shall have Mosley and his supporters behind us. It is possible to be proud of our country without being bellicose."

Williamson's idealism appeals to Lawrence. At Clouds Hill, Lawrence listens to the owls splitting the night with their screeching, runs his hands down the bark of trees. He likes the tingling sensation on his palms. Yes, Williamson, he admits, you are right, and I am on your side, but I feel that peace is not what the government wants. They won't listen to me. If they can keep me gagged and out of the way, they will. I have always been an embarrassment to them, and I am considered dishonourable because I expected them to keep their word, and give the Arabs freedom as repayment for driving the Turks out of the Middle East. I cannot bear hypocrisy. Yes, Williamson, come to Clouds Hill, where you can scold me about my comments on Tarka the Otter. You and I are too alike for Winston, and you also are probably in their gun-sights.

Lawrence knows that if Williamson comes to Clouds Hill, the press will again converge on it, and that is the last thing he wants, and yet they might just have a role to play in promoting peace. So Williamson must come. There is always anticipation when one opens a letter, but there is nothing like meeting its author in person.

* * *

On his Brough, Lawrence loves the feeling of never knowing what is round the corner on country lanes. There are a few agricultural vehicles and, of course, herds of cows. It is easy enough to hear the growl of the Brough's engine before Lawrence appears, but farmers often send ahead a labourer, who warns oncoming traffic.

One day, Lawrence is making his way goodness knows where when he sees a toothless old man with a big stick in his hand, dressed in what look like recycled potato sacks. The man waves his stick demonically, and Lawrence stops.

"You better pulls over," says the man. "Big buggers on the way. Tuck in here or they bill crush you, 'tis certain."

Lawrence has never met them on his motorcycle before, and says, "How many?"

"Hundreds," says the man.

Lawrence is irked by the man's smirk. Most people stare at the Brough enviously, but this old man, his white hair seemingly untouched by a comb for years, looks at it disdainfully, as if accusing Lawrence of smuggling into Dorset an unwanted symbol of progress.

Lawrence tucks in close to the hedge, and soon the cows appear, heading straight for him. He stays astride the machine, and holds his breath. Sure that he and his precious motorcycle will be crushed, he shuts his eyes. Voices from the back of the herd can he heard encouraging and admonishing the cows. It is Lawrence versus lurching Red Devons.

Miraculously, at the last moment, the cows veer away, their big, dark eyes fixing his, which are now open. Only one cow nudges his handlebar, but lightly. It seems an eternity that Lawrence holds his breath, and he is in awe of the size and power of these creatures. In the road, they deposit their waste, and Lawrence thinks, Oh no! It'll go all over my newly polished chrome, not to mention me!

As the last few pass, there is not a word of thanks from the farmer or his hands. Instead, they stare at him. Lawrence nods, and when it is safe to do so resumes his journey. It is impossible to avoid all the pats pocking the road for at least half a mile. But the experience triggers a memory: I am glad I saw the cows; now I know that I am truly powerless, and not the fearless warrior others think me. Not since I sat astride a camel, stick in hand, our many-coloured banners flapping above our heads, as we charged to take Aqaba, have I been so aware of the power of big beasts, and the frailty of men.

* * *

Albert Hargreaves and his friend leave their bicycles at home. Albert has a puncture, and the other boy's bicycle needs some attention to the brakes, but staying indoors is not an option when the sky is a vibrant light blue, and spring is beginning to show.

The boys have an apple in their pocket, and remember how they gathered the windfalls, and put them in sacks for their fathers. The apples are still plentiful, despite the boys raiding the supply daily. With a stick in hand to clear a path through the dense undergrowth, they set off for an afternoon of rambling, heartened by a gentle warmth on their face, and the prospect of an hour or two of freedom.

Albert says, "There's that mad bull yonder." He recognises it by the ring in its nose and its missing ear.

"Let's go that way. Might see that hawk," says the other.

Both are content to meander where they will. Neither has heard a cuckoo yet, but they have spooked, with their whooping, great clouds of starlings. They see more on foot than on bicycles, and swap ghost stories, and jokes neither knows how to tell because they do not really understand them. It is good that it is Sunday, and that Monday is yet an adventure or discovery away.

"Shall we catch a rabbit?" asks Albert.

"No," replies his mate. "Takes too long."

The longer grass is wet, and soon their shoes and socks begin to squelch, so they agree to return home along the road. They see a gate, and head for it. The gate is tied with string, and they begin to climb up it. On the top bar, they swing their legs, trying to dislodge each other. There is nothing better than to idle away time, at the age of fourteen. Once, their families took them to listen to a band playing in a big park in Dorchester, but they were soon bored. Feeling awkward and packaged in their best clothes, they grumbled, and eventually pleaded to go home. Now they sit on the gate, and savour the quiet, the solitude, their almost secret existence.

That is until they are surprised by the throaty roar of an approaching motorcycle. It comes upon them quickly, and the boys wobble so much on the gate that they nearly fall off. As he passes, Lawrence has only a second to glimpse them. That could have been a deer stepping into the road, he thinks, and a collision at my speed would do none of us any good. He slows down until he is more composed, then the road is all his again.

"Jesus!" cries Albert. "That scared me."

"We would have been killed if we'd been down there."

"The rider, too. You stand no chance at that speed, and he couldn't see us till the last second."

The noise dies away, and the boys slouch home. Each tells the story in his own way.

"That sounds like our famous neighbour," says Albert's father. "Stay out of his way."

"Why?" asks Albert.

"Because he has killed many men, and may kill you. One mistake in the twisting road, and you are all dead."

Alone again, the boys talk about what it might feel like to be dead, but secretly they hope to own a Brough, one day, just like Lawrence.

"I was just thinking," says Albert.

"What?" says his friend.

"It's a good job we weren't riding our bikes when he came."

"True. At his speed, he'd go flying over his handlebars."

* * *

Several days pass, and the longer the woman stays away, the more relaxed Lawrence becomes. As he is not invited to her father's funeral, he does not contact her to enquire if all goes smoothly. There is a chance, he calculates, that if he asks, she will feel compelled to invite him, and he does not wish to expose himself to the public gaze, or to give those with a particular interest in him information they might use against him.

Nevertheless, with her failure to make contact after three further weeks, he fears she might be in some difficulty, on his account, so goes to her cottage. It is necessary to go under cover of darkness, and the cottage sounds empty when he knocks. He does not wish to alarm her, but knocks on her window in case she has fallen asleep. A sign that she is safe and well is all he wants. In his pocket is money she might need. But she is not there, so he returns to Clouds Hill.

On the following three days, he knocks and gets no reply, so he goes to her neighbour's cottage. Peter is wearing his dressing gown. The night before, he could not sleep due to his angina, and he catches up on his sleep in the morning.

He opens his door a little, and says, "Yes?"

Lawrence sees that he has called at an inconvenient moment, and says, "I do apologise. Forgive me, but I was wondering if you could tell me if the lady in the next cottage has gone away for a few days. I am a friend, and have called several times to no avail."

Peter guesses that the man is more than a friend, and does not recognise him. Certainly, he has never seen them together. There is little rural crime, in these parts, but he is naturally cautious, and does not wish to let a stranger know that her house is empty, that its owner has gone away.

"Keep an eye on it, please, Peter," she had said. "I don't know when I'll be back."

Peter had put the tears in her eyes down to the grief she must still be feeling at her father's death.

"Of course. Do you want me to have a key here? You know, just in case?" he had asked.

"No, that won't be necessary, but thank you."

"Is there an address you can be contacted at?"

"There is, but I don't want to have to worry about anything, so the next time you see me is when I get back."

She did not tell him that there is a strong likelihood she will never return, though he guessed that there is more to it than meets the eye when she pecked him on the cheek, and beat a hasty retreat.

Peter looks at Lawrence, and closes the door a little before saying, "She's a grown woman, and can come and go as she pleases without reporting to me."

Lawrence is quick to understand that, though the man knows what has happened, he will not say.

"Then I beg your pardon for disturbing you."

Lawrence returns to Clouds Hill, and tries to read but cannot concentrate. She has gone of her own accord, or has been forced. Either is plausible, and he rarely jumps to conclusions. I did say that if it all gets too much ... Then again, if they have relocated her to provoke a reaction, then she cannot report to them about my to-ings and fro-ings, he reasons. She must have gone of her own volition is the most likely scenario, he concludes. Ah well! I have only myself to look after now.

Then he remembers that he cannot put off a letter he has been meaning to write but has neglected. Churchill knows that Lawrence corresponds with this person, and the world knows that Churchill cannot bear her. This encourages Lawrence, who has something important to ask her and is confident that she will not disappoint him.

He begins his letter, and, by the time he has finished it, has asked far more of Lady Astor than ever before.

* * *

Lady Astor finishes writing her letter to Bernard Shaw before reading Lawrence's. His are usually to linger over, as they remind her that there is a life beyond politics, a spiritual one that gives her the strength to maintain her convictions, no matter how big the feet she treads on.

She sits in her favourite chair by a well-fed fire, and reads. Immediately, she sees that there is no bounce in his sentences, no endearing address such as Milady, which she loved when he first used it. The letter is to the point, and while not desperate in tone, conveys an obvious urgency.

She thinks of bringing him to Cliveden, but doubts her husband would agree to that. Besides, Lawrence specifies her house in Plymouth. He must have a key, and come and go as he pleases, but he does not explain why he is giving her notice that he is now likely to take her up on her long-standing offer of her house as a refuge.

Privately, in other conversations, she has learned of his fear that the SIS are monitoring his every footstep, and suspects that Churchill, of all people, is behind it.

"You don't surprise me. You and I are two of a kind," she had said, after Lawrence's first intimation. "He's had me watched ever

123

since I was elected and slapped him down in the Commons. I see it as a badge of honour, and don't take it too seriously."

Lady Astor then does as Lawrence requests: throws the letter onto the fire, and watches it curl at the edges and disappear. It was what Lawrence did *not* say in it that told her he is sure his letters are intercepted and read. He is not specific in his request to come, at a moment's notice, to Plymouth. There is reference to what she had said about it, when they had last met, and how it was a good idea. This lack of clarity she knows to be a code for things are gathering pace, and that he needs her help.

So, in the spirit of intrigue she has come almost to enjoy when she feels she is engaging the enemy, she sends him a key and no note. She thinks, that will infuriate Churchill, but I cannot bear to think of Lawrence all alone in his tiny Clouds Hill. We are soul mates, he and I, and though it is an enormous waste, I am done with trying to marry him off. Besides, there is not a woman on earth who would put up with his flirting with me, and I am not going to deny that I look forward to his letters. If only the country did not have this dark cloud over it! And if it comes to war, then we shall need men like Lawrence, though we should avoid it at all costs, and that is where Lawrence can do his bit.

She has kept all his other letters. Indeed, there are boxes crammed with missives from all sorts of people: constituents, fellow MPs, relatives. But it is Lawrence's she values the most, knowing they are truly personal.

She checks that nothing remains of his last letter in the grate. At her desk again, she is unsettled. Part of her sees his request to go to Plymouth, at a moment's notice, due to circumstances – and she thinks she knows what they are – as a kind of retreat. Not exactly a sort of running away from the enemy, but not a strategy. Has she encouraged him, or has his retirement from the RAF emasculated him? But she will not desert him, not in his hour of need.

She must inform her housekeeper, and stress the need for discretion. No one else must know he is there. Privacy is everything to him, and, goodness knows, that is hard to come by for someone famous.

In true Lawrentian style, she sends him a telegram, knowing that he will appreciate it. Her assent to receive him is encoded, and she smiles at what she thinks is her cleverness. She wonders if she is not being too complacent, if he will laugh or curse her lack of judgement. The idea comes to her without warning, and she follows her instinct. The telegram reads: **A canny roast awaits you**. She rises and does a little dance around the room. If he does not decipher that, she tells herself, he is not the man I thought him!

CHAPTER FOURTEEN

Charlotte Shaw peers over the rim of her teacup, eyes sparking mischievously.

"What?" says Lawrence.

"Nothing."

Lawrence smiles. In that nothing is everything: her husband's skill, which she had insisted he demonstrate, editing Seven Pillars of Wisdom, the power she feels at refusing to consummate her marriage, and the joy of being free to visit Clouds Hill.

"Then it suits you, this inane grinning about nothing."

"The tea is excellent."

"I've had practice. Bernard was really indisposed?"

Charlotte puts down her cup and saucer; the tea is so refreshing that she does not want to drink it all in one attack. The teapot is big, army issue, brought from the Camp for his former chums.

"He *said* he was."

"And he doesn't mind you coming on your own?"

"I'm a grown woman. The hotel in Wareham is quite adequate, not one of those backward-looking ones that frown at single women."

"But you're not single."

"Pedant. I mean on their own."

Lawrence nudges the plate of biscuits towards her, but she pats her stomach, and Lawrence blushes.

"There's nothing else," he points out. "I live a Spartan existence."

"I didn't come for biscuits."

Lawrence hides behind his cup for a few sips, never copes with face-to-face flirting.

Charlotte loves his frank letters so much that she keeps them under lock and key. Bernard knows they write to each other, and finds it perfectly normal, there being a strong, literary connection between them.

"No, not for biscuits. I don't normally have any in. I'm not good at hospitality, you see. I've lived such a nomadic life that social niceties have never entered my repertoire."

Charlotte recalls that it was she who sorted him out some basic cutlery and crockery.

"I know."

"Of course," says Lawrence, "And believe me, Charlotte, I am trying."

Charlotte pats the seat next to her on the settee. Lawrence obeys, knows that the moment when he must explain the strength of his exhortation to visit is near.

She places her hand on top of his, her invitation to him to open up, and she will do all that she can, even if it is only to listen.

Lawrence leaves her hand there a while, so she is not offended by an instant recoil, but, after a minute or so, slides his hand away to pick up his tea.

"It's all the letters I've put out there. When my time comes -"

"Don't talk so. Middle age is no age at all," Charlotte protests.

"I'm being practical. This new life I have, this curse I must bear, has been shaped by what has happened, and how the world sees me will depend upon what others say about me."

Charlotte is slightly irritated by what she considers to be a little self-indulgence, and finishes her cup in a business-like manner. The cup rattles in its saucer, and Lawrence knows she is nettled.

"You can't stop others talking about you when you're dead and gone. Not even you can do that."

Lawrence is superficially wounded by this barb.

"But you see, Charlotte, I am worried about the ammunition I have given them. I fear that many of my letters are in the hands of the Secret Intelligence Service or collectors hoping to make money out of me by writing my unauthorised biography."

"So what? Let go. What you've written and sent is now out of your control. As for your letters, I keep mine under lock and key."

He feels calmer for her reassurances. She is so much wiser than me, he thinks. Mother would not be so understanding.

"Why do you keep them?" he asks.

Charlotte looks away. There is no use denying their special place in her heart.

"No one writes like you. I suppose it is the ease with which you communicate. You seem to know what I like to hear. There's no stuffiness in *your* letters. They are conversational. You might well be in the room when I read them. You are a fine writer."

Lawrence is embarrassed by this high praise, and says, "More tea?"

He stands before she answers, lifts the pot in anticipation of an affirmative answer. Charlotte pours milk into her cup, which she offers up to him. The tea sloshes into it, and each thinks what to say next.

"Thank you. This tea is so refreshing. I must write down the blend."

"The letters were meant for you alone. Will you burn them?"

"I shall not."

She smiles teasingly, making him feel more vulnerable.

"I have written so many that my legacy is in danger of -"

"Legacy?" she interrupts. "Stuff and nonsense and pomposity! Your legacy is already assured in the hearts of the people. Seven Pillars is your crowning glory, and worth a thousand times more than your letters."

Lawrence knows what she means, but because he has written it, it has become his death warrant, and he has signed it himself. Now that the version of events people will believe to be the truth exists, he is more powerful and persuasive than ever.

"No, Charlotte. You don't understand. Seven Pillars is an enormous accusation, indelible evidence of how we raised the Arabs' hopes as high as Mount Ararat, and them smashed them in Paris, the best opportunity of all."

He goes to a box, and takes out photographs he has never shown her before. In silence, she looks at them, and knows what he means.

The early ones seem to agitate her, and Lawrence says, "Do you recognise anyone?"

"Oh yes," she says. "They are men posing in chairs round huge tables. I'd recognise them and their like anywhere."

There is nothing that Lawrence can say that can change her views on the grey men in dark suits. Such images, of course, are familiar to her, but she has never seen any of Lawrence, and if she has, she has forgotten them.

"Paris is such a long time ago, but there I sowed the seeds of my current anxiety."

Charlotte continues to examine each slowly, and adds it to the pile she has begun. It occurs to her that he has gone to great lengths to acquire them. There are so many, clearly taken by different photographers from all the delegations, and she does not wish to look at them all.

"Are there many of you in the box?" she asks.

"Keep looking."

Soon she comes across one. Emir Faisal is in the middle, hands clasped just below his dagger he ensures is on full display. Lawrence is wearing his military uniform and an Arab head-dress, and is looking over Faisal's shoulder.

"Magnificent! Wonderful!" she cries, looking closely at Lawrence's smile. "You knew exactly what you were doing." The smile is half for the camera, half for himself. He has never noticed before, but he can see clearly that he is trying to gauge the reactions of onlookers.

"I knew the message I wanted to convey, but I did not want the effect to ripple down the years. I would do the same again, but these photographs have made me enemies on these and French shores. Some of these haunt me."

"Burn them. I will do it if you can't."

"No."

"Because they show what a great fellow you were?"

Only Charlotte can get away with saying that. It is partly true. He cannot deny it.

There are other photographs, some with important-looking men in long coats and tall, black hats. Lawrence tells Charlotte that he was careful to ensure that Faisal was always in the middle of the group, and that he himself was standing behind Faisal's left shoulder, showing his support.

"Faisal is so handsome," remarks Charlotte.

Lawrence is concentrating on the photographs, and says, "You will note that I have no photograph of us with David Lloyd George, Clemenceau, Wilson or Orlando. They were careful to avoid that, at all costs."

"But not as beautiful as you," adds Charlotte, taking Lawrence's hand and kissing it.

"You flatter me."

"Of course. But is this not Gertrude Bell? What on earth is a woman doing promoting Arabs in this world full of scheming men interested only in their own nations?"

"You should have been there, Charlotte. You would have done the rounds to greater effect than me. But I doubt even you could have stopped France gaining control of Syria."

"Have you any photographs from the Cairo Conference?"

Lawrence dips into the box, and eventually tips the photographs onto the floor.

"This is Winston and Clementine on arrival. Our plan was approved, and some of my promises to Faisal were kept, but there were mistakes. Winston passed the buck to me – after the best chance had gone in Paris."

"Darling, you cannot be blamed. The Arab rebels fighting in Mesopotamia could never have been made to obey Faisal as a ruler."

Lawrence looks at Charlotte, and says, in a strangled voice, "You mean well, but it was not the plan I wanted. It was too little too late, though Winston still insists it was the best we could have hoped for."

"He needed you. No one else could have done better."

"But all these years on, the vultures are gathering. They think I am an ass, that I am not on their side. There's not a Jew in the whole world who has a good word for me."

Charlotte opens her arms and wraps them round him. As she rocks him, he says, through tears, "I am on the side of justice," and Charlotte says, through kisses on his head, "Of course, you are, my darling. Of course, you are."

When she has quelled his sobbing, she turns to building his confidence by praising Seven Pillars. She repeats her husband's critique: that it is a fine piece of writing, regardless of the painful truths in it, as good as anything he has read. Lawrence raises his hand feebly in protest, but knows that is Bernard's genuine opinion, having heard him express it himself.

"So you see," argues Charlotte, "that you must write, write, write. Isn't that what you really want to do? Follow your instinct. You must."

"But don't you see that I can never reach that height again? It was not Oxford that taught me how to write like that. I was proficient enough before I went up. It was my involvement in the Middle East that gave Seven Pillars its flesh and bones. One is always affected by such experiences, and is never the same."

"You mean, the cream always rises to the top? There is something in what you say, but you still need talent to write like that. Let it drop, this self-flagellation. It is beginning to drag you down. You'll earn money from writing again, but choose a noble theme. You've done war. Try love, unrequited, preferably. You'll find it stretches the plot a little further. But, of course, you're well enough read to know that. Have you tried poetry?"

He considers showing the new Hardy poem to her, but thinks better of it. He has one he wrote, the week before, and excuses himself to fetch it from downstairs.

It takes a minute or two to find it, and he reads it to himself. She will, no doubt, praise it to the rafters, even though it is nowhere near Hardy's standard. It is too learned, with unnecessary, classical allusions, and lacks genuine, human emotion. However, let her see it. She will soon understand his hesitation to pursue poetry.

When he returns, Charlotte is sitting, at an angle, on the edge of the settee. Lawrence cannot see her face, which is turned towards his gramophone. Her fleshy, pink shoulders are bare, and her unbuttoned blouse has fallen from them, down to her elbows. The poem now seems unimportant. When she had been rocking him in her arms, he had smelt lavender water. In her plumpish cocoon, he had melted into her, as he had his mother, when a young boy.

"It's my shoulders, you see. A touch of rheumatism, perhaps. I don't know, but would you ease the ache? I would have Bernard do it, but he scowls and refuses. I've stopped asking. Anyway, he isn't here. My physiotherapist has me lie on his couch, but this settee will do. The leather is soft."

She looks over her shoulder. His face is a picture. He should refuse, but how can he after all she has done for him?

"The poem ..." he begins.

"Later."

She beckons him with her head, but not seductively. That would not work. We all need physical contact, and, Heaven knows, I have lacked that, she reminds herself.

Enthralled, Lawrence goes over to her, almost holding his breath. She takes his hands in hers, and places them clumsily on her shoulders. Her skin feels hot, and he presses his fingertips lightly on it. "Harder," she says, and when he complies, she deliberately interprets that as an instruction to lie on the settee, on her front. Lawrence hopes he can be as professional as her physiotherapist. She murmurs appreciation, guides him left and right, up and down, and soon he knows how best to please her.

In a few minutes, however, he becomes aware that she is not moving. Her right arm has slipped over the side of the settee, and, for a moment, he wonders if she has died. Then she snorts, confirming that she has fallen asleep. He nips downstairs, fetches a blanket, and covers her. In his chair, he watches over her as a parent a sick child. He looks at his hands, and the tingle in his fingertips feels like the one he experiences when he rubs tree bark.

Her snoring settles into a rhythm. What will she do and say when she awakes? There is something decadent about him watching a voluptuous, sleeping woman, he thinks, but what would Bernard think? Nothing, probably. And Lawrence wonders about his friendship with her, asks himself how it has developed to the stage where he can ease her pain, and she his.

When she awakes, she looks at him with one eye, and lifts the blanket. He goes over to her, and she makes room for him to come back into the cocoon. His back to her, he, too, sleeps again, her warm breath between his shoulder blades.

This time, it is Lawrence who awakes first, and he does not move for fear of disturbing her. She lies against him, her arm hanging limply over him. There is no feeling of guilt, on Lawrence's part. He sees it as an act of kindness to a suffering friend, but what if she wants this new intimacy to continue?

He feels her stir, and is glad. She reaches for his hand, and intertwines her fingers with his.

"You sent me to sleep," she says.

"That is what most women say!" he jokes.

"I mean with your hands. The ache has gone."

"There is no charge."

"But a debt to be repaid."

Lawrence sits up, and looks down on her. Her hair is flattened on one side where she has been lying on it. She maintains eye contact while she buttons up her blouse.

"How long have we been asleep?" he asks, looking at his pocket watch. "Guess."

"Half an hour?"

"An hour."

"I feel better."

"I'll make fresh tea. Can I offer you ..." but he cannot remember what food he has in.

"I told you, I didn't come for food."

She kneels and starts to put all the photographs back in their box. As he watches her, he envies Bernard, but is puzzled why, though they are married, their relationship has faltered in this way. Lawrence does not know what is missing between them, but considers the relationship between Charlotte and himself to be perfectly natural. Yet he does wish she would burn all his letters – without delay.

In her hand, she holds back one of the photographs.

"May I keep this? You are so handsome in it," she says. "It could go on the sideboard."

"What would Bernard say?"

"Nothing. He won't even notice it's there."

So Lawrence agrees. It is the least he can do for the time she gives him.

"Keep it."

Charlotte then tells him she is going to make another pot of tea, and insists Lawrence stays where he is.

"It's my turn to be Mother now."

And Lawrence is quite content to admit that Charlotte is more than a run-of-the-mill friend. Much more, more than letters can tell.

CHAPTER FIFTEEN

So you are not dead after all! thinks Lawrence. He puts Field Marshall Allenby in his seventies, though the image he retains of his former, now retired, commanding officer is of a younger soldier, immaculately attired, moustache trimmed short. Lawrence imagines Allenby saying, "We could not have taken Damascus without you. And it is my pleasure to meet you again. I have not forgotten you."

Lawrence reads Allenby's letter for a second time, knows how highly Allenby rates him. This time, Lawrence detects something unsettling in the concise expression of his invitation to dinner. There is an attempt to sound pleased at the prospect of meeting him again, but also a lack of enthusiasm expected from someone who has not been in touch for a long time. London, too. Why at a restaurant in Camden? Lawrence has never heard of it. Mean sod, he thinks. No slap-up dinner at The Dorchester, then. Furthermore, he has signed the letter Bloody Bull, his nickname, instead of Allenby.

For the next hour or two, Lawrence revisits the letter, knows how keen Allenby was for him to head up the Secret Intelligence Services, after the war. "There is no one else to touch you. I'll speak up for you. We need someone like you," Allenby had said. Why did I turn you down? wonders Lawrence. You who helped to shape the Middle East.

Allenby is decisive, clear in his communications, but this letter is untypically taut. He knows Lawrence will spot the absence of genuine warmth. So Lawrence takes the invitation seriously, and sets about decoding the real message, starting with methods he shared with officers he could trust. Allenby was one of them, and there it is, the warning. Lawrence takes the first letter of each word in the very last sentence: **D**o **a**nswer **n**ow **G**ermany **e**nrages **r**elentlessly.

There is no address to which he can send a reply, and this tells him that he has no choice, no time for questions. He must turn up at The Camden, at 7.00pm, Sunday next. Knowing that Allenby trusts him to work out how imperative the meeting is, Lawrence decides to go on his Brough. He is less recognisable on England's roads than on public transport, and can come and go as he pleases. There is no chance of him returning to Clouds Hill afterwards. A mechanical failure in the dark, and the overnight closure of petrol stations, would be disastrous.

Sunday comes soon enough, and he sets off early. He had contemplated leaving on the Saturday, and taking a room for an extra night, but he does not wish to spend money unnecessarily, it being in short supply.

The guesthouse he selects has a rear yard, where he stands his motorcycle. In Camden, no one bats an eyelid at his precious Brough.

"Is The Camden far?" he asks the porter behind the front desk.

"No."

Lawrence expects him to give its exact location, but the porter does not expand until prompted.

"Where is it?"

The porter stares at Lawrence's blue and blood-shot eyes, and is intimidated.

"Down the road, third left, second right, and you can't miss it."

"Thanks. And my room?"

"Follow me."

When they get there, the porter opens the door, and switches on the feeble light, which washes the simply furnished room brown. Lawrence steps inside. There is no need for him to check that he has all he wants; his life has been without material comforts, and these are the last things on his mind.

"Is there anything else?" asks Lawrence, when he sees that the porter is loitering.

Lawrence is tired, wants to sleep before his dinner with Allenby, and forgets that it is customary to tip.

"Nothing," says the porter, closing the door noisily behind him.

Lawrence sleeps for three hours. In his bag is a change of clothes. The shirt is more creased than he would like, and he wonders if the guesthouse has an iron, but he simply hangs it up. He knows that Allenby, in normal circumstances, would be immaculately turned out. All his years in the British Army have taught him the importance of high standards in all he does. Yet given the strain in his prose, and the choice of place to meet, Lawrence suspects that Allenby will be attired to ensure anonymity.

Lawrence washes in tepid water, for which he is paying more than he would like. In the morning, he will use that to negotiate a reduction. In his clean clothes, he does not feel too bad. Usually, he nicks his chin, as he shaves, but, miraculously, he escapes unscathed, despite the fact that he has come without his leather strop. While crossing the desert, he had used his precious water ration to shave, to the amazement of the Arabs, who put it down to him being an English gentleman, but he had said, "No, you are mistaken. I must go into battle looking my best!"

"Do you have a key to the front door? I may be late," he says to the porter.

Without speaking, the porter slides one across the counter. There is brief eye-contact between them, and Lawrence makes a note to complain to the proprietor. There is no excuse for such surliness.

After a quick check that his motorcycle is safe in the yard, he sets off for The Camden. Even in the darkness, it is possible to see that this part of the district is faded glory, and he begins to wonder how two such prominent war heroes have come down to this.

The maître d'hôtel greets him and checks the bookings, and cannot find the name Allenby. How stupid of me! thinks Lawrence. He would never use his real name. Fortunately, Allenby has been keeping an eye out for him. Their table has an uninterrupted view of the entrance, and Allenby steps forward to greet him.

"This is the guest I was telling you about," says Allenby to the maître d'hôtel. "He'll have water, I think."

Lawrence smiles. Allenby remembers that he does not drink alcohol.

They shake hands briefly, as if they have only just seen each other, the day before. Allenby indicates an empty chair. The dining table appears to be his desk, and the restaurant his office.

Lawrence notices that Allenby moves a little more stiffly, but there remains that unmistakeable purposefulness in language and movement.

"Your billet far from here?" asks Allenby.

"Five minutes on foot. Nothing flash. You know me."

Lawrence sees that Allenby's smile is forced.

"I've already ordered for us. I hope you don't mind. It's on me."

"That's kind. Not a conventional reunion, then, tonight?"

Allenby looks round the room. It is safe to talk, but he does not begin, as their meals arrive. Why the rush?

"Not exactly. You see, though it is a few years since we actually worked together, I have never forgotten you. You know how I valued your loyalty as well as ability. But those days are history. Gone for ever."

He picks at his roast beef, while Lawrence sets about his with a vengeance.

"But you didn't bring me here to tell me that."

"No, and you know from my letter that I would not bring you all this way simply to buy you a meal. The fact is, Lawrence, that though I am a man of leisure, these days, you never actually leave the Army. You may have discovered that already."

"I've tried to leave, but my past barks at my heels like a rabid dog."

"From time to time, I hear things. It's inevitable. Mostly, it's inconsequential stuff, but sometimes I hear something I cannot ignore."

"About me, you mean."

"Yes, about you."

Just then, the waiter returns to see if everything is all right with their meal.

"Do you have any mustard?" asks Lawrence.

"Certainly, sir."

They only resume their conversation when the mustard has been delivered.

"I'll come straight to the point: they are out to get you," blurts out Allenby.

"I know," says Lawrence. "I've known for some time."

Allenby chews slowly. There is nothing wrong with his beef. Indeed, Lawrence devours his as if he has not eaten for a week.

"I thought you might. You know, if you'd followed my advice, and thrown your hat into the ring, you'd have been Head of SIS, with your finger on the pulse of these matters. As it is, they're now out to eliminate you. Disappear, Lawrence. Don't you have a place you can go? Surely, you have a Bedouin tent somewhere."

Lawrence is irked by Allenby's simplistic view of the possible ways of avoiding certain death, and of his love for the desert.

"I live at Clouds Hill now."

"You know it's come from the highest level, don't you?"

"I expect so. He's not fussy whom he kills."

Allenby looks surprised, but Lawrence is sure he knows. It is the most open secret of all who claim to know Churchill personally. Lawrence believes that Allenby knows too, and that George Smith-Cumming suffered a similar fate.

"I don't understand."

Lawrence puts down his knife and fork for emphasis.

"Stop pretending. We're all caught in the same web. Now it's my turn. Winston, of course, won't bloody his own hands personally. You are exempt because you kept your nose clean, and were – *are* – the archetypal military leader."

"The Army needed both you and me. You were the maverick, I the commanding officer, but I haven't dragged you all this way to rake over the ashes of the past."

"Who told you I was next in line?"

Lawrence resumes eating, and Allenby shakes his head.

"You know I can't tell you that."

"Why not? You've brought me all this way to tell me only half the story? You want to save me, so tell me, do you know anything else? The how, the where, the when? Come on, sir, give me a fighting chance."

The use of sir re-establishes a connection with the past. It was not planned, but Allenby welcomes it.

"All I know is that you'd better leave the country. I can't name my source, but he's reliable."

"Intelligence?"

Allenby does not reply, so Lawrence takes that as a yes. Lawrence realises that there is nothing further he can prise from him. They finish their meal, and decline a dessert. Allenby pays the bill, and asks for his coat. There is mutual understanding that they need to keep their meeting focused. There is a moment when Allenby insists Lawrence goes first, but Lawrence wins the day.

Lawrence follows closely, and when they are out in the deserted street, Lawrence orders, "Keep walking, and then turn into the doorway on your right. Don't look round, even if you're sorely tempted."

Allenby feels the barrel of Lawrence's pistol between his shoulder blades. If Lawrence pulls the trigger, the bullet will go straight through the heart.

In the doorway, Allenby puts his hands on his head while Lawrence quickly searches him. Allenby says nothing during the search, but assesses the likelihood of Lawrence shooting him as high. Lawrence's finger is on the trigger, and the barrel is now sticking in Allenby's chest. This is no time for heroics. Everywhere is felt, and Allenby winces when Lawrence rummages between his legs.

Then the moment of immediate danger passes, and the gun goes back into Lawrence's pocket.

"I expected no less. I trained you well. Is it loaded?" Lawrence shows him the bullets in the chamber. "I see. And if I'd had a gun?"

"I'd have killed you."

"You always were a ruthless bastard."

In the poor light, Allenby cannot see him suppress the birth of a grin.

"I'll take that as a compliment, sir."

"I'm not looking for gratitude. I've always had a soft spot for you. When you walked in the War Office in Cairo, I always felt better. Some of those intelligence officers couldn't hold a candle to you. *I* should die before you."

"I'm truly humbled, but I'm more of a prodigal than reliable son, and I'm apt to disappoint, these days, I'm afraid."

Then the lights of a car flood the road. Both men watch it slowly stop in front of them. Lawrence's finger is on the trigger. Is this a trap, after all that Allenby has said? Allenby senses Lawrence is edgy. The hand in the pocket says everything, but this is the cab Allenby ordered, earlier in the day.

"It's for me. Can I give you a lift back to your bunk-house?"

"I'll walk," Lawrence says.

Though he is convinced of Allenby's motives, he prefers to make his own way, and watches the low loader drive into the night. Allenby did not offer his hand, knowing that Lawrence was glued to his pistol.

When the car is out of sight, Lawrence doubles back to The Camden. The maître d'hôtel recognises him immediately, and wonders if he has forgotten something.

"No, I was wondering if you could let me know in whose name our table was booked. Mr. Allenby and I enjoyed our meal, and would gladly recommend you."

The coin Lawrence offers does the trick.

"Certainly, sir."

Lawrence stands close to the reservations book, so that he can see the names. The light is subdued, and the maître d'hôtel works his way down the bookings with his forefinger.

"The name that's written here is Hugh Sinclair."

"Thank you," says Lawrence. "Of course."

"My pleasure," says the maître d'hôtel obsequiously.

Lawrence does not return to the guesthouse the way he came but finds an alternative, more circuitous, route back. Behind him, he senses a follower, so stops, and waits till the possible threat has passed.

There is no need to use his key as the front door is unlocked, and the porter is sitting there, reading a newspaper.

Without speaking, Lawrence places the key on the counter. The porter looks smug, as if he knows something he should not, and bids him goodnight.

Lawrence opens his bedroom door, and enters. The light bulb buzzes when it is switched on. The next thing he does is lock himself in. Damn! he curses. I never checked the Brough, but I am too tired now. Then he goes over to his bed, and sees a piece of paper on his pillow. He reads it, and discovers that he needs to be on his guard, not let things slip. The note is written in jest, but Lawrence is sad that Allenby has exposed his deteriorating standards:

You told me your digs were not more than five minutes away on foot. My cab-driver knew this place to be the only one near The Camden, and he brought me here. I asked the

porter if I could leave you a note, and it cost me a shilling.
You booked in the name of John Hume Ross. A bit silly that!
I could have paid him ten bob to let me wait in the dark for
you, and I could have shot you, the moment you walked
through the door. This time it's me. The next, it could be
your assassin. I came in good faith. Remember that, if not
your training.

Yours ever,

Bloody Bull

The next day, Lawrence negotiates a reduction for the tepid water, and then retrieves his Brough, on which he is glad to roar away.

"Strange bloke," the porter tells the chambermaid. "Face rings a bell. Don't get his sort staying here. Took no breakfast. A dead-ringer for someone, but I just can't think who. Polite in a threatening way, if you see what I mean. Can you change the sheets, please?"

The chambermaid trudges up the stairs. On Lawrence's bed there is another note, and she reads it. The handwriting is florid, and it takes her a while in the dim light to decipher it.

Down at the counter again, she gives it to the porter, for whom it is intended, and she watches his lips move as he reads it.

A mile or two out of London, filled with a great sense of escape, Lawrence laughs and shouts demonically into the wind, but the gibbering porter, behind his desk, does not hear him, and trembles as he has never done before. Lawrence waves his hand in the air, as if he is wielding a sword, flashing in the sunlight, at an invisible enemy, and hacking him to death.

"You going to tell the police?" asks the chambermaid. "He can't get away with writing that. What you do to upset him?"

The porter does not answer. Has he not agreed to a reduction for the tepid water? In his trembling hand is the unexpected, threatening note.

"I ought to."

"Then do it," encourages the chambermaid.

"I can't," stutters the porter.

"Why not?"

"Because he says he's killed hundreds of Turks, and he's got away with that, hasn't he?"

"But you're not a Turk," she says.

"I know, but what difference does one lousy porter in Camden make? No actual crime has been committed. Listen, girl. Do you know what this word means?"

The chambermaid reads in the note that Lawrence has removed the testicles of many sheep and goats to make a meal in the desert. She stumbles over the word testicles, not having understood its significance, the first time she read it.

"No."

"He's implying that I was close to becoming like those sheep."

"Oh," says the chambermaid. "Then it's a good job he's gone! Now, I'll make you a strong cup of tea, so you just sit a bit."

"Thank you, dear," says the porter. "Who would have thought that? Truth is, I never knowed who he was."

The chambermaid looks in the guest book, and says. "He's John Hume Ross. That's who he is."

"Well he's not, and I'd be disappointed to be threatened by a madman who goes by that name."

The porter then points to the signature on the note.

"T. E. Lawrence? Am I supposed to know who that is?"

"It's Lawrence of Arabia, not any old murderer! I've been trying to think where I've seen him. It's his eyes, you see. They're a dead giveaway. Blue as the Med, they say. Not that I've ever seen the Med, but once seen, never forgotten is what I hear."

The chambermaid shrugs, never having heard of him or his culinary expertise in the desert.

For the rest of that day, the porter jumps whenever the front door opens, fearing that Lawrence has returned to keep his promise to emasculate him, and, after a few days, when the porter's fears have gone, he is proud to tell his story. Indeed, the proprietor is so impressed that he considers having a plaque mounted on the outside wall, marking the building where T. E. Lawrence slept the night.

The porter is a slow reader, who usually flits from page to page of his newspaper. Had he looked more closely on page two of the one he keeps below the counter for quieter moments, he would have seen the photograph of his recent guest, caught in an aggressive pose at Clouds Hill. He might also have read the accompanying article written by a reporter called Stephenson, who claims to have had his jaw broken by him.

CHAPTER SIXTEEN

L awrence inhales the cold morning air, at the top of the hill, and sips his hot tea. He has taken it outside as a dare to himself, as he feels he has unwittingly slipped into a rut, and needs to introduce variety into his routine.

The list of people to whom he owes a letter is daunting, and he has almost given up hope that he will ever catch up. Besides, the cost of postage is prohibitive on his now slender budget. The day before, he had sat down and made himself look at his financial position, which he knows is dire. There is no short cut to replenishing the coffers by writing. Inspiration cannot be turned on and off like a tap, and when he has consciously tried to compose, nothing worthwhile has been produced.

He decides that a popular edition of Revolt in the Desert is not the answer. Seven Pillars, as it was originally composed, is becoming more emaciated with every abridgement. Lawrence would sooner lock it away, and never set eyes on it again, rather than reduce it to a pale imitation of the Oxford version. Sometimes, he regrets ever rewriting it, after he left it at Reading Station, and it was lost. There was a time when he was sure that someone would ask for a huge sum of money for its return, and he decided that he would not pay a penny. Since then, several people have suggested to him that, subconsciously, he had really wanted to generate more publicity for it in the national press, and that the idea had backfired when it was not returned. He always denies that this was the case, but often wonders whether life would have been simpler if he had not rewritten it.

He turns three hundred and sixty degrees, and feels himself immensely lucky to live at Clouds Hill, with Pat, ever-reliable Pat, just over the road. Few people have what Lawrence has, even if they have more money. So today he will luxuriate in Clouds Hill. There are jobs he can be getting on with, and he will set about them soon, and his treat will be an hour's run out, in the afternoon, after which he can read to his heart's content.

He begins by sharpening his axe, and oiling his tree saw, both bought cheaply at Bridport market. There is something especially satisfying about preparing the axe, and then hearing the steady rhythm of the thuds as he fells a tree. The sound reverberates around the hill, and reminds him occasionally of the distant firing of big guns. Pat often tells him that he has heard him chopping and sawing, and wonders how Lawrence can keep it up for so long.

"Economy of movement, exploitation of swing. If you push it, you get no further than if you let gravity have its way," explains Lawrence.

"Sometimes, it sounds as if you are at war with the woodland," says Pat, suspecting that for Lawrence it is therapy, as well as replenishment of his stocks of wood for the fires.

After sharpening his axe, he wanders, tries to identify growth he can use. Soon, he becomes aware that he is stalking a victim, and is excited when he finds one. Using his saw, he cuts up the wood into pieces that will fit easily into his grates. He is careful to remove twigs from the faggots, like a butcher preparing a joint of meat for a valued customer.

The physical act of chopping, sawing, and stooping to pick up, erases most of Lawrence's thoughts. He asks himself if this is all he wants: simple self-sufficiency, as humans have always practised. If he throws himself into a *modus vivendi* requiring little money, he feels he will be happier, might even ignore the press, who still turn up at Clouds Hill.

When the logs are piled up inside his garage, he feels more secure. They should see him through to the summer, when they will be burnt only on unexpectedly cold evenings. They have cost him only the effort of harvesting them. Now he can reward himself with some Elgar, while he closes his eyes, and drifts away to Worcestershire. Then the water will be hot enough for a bath.

The music ends, and Lawrence begins to doze in the bath. Some sensor within him jolts him back to full consciousness, and as he convulses, he kicks out, and splashes water over the side. He had been thinking that if she had wanted him to know where she was, she would have contacted him by now. Occasionally, her disappearance returns to upset him, and invades his dreams and waking moments.

He feels so glowing, after his bath, that he decides to go to Sherborne, where there is a good bookshop, someone mentioned, and it is some time since he last visited the abbey. Given his lack of funds, he should not spend too much on books, but he considers them an investment in his mental well-being. Without them, he is nothing.

On his way to Dorchester, he takes blind corners far too quickly, but his *joie de vivre* is greater than his need for self-preservation, that day. Soon he reaches Dorchester, then goes through Charminster, and on to Cerne Abbas, where he stops to see the priapic giant. Many times, he has tried to guess its origins. His love of history tempts him to intellectualise its significance, but his imagination persuades him that it is more an expression of humour than a tribal warning to others.

On the outskirts of Sherborne, he is tempted to visit the castle, but finds instead a teashop, where he eats a slice of apple-cake, and drinks tea. All this is so far removed from life at Clouds Hill that his habitual anxiety evaporates.

"Is the abbey open today?" he asks the waitress.

"Might be, might not, though, no doubt, it is probly writ on the door," she replies. Her smile suggests she thinks she has been helpful, but Lawrence is none the wiser.

However, on the next table, two schoolboys in uniform overhear his exchange, and one says, "Yes, sir. There was no service on when we passed. It's open."

"Thank you," says Lawrence. "You have no lessons today?"

They look at each other sheepishly, and finish their drink hastily. Is Lawrence a master they do not know? The prospect of lines for skipping lessons prompts them to leave before their helpfulness gets them into trouble.

Lawrence casts his mind back to his time at Oxford High School, but cannot remember if he ever absented himself from lessons. I doubt it, he concludes; I would have remembered the thrashing.

A world of learning awaits the boys, yet they skip away from it. There has never been a time when Lawrence has tired of expanding his mind, either at school or university. He considers himself lucky. With the odd exception, he had inspiring masters, and believes he might be of some use in a school like Sherborne, be able to give something back to the system that gave him a priceless education.

After his tea, he strolls to the abbey. A service has taken place, that very morning, and he enters, and looks up at the vaulting ceiling. On his travels, he has often visited archaeological ruins, and gasped at the skill of the architects and builders, and now he is in awe of the beauty created by the many stonemasons who built the abbey. He feels secure in the warm womb of golden stone, and though his heart feels untouched by God, he is inspired.

He strolls down the aisle, marvels at the windows. There are two other people there, and he nods to them. He thinks they look more European than British, as they do not understand the nod but look at him oddly, as if they think he has an unfortunate facial tic.

Lawrence's exit coincides with that of many boys from lessons. For him, it is a marvellous sight. The boys chatter animatedly, and he feels somehow more alive for coming across them. A master follows them, and sets Lawrence thinking that he himself might have something to offer them. His love of history and knowledge of ancient civilisations are, he believes, as great as anyone's, but do I have the patience, the energy to enthuse them? he asks himself.

He approaches the master, and asks the name of the Headmaster.

"Alexander Wallace. Relatively new to Sherborne. Promising. Most promising."

"And how do I find him?"

The master gives him convoluted directions, and Lawrence thanks him profusely. Lawrence surprises himself when he knocks on the door, but he has faced death, and a polite enquiry does not intimidate him. The corridor has the sweet scent of pipe tobacco and wood polish, and he is transported back to his tutor's room at Oxford.

"Come!" is the call.

Lawrence opens the door, and Wallace looks up from his cluttered desk.

"I don't think I know you," he says.

"I'm Shaw. I've come to ask you whether you require a Classics or History teacher. I've never taught before, but feel I can be of use."

"You have no teaching qualification? I'm afraid our masters are extremely well qualified. What is your background?"

Lawrence almost freezes. Some economy of the truth is required here, but he has always been able to think on his feet.

"Oxford High School and the University of Oxford."

"So you're an Oxford man."

"I am, indeed."

Wallace offers him a seat, then asks his secretary, in the next room, to fetch the Head of Classics from the Senior Common Room. While they are waiting, Wallace tries to find out more about his visitor, and is fascinated by his vivid descriptions of Karachi, Aleppo, Paris, Cairo. Lawrence makes clear that he has travelled when in the British Army, but does not elaborate on his role. However, he knows they will find out whom he really is soon enough, and decides he will be truthful, when the time comes. He has been found out before, and the shame that follows the duplicity is most uncomfortable.

The secretary confesses to the Head of Classics that she does not know why he is required, and he wonders whether he is trouble. Lawrence stands when the master enters.

"Ah, there you are. Come in, come in. This here is Shaw, who is looking for a teaching post. He's History and Classics, an Oxford man before he joined the military. Currently, Shaw, there is no vacancy, but someone we know is close to retirement, and might be persuaded to go early. Still, that is pure speculation. Have a chat, the two of you, and then we shall see where we go from there. Meanwhile, there are a few matters to which I must attend elsewhere. There is always something to do at Sherborne. Always!"

Lawrence smiles. This is not how he had envisaged his day, but a salary in exchange for some of his wisdom might be just what he is looking for.

"I'm not a qualified teacher," begins Lawrence, believing he ought to make that clear at the outset, "but I am a Classicist, and know Middle Eastern history quite well."

"A man after my own heart. Now then, where shall we begin?"

They talk about the Roman and Ottoman Empires, and Lawrence takes him through the great classical, literary works so thoroughly that the Headmaster, on his return, has to remind his colleague that his class awaits him.

"Well?" asks the Headmaster, outside the room.

"A brilliant mind, but we can't touch him. The governors would not tolerate it. He would be an unwelcome distraction, I fear, despite his obvious intelligence."

"What on earth are you talking about? He's an Oxford man. He knows his stuff, doesn't he?"

The Headmaster is becoming annoyed at this unexpected obstacle, there being nothing he would like more than to see the early departure of a master who falls asleep in lessons, and has taken to drinking craftily when the boys are not paying attention, which is often.

"Oh, yes. He can run rings round me, but don't you read The Times? Extraordinary that such a figure should want to work at Sherborne. Apparently, he's out of favour in high places, even though he's a bloody hero."

"The Times?"

"Yes, Wallace. The Times, no less. He may be Shaw but he's also Lawrence. There are rumours that he's for peace, at all costs. The governors would see him as subversive, a bad influence on the boys."

"Well, we can't have subversion at Sherborne. It is true that we have a close association with the rule of law, and we are patriotic. But put me out of my misery. I have to go in there and, if what you say is true, let him down gently. Who is this Shaw that has turned up unannounced?"

"It is no less than Lawrence of Arabia. Shaw is his adopted name."

Amazed, the Headmaster shoos the master off to his class.

"Ah, Mr. Shaw. I've had a word, and we are most impressed with your intellectual abilities. Our boys would certainly benefit from your tuition, but I'm afraid to say there is no vacancy. I've been to see the colleague to whom I referred, and he's adamant he wants to stay till the summer. So I'm afraid I'm going to have to disappoint you, on this occasion," says the Headmaster, when he has made up his mind to avoid the adverse publicity that would ensue if he appointed Lawrence.

Lawrence smiles weakly, can do nothing but accept the decision. In Wallace's eyes, however, he sees a hint of regret. If truth be told, Wallace quite likes the idea of shaking up the Senior Common Room, but it would come undoubtedly at a high cost – his own position, which he values above everything else.

As he goes out into what feels like a brighter day than on arrival, Lawrence can hardly believe that he has been rejected following an impromptu interview. There is some consolation in the fact that he lacks a formal teaching qualification, but he is nevertheless hugely disappointed that his substantial knowledge of history and the classics are not able to persuade the Headmaster that he is worth employing in some capacity. But by the time he witnesses the schoolboys' horse-play on the green in front of the abbey, at lunchtime, he begins to feel that he must have forgotten what it was like to be that age, that his powers of empathy have waned. Indeed, he concludes that, though he has been turned down, he has had the narrowest of escapes.

He finds the bookshop he has heard is an Aladdin's Cave, and enters. Immediately, he feels more secure. The sounds of the street are locked out, and the piles of books, some as tall as himself, afford him the privacy he would be denied in the classroom. The bookshop has several rooms found by leaving the one into which he entered from the street. It is so quiet that he might be the only one there.

Where to start? He holds his nose to a stack of plays by Shakespeare. Ah! That unmistakeable scent of ageing vellum soothes his soul, and the disappointment of rejection vanishes.

"Just in," says a woman, who has popped up behind him. "Looking for anything in particular?"

Lawrence is so surprised that he loses his balance, and is forced to grab the small bookcase containing what looks like a complete set of Dickens.

"I did not see you," explains Lawrence.

The woman smiles. Her face is that of a friendly owl, and her nest, where customers pay, is behind ramparts of books yet to be placed alphabetically on shelves.

"I dropped my bookmark. I heard you come in, but I was on my knees, almost within touching distance of it." She brandishes the strip of leather she fashioned from the tongue of an old battered boot. "But, dear me, I've lost my book now!"

Lawrence assumes she is the owner, and is amused.

"You have plenty of others from which to choose."

"Indeed. One can never have enough books. Some days I even have to *make* myself part with a book to a buyer. You see, my books are my children. I have a very big brood!"

Lawrence laughs and says, "Only they don't make as much noise or answer back like real ones."

"Well, I concede that they aren't noisy, but they do answer back in their own way."

Lawrence thinks he understands, and agrees.

"They certainly provoke."

"Are you a fiction man? Poetry? Or drama, perhaps? We also do maps and biography. I'm quite happy to show you where things are, but people prefer to come across things by chance. It's part of the fun."

"I'm content to just browse, if I may."

The book-seller gives a cry of delight at rediscovering her book, and lets Lawrence begin his adventure. The real pleasure for him is touching the books. He likes to run his fingertips down the spine, like a blind man reading Braille. Some pages have deckle edges, which he likes especially. There are familiar names wherever he looks, and he is so enraptured by their titles that he wishes he could swap places with the book-seller. He would be safe behind the defences she has built. Of course, he does not look for any book about war, but comes across many, and there are references to him in almost all.

The pity is that he would have to build an extension at Clouds Hill to accommodate all the books he wants to buy and read, and he cannot stretch to anything like a first edition of Collins or Stevenson. So he must choose carefully. His purchase will be a compromise between the appeal of the text and a modest budget of five shillings, four if he decides to have a bite to eat before returning to Clouds Hill.

He settles on a small edition of A Pair of Blue Eyes, by Hardy. The title amuses him. On the first page is a dedication, and he wonders how the novel has found its way into the shop. He cannot imagine it is so poor a story that someone would wish to sell it. After all, it is by Hardy. As a matter of principle, one never sells Hardy after reading him.

"An excellent choice!" the book-seller enthuses.

"I think I've read all the others."

"A man after my own heart."

Lawrence blushes at this establishment of a connection between them.

"Have you a bag?" she asks. "They say rain for later."

He tries his coat pocket, and the book fits.

"Perfect!"

He pays and takes the change. There is little more to say, but the book-seller smiles widely, which Lawrence interprets as a wish to say something more. When she does, he breaks the habit of a lifetime.

"Come round the side," she invites. "Believe it or not, there is a desk I work on."

Lawrence squeezes through two piles. She opens a book entitled The War in the Desert, by an author of whom Lawrence has never heard.

"Will you sign this for me? Perhaps, you could write a little message for me, something like, *I came, I saw, I conquered,*" she proposes, her mischievous grin disarming him.

"*Veni, vidi, vici,* as per the original? I don't know your name, though."

"Better put it in English. My name's Tilly Bates, but just write, *For Tilly, with love. I came, I saw, I conquered.* Then put, *T. E. Lawrence, your Arabian knight.* That's with a k!"

She giggles, and Lawrence follows her instructions to the letter.

"There!" he says. "Done."

At the door, she calls. "I think you're marvellous. *Bloody* marvellous."

Out in the street again, Lawrence thinks, if you say I am, who am I to argue?

Inside the bookshop, his admirer clutches the book to her breast, and says, "He must have known my heart was a desert, and now there is an oasis in it, and I shall drink from it whenever I am thirsty."

CHAPTER SEVENTEEN

Lawrence hears a knock on the door. Trained to be suspicious of unexpected events, he quickly fetches the Colt he keeps by his bed, at night, and never far away from his hand, during the day. He becomes a cat, and walks almost on tip-toe, silently, wanting to give the impression that he might not be in.

It is mid-morning, not the usual time for taking someone by surprise, or for clandestine activity, so Lawrence calls to his visitor, "Hello? I won't be a moment. Who is it, please?"

The delay in answering suggests something is not quite right, but he eventually hears, "Morning, Mr. Lawrence. It's Special Branch. I'm calling about your security here at Clouds Hill. It's my understanding that you've put in a request for protection."

The voice is clear, friendly, and business-like, and Lawrence wants to believe that the stated reason for coming is genuine, but he knows there are many ruses enemies might use to gain access to him.

"And your name?"

"You know I can't divulge that, but my orders are from the highest authority."

"Are you on your own?"

"Yes, sir."

Lawrence is not fooled by the easy use of sir, and is not yet satisfied that it is safe to open the door.

"How did you get here?"

"Car, sir. I don't drive personally, but I have a driver. Perhaps, you would like me to step back to a position where you can speak to me more comfortably. My hands are on my head now, as you will see if you open the door."

"Just you and your driver?"

"Yes."

"And there is no sniper on the hill, waiting to take me out, the minute I open the door?"

"No, sir. As I said, I've come to discuss your protection, not your assassination."

When Lawrence hears footsteps on gravel, he knows the man has moved from the bare soil in front of the door, yet Lawrence hesitates, prompting his visitor to say, "My instructions come directly from Walter Thompson, whom I believe you saw on your last visit to Chartwell. He told me you'd be ultra-cautious."

Lawrence tries to recall the man who sits outside any room Churchill graces with his presence. As a bodyguard, Thompson is Churchill's shadow. No, Lawrence has no recollection of Walter Thompson, at Chartwell.

Lawrence opens the door, and points his Colt at the man with his hands on his head. The man does not flinch, and says, "Search me, if you like. I'm clean."

"Then you are not Special Branch," says Lawrence, letting the man see that his finger is on the trigger.

"My gun's in the car. Walter said you'd shoot me if I had it on me."

"He's right."

"May I come in? I want to tell you our thinking on round-the-clock police protection. Walter says you might be twitchy about it, but has it on good authority that you've written to ask for something to be done about the press and the threats from other hostile groups. There's been damage to your property, I believe."

Lawrence lowers his gun. If there is a sniper on the hill, then now is the time to kill me, he thinks.

"You'd better come in," he says, convinced that the man from Special Branch is genuine.

He turns his back on him, and lets him into his cottage.

"Cosy," the man says, as he passes Lawrence, who is pointing the way up the stairs.

"There's just me."

Lawrence offers to make tea, but the man declines, and explains that time is pressing.

"Intimate," he observes, looking round the room. "Our information is that there has been damage to your roof, and that you can't go about your business due to harassment by the press. We'll post a uniformed officer at your gate. Naturally, the officers will work shifts. They have been told not to speak to you unless there is an issue related to your safety."

"You mean I can't make them a hot drink?" asks Lawrence.

"They will work shifts of four hours, to maintain maximum concentration. There won't be time for refreshments."

"A bit harsh, but I understand. Local police?"

The man is disappointed that Lawrence asks questions he should know will not be answered.

"I'm afraid I can't comment. If you have any problems, ring this number. You won't be able to speak to me directly, but I shall visit you when I receive a message."

"I see."

"The protection begins today at 2.00pm."

"Will the officers be armed?"

"Yes, and trained to shoot to kill if necessary."

Then they are not routine police officers, knows Lawrence. They are more likely to be from the Army but dressed in police uniforms. Dorset Constabulary is not known for its shoot-to-kill policy.

Lawrence thinks that though the reporters are a nuisance, they do not deserve to die for a missing roof-tile or two, and he conveys his concerns.

The man then reveals more details behind their operation.

"The fact is, sir, that there are others who would do you harm. I can assure you that our measures are appropriate for the level of threat you face."

"Intelligence turned anything up?"

The man does not confirm this. Lawrence really ought to know better. Is he so ring-rusty that he expects such openness?

"You should proceed with caution, sir. It will come as no surprise that Zionists see you as a threat to their ambitions for a Jewish state. There are also people in the Middle East who are disillusioned that more was not done for them. I hope you don't mind me being frank, sir. You'll understand, I'm sure."

"It is not Arabs or Jews I fear," says Lawrence flatly.

The man does not comment. Lawrence must content himself with the suspicion that Special Branch has become involved because of specific intelligence.

"I will, of course, co-operate, but I will not be a prisoner in my own home."

The man has nothing further to communicate, and they do not shake hands.

Lawrence escorts him to his car, and, as promised, a police officer is delivered to Clouds Hill at the stated time. In his arms, he cradles a machine gun, confirming Lawrence's theory that he is being protected by soldiers and not police officers. Wanting to start on the right foot, Lawrence merely nods to him, and is sure that, though no verbal salutation is exchanged, the officer moves his head slightly in acknowledgement.

Pat Knowles is just thinking about what jobs he has to do, that day, when Lawrence makes his presence known.

"Come in," says Pat. "Drink?"

"Yes, please. I've come to let you know that there is a uniformed presence at my gate. He has a machine gun, so don't argue with him!"

Pat goes straight to the kettle, and calls, "I've no intention of arguing with anyone today."

Lawrence wishes he was more like Pat but is not, and, therefore, Pat has a therapeutic effect on him. It is Pat's acceptance of him as a global celebrity that binds them as loyal friends to each other.

Pat carries in the tea tray with his customary concentration. There is a packet of biscuits on it, but Lawrence does not like to presume they are for him.

"Help yourself," invites Pat, eventually.

Lawrence takes two, and hot tea follows. Standing on no ceremony, he dunks his first. For a moment, he is back in the barracks with his mates, daring himself to leave the biscuit in as long as he can without losing the submerged half.

"Just what I need," he says.

"Help yourself," Pat repeats. "I shan't manage them all myself."

Pat knows what is coming. The signs are all there: an impulsive arrival at an unusual time, for Lawrence; the barely controlled agitation; the announcement of an unforeseen event. So when Lawrence throws his arms up in the air, and allows his hands to fall and slap his thighs, Pat awaits the declaration he knows is imminent.

"That's what I like about you, Pat."

"What, precisely?" asks Pat. "I shall sit here and listen as you rattle off my many qualities."

Too tense to appreciate Pat's gentle humour, Lawrence says, "It's just that you are so content with your life."

"It's not always been a bed of roses."

"Mine is now an overgrown patch of tangled briars."

"As you're retired, you should be more contented. Give it time."

"That's just the point, Pat: I can't. I've danced with the devil, and I think he's demanding the last waltz with me."

"Be positive. Look what you've achieved."

"None of my achievements has brought me security. Some people, though, have made a fortune out of me. Look at Lowell

Thomas. He dogged me for months in the desert, and made thousands from his film of me. Then add to that all the glamorous photographs …"

"And you never posed for them? Never felt you were preparing the way to immortality?"

"It was all for the cause, Pat, I swear. Every single, last click of me was to bring to the world's attention the plight of the Arabs."

Pat senses that Lawrence is now being sucked into the quicksand of negativity. Let him go where he wants, and I'll roll with it, is Pat's policy, at such times.

"I know you never did it for the money. You don't have to persuade me of that."

"You're right, Pat. One does not think of wealth when sand is in your face, and bullets are whistling past your ears. But Thomas' film has toured the world. Think how my life might be now with just a tiny fraction of the revenue from it. Allenby, too, has had nothing except his Army pension."

Pat has no wish to come into conflict with Lawrence. There is clearly unfairness in the fact that such a self-promoting man as Thomas, with the assistance of his cameraman – Harry Chase – can exploit Lawrence's fame with impunity. However, Pat wants to encourage Lawrence to look forward. Constantly dwelling in the past serves no purpose.

"You can't change any of that. Try to take from the reality what you can. Your name will endure eternally, and your deeds will be remembered in a thousand years. Do what makes you happy: write. In the name of every God in the hearts of all men: write as only you can."

During Pat's exhortation, the shadow of the consequences of his friend's opposition to the government grows ever darker.

Lawrence sometimes looks at himself, in photographs, films, and posters, with incredulity. The images are of an *alter ego*, and there are so many of them that it is a miracle that Pat sees him as a man changing wardrobes for specific purposes, and not one in an endless search for a true identity.

"But it's this living on tenterhooks, in a perpetual state of high alert, that exacts a toll. They will strike when they can take me by surprise. I always tried to collect the best intelligence about the enemy, but I had troops, at the time. Now there is just me. Oh, I have one or two who tell me what they have heard, but there is never anything concrete. When I left the RAF, I was prepared to accept that there would be a transitional period, but Clouds Hill should be unassailable, and, from Day One, it has been anything but that."

Pat sighs. There is nothing he can do but listen and put a gloss on circumstances. What he cannot do is restore him to full mental health.

"Take joy in small things," Pat advises philosophically, as if he has himself found the secret of true happiness. "A cup of tea, a biscuit, the first word of the first sentence of the first paragraph of the first chapter of the first volume of the greatest story ever written."

At last, Lawrence smiles. The idea that he can alleviate his depression with a biscuit is ludicrous, but he does not want to hurt Pat, who is genuinely concerned for him.

"I try, I really do, but my head is so full of maps and boat designs and orders given by incompetent officers in the Tank Corps and RAF that my brain is cluttered. That is when I feel most worthless. Tell me if you think me arrogant. Was it arrogant of me to think only good would come of standing by Faisal and his people, when I was up against not only the Turks but the global interests of the British Empire?"

Pat is no judge of this, being what he considers to be an ordinary, Dorset man, with his feet firmly on the ground, and suspects that Lawrence's survival depends on letting go of whatever did not go his way.

"No, it wasn't arrogant, but we live from second to second, minute by minute, and so on. Is it not time to forget all those maps of other places? Draw a new one. Start with Clouds Hill in the middle. Add to it all the places you like in Dorset. It will be smaller than the map of the Middle East, but it will anchor you here."

Lawrence looks at Pat gratefully, and feels that he does not deserve his friendship. Drawing the map would be easy, but how does he tell Pat he does not know where to mark the spot where they will kill and bury him? And he does not dare tell him that he does not have the strength to go to war again.

"You make it sound so simple, Pat. I should only ever listen to you, and not all these voices whispering in my ear."

Pat automatically replenishes the cups when Lawrence goes to take a drink and finds his empty. Lawrence leans forward to pass it, and feels the weight of the Colt in his jacket pocket, but he does not let Pat know it is there. What man would take a gun into his best friend's home without permission?

"What voices?" asks Pat.

"Williamson, Mosley, Lady Astor. Others."

"And what do they whisper?"

"Temptation. They would have me go to Germany to see how Herr Hitler is restoring pride to a damaged Germany. Williamson, particularly, sees him as the saviour of a decadent Europe."

"And you?"

"I am a thorn in the side of our government, who trace my every step, read every letter I send. *I* am the enemy. I imagine they see our little group as fascist."

Pat nearly suggests Lawrence should go to see a doctor, but what can pills do but send him to sleep? If only he could settle to something on paper. Lawrence himself knows why he cannot, and when Pat returns to that theme, Lawrence says, "Whenever I search for the first word of a new story, I am filled with a disturbing narrative that will not sit quietly on the shelf, and I know that someone else will write the final chapter anyway."

The conversation turns this way and that. Lawrence even expresses relief that as he has no wife or children, he will, at least, leave no widow, or children fatherless.

"Who knows? You're a relatively young man. There's still time for a family," remarks Pat.

Embarrassed, Lawrence shakes his head. How can such a man offer stability to loved ones when he is used to living in lots of different places?

"I don't think so. I've led too Quixotic a life to contemplate that."

"You have no regrets on that score?"

"What is the point? I am what I am."

From Lawrence's tone, Pat sees they have strayed onto uneven ground, and changes the subject.

"Is there any chance your hunch is wrong?"

Lawrence does not want to tell him about Allenby at The Camden. Pat is going to have to take his word for it.

"None. That is why I carry this," replies Lawrence, patting the Colt.

Pat is puzzled about the armed police officer. Why would they go to the trouble and expense of assigning a guard if they wanted Lawrence dead? Surely, they would just shoot him, would they not?

"No, they would not. Bullets are messy, and the lines of enquiry would drag in people who want to stay out of it. If bullets were the answer, I would be dead by now."

Then the rattle of machine gun fire jolts Lawrence from his sedentary position. There are three bursts loud enough to make him throw himself flat onto the floor. He takes out his Colt, and his hand shakes. With his empty hand, he holds onto the rock. Above, a buzzard drifts in circles. Pat looks on helplessly as further machine gun fire causes Lawrence's head to sink into his neck and shoulders.

Deciding that he cannot stay there, Lawrence crawls to Pat's door, and Pat watches him open it and, in short spasms of movement, go into the lane.

"Thanks for covering me. Did you get any?" he calls to the guard outside his cottage.

"Who?"

"The snipers on the ridge."

The puzzled guard looks at Pat, who takes his friend by the arm, and leads him back to his house.

"Come on, old chap," says Pat. "There are still some biscuits left, and I'll make a fresh pot of tea."

"You just get one look at them sometimes. Thanks for covering me," Lawrence says again to the guard.

Pat goes along with it, anxious to get Lawrence to safety, where he can manage his trauma more easily.

"I don't think I got any of them. Still, we all have an off-day, don't we, Pat? All of us. It's target practice for me tomorrow. I'm losing my touch."

"We do, indeed," Pat agrees.

Pat takes the Colt gently from Lawrence. How his hand shakes! he notices. Lawrence fits himself tightly into Pat's chair. They cannot see me here, he thinks. None of them. Except that damned buzzard, who will have my flesh soon enough. But not today. Not in the endless desert. There, Colonel Lawrence is invincible.

CHAPTER EIGHTEEN

Lawrence contemplates the absence of real happiness in his life. Flitting to London and the Midlands to escape the pursuit of persistent reporters is anything but pleasant. Yes, he loves the thrill of high speed on his Brough, but he can never forget that he is running away from someone.

Lack of money is now the main source of stress in his life, and reminds him that he can no longer be as philanthropic as he used to be. Being single, he never hesitated to give it away to anyone with a desperate, genuine need of it, and he expected nothing in return. Years ago, he selflessly sacrificed two thirds of his daily pay to help the sister of a friend.

* * *

Greyham Bryant leads him round the edge of the dance floor, Lawrence still throbbing from the exhilarating motorcycle ride that has taken them to Skegness and back, that day. The band plays a jolly tune, and the hall is a mixture of RAF personnel from Cranwell, and women from Newark, some of whom have connections with the base. Greyham scans the floor for pretty girls. Lawrence loves the music, less so the raucous gatherings of young men, hair slicked back, in their freshly ironed uniforms, and trying to pick out a girl for the night. Local men resent the effect the RAF image has on women, all of whom would prefer a uniform to a butcher's apron from Newark, but a pound of stewing steak has its compensations when you belong to a large family that needs feeding.

"Ruby's here somewhere," shouts Greyham into Lawrence's ear, as Lawrence leans forward.

Lawrence nods. The drummer beats out a quickstep, and he clicks his fingers to the rhythm. His body absorbs the sound, and moves to interpret it. No great dancer, he is in the mood to make the most of the evening. It has been a good day, and excitement in a dance hall rounds it off perfectly.

"It's hot in here," he remarks.

"I'll get us a pint of mild," says Greyham.

"I'll have a shandy, if you don't mind," says Lawrence.

"Shandy? On a Saturday night?"

"A Brough can be dangerous in the hands of a drunken rider. I'm happy enough with a shandy."

"As you wish. Wait here. I won't be a minute."

The number finishes, and women brush past Lawrence so closely that he can smell their strong perfume, and is reminded momentarily of the heady scent of a backstreet in Aleppo. There he is, early evening, in the growing crowd, his senses bombarded with the unforgettable sounds and sights of merchants, and the aromas of herbs and spices wafting from windows high up on buildings giving protection from the yet fierce sun. Now, back in the dance hall, one or two women give him a furtive glance as their bodies press against his. It is not difficult to understand what their eyes are saying, and he looks vaguely to the far side of the hall, where one man curls his arm round the waist of a woman in a blue dress. He bends down to her, and whispers something so provocative that she slaps his face. His friends laugh, and eventually so does he, but the shame of rejection stings longer than his cheek.

Greyham returns with the drinks, and says, "Ruby's on her way."

Her brown dress is faded; it is the only one she has now. She had two others, but they had seen better days, and she had cut them up to make dusters and dishcloths. She is, thinks Lawrence, rather thin, and plain in an attractive way. Unlike her two friends, she wears no jewellery. In her face are the unmistakable signs of the life of the suffering maid Greyham had described.

Lawrence waits to be introduced. There is no nearby table on which he can place his shandy. Greyham is proud of the fact that he has brought her to live at Newark, where he can look after her. An orphan, she was acutely unhappy in a family indifferent to her basic human needs, and when he saw how thin she had become, he rescued her.

"This is Ted, Ruby," says Greyham.

Lawrence offers his hand, and Ruby takes it in hers, which is hot. His grip is rather too weak for a Cranwell man, but she likes his face, which, she thinks, is unlike any other she has seen in Newark. Too good for me, and a bit lah-di-dah, the way he speaks, but decent enough, she thinks.

"Ted is a motorcycle buff like me," Greyham tells his sister.

Ruby is too young, inexperienced, to make small talk, but she is saved when the band starts to play a tune slow enough to convince Lawrence that he can manage a shuffle with her on what suddenly becomes, as if by magic, a floor with no room for fancy steps.

Greyham keeps an eye on them. Lawrence is the perfect gentleman, and asks her what she now does.

She sighs, and says, "I used to be a maid, but it didn't work out. I do a bit of this and that, but nothing regular. I want to be a secretary. The trouble is, the course is too expensive, and I've no money. Greyham is as good to me as he can be, but there are no bottomless pockets, these days."

Lawrence has heard her story, in graphic detail, from Greyham, and feels great sympathy for her.

"Yes, these are difficult times."

She moves a little more closely to Lawrence. That evening, she has been asked to dance only twice, once by a man who unashamedly asked her if she wanted to go outside with him, and by another who was twice her age and reeked of beer and cigarettes. She knows Lawrence is different, having heard her brother speak of him at length, and feels safe in his hold.

"You do the same here as Greyham?" she asks.

"Not allowed to say. We sign an oath not to talk about our work," explains Lawrence.

"Well, Greyham tells me most things he does."

Lawrence laughs, and says, "It's a good job you're not a spy, then."

"I'm his sister!" declares Ruby.

"I know. It was just a little joke."

"Oh," says Ruby. "I bet you think I'm stupid now."

"Not at all. I'm sure you'd make a smashing secretary."

She shakes her head. Living on a meagre budget has dented her confidence so much that she has almost given up thinking about it.

"A secretary's a good job, in a nice, clean office. Not much to ask, is it?"

"Not at all. Don't give up hope. Follow your dream, and something will turn up."

It does – with a little help from Lawrence. By the end of the evening, he makes up his mind to help her financially. Anyone else and Greyham would question their motives, but Lawrence, he knows, is philanthropy personified, and, after Greyham mildly protests, and sleeps on the idea, he shakes his hand. They discuss how they will let Ruby know, and Greyham thinks it best if he himself raises the subject with her.

"It must be for a short time only. She must stand on her own two feet, like the rest of us," he says. "It's awfully decent of you."

"I'll have it sent directly from my salary. She'll need new clothes, I imagine, and to enroll on a good secretarial course."

"The fact is I can't do what you're offering to do for her. How can I ever pay you back?"

"You don't have to. I won't accept a penny. There is one thing I ask, though: no one else should know of this. People do not always look favourably on this type of arrangement."

Greyham is puzzled, so Lawrence explains in simple terms: "She will not be a kept woman. That is not my intention, but some may comment on any material changes they notice. There are gossips that stand on doorsteps, keeping an eye out for her comings and goings. Poverty does that. You must have seen it. That's how some women survive. They don't do it for the love of it."

"I see," says Greyham, comprehending Lawrence's concern. "Let me speak to her. I'll have to tell her the truth, of course."

"Yes, whatever you think."

"And she must meet you, from time to time, to let you know how she's getting on."

"She's not a project, Greyham. I don't want her to think she has to report to me. Just let me know if she's making a fist of things. But we should speak, Ruby and I. This is something she has to feel comfortable with, too."

"All right," agrees Greyham. "I'll see her."

He takes Lawrence to her lodgings. Ruby already has her hat and coat on, and does not invite them in as she does not want Lawrence to see the penurious state in which she lives. Over the road, a woman is standing on her doorstep, watching Greyham tuck Ruby's arm into his, and tutting.

"Afternoon!" he calls to the busy-body.

Ruby tugs on his arm, not wanting trouble. The street is full of people, like her, struggling to get by, to find enough kindling to have ten minutes by their fire, or enough beef dripping to spread on a slice of toast.

She thinks Lawrence might be there because he has taken a shine to her, and she is a little wary.

"What do you think of him?" her brother had asked, when he had told her they would call for her to discuss an important matter.

"He's not from round here, you can tell."

171

"Inverted snobbery!"

"Such big words! Far too big for me."

"Did you like him at the dance?"

"I suppose so. He's handsome enough. You're not match-making, are you?"

"No, but he's a kind man, and wants to help you. Just listen to what he has to say."

"I will," she had said.

Lawrence says he will treat them all to a cup of tea and a scone, and they find a shop near the marketplace. There is an air of unspoken business, and when they are on their second cup from the large teapot, Lawrence begins.

"Ruby, Greyham has told me all about your circumstances, and, to get right to the point, I hope you'll let me do something to help you."

It is hard for Ruby to look at him, but she does not want to let her brother down, so holds her head up.

"Thank you," she says, not understanding what he is really offering. "That's very kind."

"Your secretarial course, and a few home comforts to make life a little more bearable. That sort of thing."

She looks at Greyham for confirmation that it is money Lawrence is offering, and Greyham says, "It's a chance to do things, Ruby. It won't come this way again. There are no strings attached. I'd bite his hand off if I were you."

Ruby can hardly believe her luck. Her life has been so lacking in opportunity that she cannot summon the pride to turn him down. She feels numb rather than grateful. Life has relentlessly imposed vicissitudes on her, and she does not find it difficult to accept his offer.

"Well, if you're sure you can spare it, that would be helpful."

"And you will enroll immediately?" asks Greyham excitedly.

"I'll enquire just as soon as I've finished my tea."

Lawrence sees that Greyham is keen for her to begin, but makes it clear she can do it in the coming days. Looking at her, he notices there is something missing: that look of hope that accompanies a stroke of good fortune. The smile he supposes is what she intends lacks the usual definition expected at hearing good news. As she takes a bite of her scone, there is a degree of restraint normally reserved for something less sweet. The fact that his offer makes possible other opportunities to eat in a teashop is lost on her, and she does not refer to any plans the money might encourage.

Greyham points to the strawberry jam on her chin, and she glances at Lawrence, who makes her a little nervous. She is not sure what her brother sees in him apart from his shared love of fast motorcycles and the RAF.

They all get along fine, though the men are conscious of the decision that has been taken, and limit their reference to everyday matters. Greyham feels he ought to pay the bill, and Lawrence allows him, to avoid appearing too beneficent.

On the way home, Greyham takes Ruby's arm again, and Lawrence notices how protective he is.

"Thank you," she says, when they arrive at her lodgings.

"I hope it helps you," says Lawrence.

"I'm sure it will," says Greyham.

On their way to their motorcycles, Greyham says, "You know, you can pull out, at any time."

"A few months will make such a difference, enough to put her back on her feet again."

Greyham sighs, and points out that she has never been on them in the first place, and that confirms to Lawrence that he is doing the right thing. All he asks is that Greyham keeps an eye on her, sees that the money is well spent.

"Of course, I will, but she's good at making ends meet. She's had to be – all her life."

Lawrence makes the arrangements for two thirds of his daily pay to be sent to her, and Ruby leads a much changed life, one closer to that she might have had, had she not been so unlucky.

* * *

173

Years later, there are days when Lawrence makes himself put all the money in his wallet and pockets on the table. He knows that he should take a more mature interest in budgeting, but procrastination has led him to neglect things, and to being haunted by Micawber's mantra that if you spend more than you have, you will be extremely miserable.

He knows, by listening to his body, that he can last the day without eating again. There are several edible items he can call upon, if he is seized by uncontrollable hunger, but he decides that he will spread them over the next few days. There is no immediate need to spend any money. But more than that, he must rise to the challenge of self-deprivation. This has been missing from his life for a number of years. The exquisite restraint that only a desert campaign can impose had made him feel he could do anything. It had sharpened his will, and now he must find it again.

The fuel for his motorcycle is an unavoidable expense. There are sacrifices to be made, but he cannot give up his jaunts. In a way, they are as good as food to him, energise him, so that he feels all things are possible.

So the challenge he sets himself is not to spend a single penny for a whole week. His fuel tank is nearly full. If I cannot refrain from spending for seven days, then I am a shadow of my former self, as I went months without spending anything on my personal comforts, during the war, he reminds himself.

That is what makes us all soft, he contends. We are not abstemious enough. Unless we suffer, we cannot atone for our sins. Pain alone adjusts our moral compass.

He leaves his money where he can see it. When he goes out, it will stay there, not because he does not trust himself but because he does. He trusts himself to control his appetites. Those coins, which he builds into a pyramid, are a memorial to his self-denial.

On his settee lies his Colt. He usually warns his armed guard when he is about to fire at a target, up the hill, behind the cottage, and Special Branch has told their man not to speak to him unless there is an emergency. The guard always acknowledges with a slight tilt of the head when Lawrence shows him the gun as a declaration of his intention to practise. Now, on the settee, Lawrence picks up the gun, and will not warn the guard that he is about to fire it. He chooses a shot to the head, knowing that no one can survive it. Standing up or sitting down? He laughs. What the hell does it matter? So he sits on the settee, and points the gun at his right temple. The metal is cold. There is no last thought for loved ones. He is only too glad that the blood will not splatter his precious books, which are downstairs. There is no suicide note. His hand starts to shake as he lightly presses the trigger. He closes his eyes, and pulls it. The gun falls from his hand and clatters on the floorboards.

The last of the breath he has been holding is quietly released. It is a dead man's whisper.

"I can do it," he says. "If I have to, I can bloody well do it."

CHAPTER NINETEEN

It is time for Forster to visit Clouds Hill again. He has been extremely helpful to Lawrence, even when he has been almost unbearably critical of his writing. There has always been something in what he says that resonates.

Lawrence recalls the first time Forster came. Chastened by his critique of his writing, Lawrence has learned so much from him, yet is still gripped by a paralysis of the imagination.

Each thinks the other an oddity, but there is a mutual, intellectual attraction. Forster is open about how much work is still needed on Lawrence's prose.

"The secret – at least, what I think is the secret – of whipping meaning into shape is to trust words to try and live together. Put words you think have nothing in common side by side. They will, in good time – believe me – make their compatibility, or lack of it, known to you, after a day or two. They will leap off the page, and trip up on your lips, be better off further down sentences," explains Forster. "Take The Mint, for example. You convey what you and your chums did, and how the officers treated you, but where is it all leading, my darling? Nowhere, I'm afraid to say. I wish it were."

Lawrence laughs at Forster's mock-horror at the lack of narrative direction.

"But you are a novelist," Lawrence reminds him. "I wanted to tell the truth."

"Only to a certain degree. There are bits where you use your imagination to raise the scene and characters above the prosaic, but not enough. A little truth can be sacrificed for the sake of a bit of taking the reader by the scruff of the neck, and shaking him into excitement."

Lawrence shows Forster his collection of books. There are one or two oohs and aahs, but also periods of silence when Forster is underwhelmed by the titles on the shelves.

"You are an interesting fellow!" exclaims Forster. "But you could do with a few more of the great novelists of the last century. You must be keeping mine under lock and key!"

"I have been more a man of action than words," explains Lawrence, "and yours are on the top shelf. As you can see, I don't have time for alphabetical order."

"But Seven Pillars is a poem, Lawrence. It might start off by being boring – forgive me, but it's true – but it becomes one of the greatest narrative poems I've ever read. And a few people out there possess it in one of the most beautiful editions ever made."

Lawrence thinks of Hardy, his innumerable verse forms, the way he matches them to mood and content, and his heart sinks. Grateful for Forster's praise, he is nevertheless conscious that Hardy is on a higher plane.

"There are poetic phrases," acknowledges Lawrence. "That's just me trying to find a form in which to write."

"What about your Odyssey? Your translation is wonderful," insists Forster, "and as a physical object it is beautiful."

Now that Forster has embarked upon a journey to keep Lawrence writing, he will not give up easily, but Lawrence remains over-critical of his own work.

"You don't understand: I do not make enough from my writing to live on. That is the truth and the pity. Praise alone does not put bread on the table."

Forster is now beginning to be really annoyed with him, and launches into a withering attack.

"Is that why you write? You are nothing more than a prostitute! You are mistaken if you think you can make money by mechanical writing. Destroy your pens and pour away your ink if that is what you want to do. You must know that inspiration gushes onto the page when we least expect it. Don't just talk about writing as something to trade. Write so that the world will know who you really are. Your *oeuvre* will be your memorial. No one will be interested in your bank balance."

Lawrence feels suitably chastised. Maybe this is what I need, he reflects: a good telling off, and removal from the seemingly bottomless well of self-pity.

"You're right, of course. Art exists for its own sake."

Forster looks at Lawrence slumped on his settee, wonders whether he is being too harsh, and lowers his voice almost to a whisper.

"Yes, we should take good care of it, and never leave it at a train station!"

Lawrence is cheered by Forster's smile, touch of welcome humour.

"It's just that writing is harder than crossing the desert."

"I never said it was easy," agrees Forster. "It is rarely that, but, as when the desert has to be crossed, so a writer has to just keep going, day after day, till he finds an oasis, where he guzzles inspiration."

Lawrence does not resent his tutorial from Forster. It is, in many respects, just what he needs. Forster is so unlike others in his gallery of visitors that Lawrence puts up with his pull-yourself-together tone. He never gets that from Graves, who is a very good friend. No, Graves is a poet, like Sassoon, who happens to be also a friend. That is what Lawrence can never understand: why two writers who hate war so much can like someone who has made his reputation fighting one. Not that Lawrence considers himself a war-monger.

"Sassoon draws upon his anger at the politicians, the generals, anyone who perpetuates war," Lawrence tells Forster.

Forster now sees the problem: Lawrence has been far too long in the military, which has taken too much out of him.

"Don't rail so much, dear fellow. You have drawn upon what made you angry. Think yourself lucky you have had such a big subject. Pity we poor novelists who scratch around in the attic of the imagination for a tinderbox to set us alight. You have, in this … charming but tiny cottage the austerity poets dream of. Now we shall have no more of this, or I shall write to Graves and Shaw, who will have strong words of their own for you!"

Lawrence can now tell that he is being less than the perfect host by talking about himself, so he changes tack.

"Tell me how Abinger Harvest is doing."

That is Forster's cue to deliver strong medicine to Lawrence.

"It is a bagful of articles, essays, reviews, poems, and a pageant play. It is me not being sorry for myself, bits and bobs I worked up when I was feeling just like you are now."

Lawrence smiles weakly. Expecting only an over-view, he has to sit through a blow-by-blow account of the contents of it, and the lesson he learns from Forster is that you can never be sure what words will fly from your pen until they are on paper.

* * *

The key that Nancy Astor sent him sits in his palm. It is cold and heavy, a reminder that he still has a friend in high places. Now he has it, he considers it the height of bad manners not to use it, and, besides, it would be the perfect antidote to Forster's visit.

Plymouth is a good ride from Clouds Hill, and the prospect of opening up the throttle of his Brough, and charging up and down long, steep hills, excites him. So he throws a few clothes and requisites into a bag, and sets off. As instructed by Special Branch, he does not speak to the armed guard. The house still needs protection, even when he is not there.

There is plenty of time on his journey to think of past association with Plymouth, where he arrived from his stint in

Karachi. He remembers his first sight of The Hoe, a symbol of England's stubborn resistance to her enemies. His heart had quickened, and, again on *terra firma*, he had looked out to sea. How far I have been and come! he marvelled. And now I am well and truly home.

As he sets off from Clouds Hill, he wonders if he should send Lady Astor a telegram, but secrecy is everything. She will know, in due course, of his arrival. Her housekeeper will inform her. This is all part of staying one step ahead of his detractors.

He pushes his Brough hard, tries to top eighty miles per hour, but in Devon there is always a bend to make him cautious. Soon Plymouth greets him, and he is peculiarly sad. He has no idea how he will occupy his time, but is sure that Lady Astor will, at some stage, demand to ride pillion. The last time, she clung on to him, whooped and screamed, shut her eyes, not quite sure if Lawrence would lose control, and create a scandal to eclipse all others in which she had felt obliged to play a part. She loved the sensation of almost flying, when her internal organs moved upwards, as Lawrence deliberately accelerated into a bump in the road.

He finds the house easily enough, and the roar of the Brough's engine is replaced by the cry of gulls above. A little sore from the saddle, he is relieved to have arrived.

The key turns in the lock, but the door does not open. He suspects that it has been bolted inside, and his suspicion is confirmed when he hears it being slid back. The door opens, and there stands a diminutive woman with sparkling eyes. She has moved to one side the stool on which she stood to shift the bolt.

"Good morning," she says.

Lawrence hears an American accent. She must have been imported by Nancy, he guesses.

"It's Mr. Shaw," he says. "Lady Astor sent me the key. I am no burglar!"

The woman's eyes sparkle more, but she does not laugh.

"Are you Mr. Lawrence? Lady Astor said something about a Mr. Lawrence, but that you were also Mr. Shaw."

"I am one and the same."

He does not feel inclined to explain why he has changed his name. It is enough for him to know he is legally Shaw, despite the fact that he will always be known as Lawrence of Arabia.

"I thought you were. You'd better come in."

"Will my motorcycle be safe here?"

The woman looks up to the sky, then down at the pavement splotched with gull excrement.

"As far as anyone or thing is safe from the birds."

The Brough has been bombed before. All that are required to restore it to its usually immaculate appearance are a bucket of water and a cloth.

"Then I'll come in, if that's all right."

The woman does not introduce herself but gives Lawrence a quick, guided tour of the house. She tells him she will call later to see if he has any particular requirements, and to attend to any pressing domestic matters. Otherwise, he can make himself at home.

"Will you let Lady Astor know I am here?" asks Lawrence.

"I will, indeed. Good day, Mr. Shaw."

The woman dons her hat and coat, and with a smile that goes as quickly as it comes, she leaves.

He finds the tea caddy, and makes himself a drink. The house is big, and he is used to Clouds Hill, where the rooms are intimate. Somehow, he now feels more vulnerable, so he revisits each room to check no one is hiding. Then he sips his tea, after which he is reunited with his Colt. His stomach floats from its usual position. He thinks of Pat, then the armed guard. When he is alone at Clouds Hill, he is never lonely, but here, in Plymouth, he feels dreadful, and wishes Lady Astor would come soon.

Late in the afternoon, his wish comes true. He sees her stroke his Brough, and he laughs.

"Now!" she demands. "Take me *now*."

They kiss: both cheeks.

"Right now?"

"Might as well."

So Lawrence obliges, as he has done twice before in Dorset. She clings to him tightly round his waist, her fingers interwoven. At the end of his earlier journey, there was not enough fuel left for a long excursion, but he does not want to disappoint her, so retraces his route so that he quickly finds a straight stretch where he can accelerate to give her the thrill she wants. At seventy miles per hour, she buries her head between his shoulders, and he feels her breasts against him. And this is how it would feel, they both think simultaneously.

Returning to the house, Lawrence drives slowly, and she thanks him for the trip.

"I really should buy one of these, but I fear I should not be strong enough to keep it upright," she says. "Anyway, I like it when you take me for a ride. It absolves me from any responsibility. There is no turning back."

"Once you have forward momentum, it's almost impossible to fall off."

"Ah, forward momentum. That is just what I want to talk to you about. I've invited one or two friends for dinner tonight. I hope you don't mind. I've ordered a cold buffet to be delivered."

Lawrence grimaces, and says, "I'll hardly be the life and soul of the party. The journey has rather taken it out of me, I'm afraid."

"Get your head down for an hour. I want you at your best."

Lawrence laughs feebly. This is the last thing he wants to hear.

"Please don't feel you need to entertain me now I'm in hiding for a week or so."

"Entertain? Who said anything about entertaining you? I need you to help me do something most important."

"And what is that?"

Lawrence appreciates her badinage, and knows that it is futile to try to curtail it. It has a will of its own.

"Save the nation. I want you to help me to change the course of history."

Lawrence guffaws, knowing his days of nation-saving are well and truly over.

"Well, if that is all, then let us set to. There appears to be no time to waste."

In the house, she refuses to elaborate till the evening. He must bide his time, though her cloak and dagger demeanour makes him uneasy. He has gone there for a period of quiet isolation. I should have known better, he curses. She is, after all, a politician.

Lawrence politely enquires after her family, Parliament, Plymouth. She skates over her family, and has very little to say about Plymouth, but she is expansive about Parliament, and shows no restraint in her criticism of the government. Her lack of confidence in its policies is seasoned with thumbnails of this MP and that, and Lawrence has the impression that the country has elected representatives who are steering it towards the abyss.

The buffet arrives accompanied by the woman who had greeted him. Lawrence watches how Lady Astor instructs her. There is salmon, beef, game pie, fruit, cheese, mustard, bread and butter.

"I must say, you've done us proud," says Lawrence.

"A movement requires nourishment. Certainly, its generals do."

"Movement?"

"Yes. One I hope will save not only us but Europe."

Then a generous slice of game pie is just what we need, thinks Lawrence.

"There will be four of us," informs Lady Astor.

In fact, the meeting – for that is what the gathering is – swells to five, much to her delight. All the guests arrive within ten minutes of each other. They all kiss Lady Astor, and greet Lawrence with particular warmth. The housekeeper sets out sherry, ale, and brandy; Lawrence settles for water.

They all make small talk, and Lady Astor urges them to fill their plates again. It would be, in this age of conspicuous want, a crime to leave food to go to waste. Lawrence wonders what she really knows about want, but the salmon is a rare treat, and he avails himself of an extra portion. Gradually, the room settles into a quietness that seems to await the introduction of the evening's business, and Lady Astor leads.

"As you are all well fed, we shall begin. The world, and particularly Europe, is in a parlous state. I think we can all agree on that."

There are general expressions of agreement, but Lawrence's lips do not move, and when Dawson looks at him, Lawrence nods, more as if he has been momentarily startled than in support.

"Indeed," says Geoffrey Dawson, Editor of the London Times.

A second later, he splutters. Talking while chewing beef is an art he has not yet mastered, so he takes a large swig of sherry, and the obstruction goes. He thinks about wiping his mouth with the silk handkerchief fluffed up in his breast suit pocket, but then reaches for his napkin, with which he dabs his mouth. So smartly dressed, thinks Lawrence. His shirt collars are like two shark's teeth.

"Couldn't agree with you more," adds Lord Halifax, who has a fire in his eyes strangely at odds with his pallid, gaunt face.

"My sentiment entirely," agrees Robert Brand, a civil servant with an impeccable career, now in danger of being ruined, behind him.

They all look at Lawrence, who does not want to appear ungrateful, so says, "There are tensions, there is no doubt."

"And we are heading for war again – unless we can prevent it. The last war, I need hardly remind you" – and here she catches Lawrence's eye – "nearly destroyed European civilisation, and we should learn from it. But peace will not come knocking. It is our responsibility to invite it into our lives."

"Correct," interrupts Dawson. "And we should embrace National Socialism, which has motivated Germany to be proud again. Mosley is right. He is full of praise for Hitler's rallies."

Lawrence wriggles a little. Where is this leading? he wonders.

Brand then says, "We need peace. Our country cannot afford another war. I should know. I've calculated the cost, and we shall not eradicate it in my lifetime."

Lawrence feels all eyes turn towards him.

"And that's where you have a part to play," says Lady Astor.

"But I have retired, done with war."

"The prize is peace. Think of that."

"What do you want me to do?"

There is something in him that still clings to the thought that he might be useful again. He is even flattered that they have invited him to hear them out. But his circumstances have changed, and he is unsure whether their project is for him.

"Join us! Mosley takes the lead, but he can't do it on his own. Williamson is convinced Hitler will listen to you. He has heard of you, will respect you as a warrior."

"*Former* warrior."

Dawson says, "It's the only way. There is much to be admired in the recent transformation of Germany. The old way is failing. If we prepare for war, there will *be* war."

Lawrence does not recall him speaking like this in The Times, and it has not always been Lady Astor's stance, but people change their view of the world.

"So here's what we are going to do!" declares Lady Astor.

She speaks at length, on the edge of her chair, and holds her audience spell-bound. Lawrence listens carefully. My word, he admits to himself, she is a fine orator. Her passion can ignite even the most sceptical of men.

By the time she has finished, Lawrence is looking forward to hearing from Williamson, who is their intermediary. I have nothing better to do, he thinks. If I go, I just might prevent the conflagration that will consume each and every one of us. That would be one in the eye for Winston, and, for that reason alone, I shall look forward to meeting Williamson, the otter man.

CHAPTER TWENTY

Henry Williamson is wading downstream when he sees a kingfisher. Slowly, so he does not disturb it as it perches on a fallen branch, in the warm sunlight, he lifts his binoculars to zoom in on its iridescent plumage. The kingfisher remains still, long enough for Williamson's admiration to blossom.

The bird shoots upwards, and plummets into the water. For a second or two, it stays submerged, until it launches itself into the air again. In its mouth, it grips a stickleback it then proceeds to swallow in two convulsive gulps, before flying out of sight.

"Marvellous!" exclaims Williamson. "Beautiful yet deadly."

In the case of the kingfisher, it is the solitary sniper's instinct that impresses him. He sees that it works alone, identifies its target, and invariably hits it.

"Man should study birds and animals more. We can fly, so what can we not do if we apply ourselves to imitating Nature?"

When he returns to his study, he records in his journal what he has seen, that morning. It is part of the routine he hopes will provide the inspiration for another story. Tarka the Otter has fired his ambitions, but he still feels in the shadow of Kipling and his animal stories.

On his desk are two letters. The first contains a eulogy from a sycophantic reader, but Williamson will thank him. Gratitude costs only a minute or two and postage. He knows from the handwriting that the second comes from Lady Astor, who has wasted no time in relaying the outcome of her meeting with kindred spirits. In anticipation of an affirmation of Lawrence's support, he carefully applies his paperknife to the envelope, and takes out the letter.

As he reads, he wishes she would dispense with her customary preamble: what they ate, what mood each was in.

The second paragraph, however, moves to the core business: the presentation of the case for making contact with Hitler. She goes into some detail about the support pledged by each of the others. Enthusiastically, Williamson delivers a commentary to himself: "Good, good. Excellent! Oh joy illimited!" She makes it clear that Lawrence sees the sense in talking with Hitler, and Williamson notes, too, that though Lawrence does not definitely agree to go to Germany, he is willing to be persuaded. And that, concludes Lady Astor, is where Williamson comes in.

"So," he says aloud, "she wants me to write to Lawrence, to arrange to go and see him at Clouds Hill. No sooner said than done. If I can play some small part in helping this country and Germany to recognise that we have more in common than not, then that will be my finest achievement."

He believes that there is no time like the present, so takes a sheet of paper out of his drawer, and begins. It is important that the letter is not too long. After all, it is simply a request to visit. There must be no lecture. The merits of the plan must speak for themselves when he arrives at Clouds Hill.

Then it occurs to him that, though he feels they know each other well, they have met only a few times. This, as much as the reason for his visit, makes Williamson excited. Lawrence is a good listener, just the man.

The letter is sent, and replying to Lady Astor, Williamson is unable to omit an account of his sighting of the kingfisher diving to catch its breakfast. He hopes that she will glean its significance, but, just in case she does not, he explains the importance of seizing the moment.

He returns to his journal, but the image of the kingfisher now blurs with that of Lawrence, so he goes to post the letter. It is no use offering advice if one does not follow it oneself.

* * *

Corporal Catchpole follows orders to the letter. There is security in this automatic response. Yes, there are times when he fleetingly questions, in his own head, the wisdom of some instructions, but he understands the need for conformity. How else would Britain have built an empire?

In recent days, he has been assigned guard duty, and, from his position, is not too far away from Clouds Hill. On fine days, it is a joy to be positioned there, but while others rotate, he stays where he is. Occasionally, he interprets this as the Army's confidence in him to guard the Camp, but sometimes he thinks they have forgotten him.

One day, he asks, "Why am I always on duty in the same place?"

The Sergeant replies, "*Sir*. Why am I always on duty in the same place, *sir*? And the simple answer is: because that's where I put you."

"Thank you, *sir*," replies Corporal Catchpole, knowing that is as far as he will get.

"Think yourself lucky you're not on night duty like some of the poor bastards," adds the Sergeant.

"Yes, sir. Very grateful, indeed, sir. Very."

The Sergeant reports to the Major that Catchpole is aware of the unusual pattern of the shifts, in relation to the others.

"Deal with it," says the Major, who looks preoccupied with more urgent matters.

"But it's Corporal Catchpole, sir. You specifically requested to keep him there. Just thought you needed to know."

"Tell him he's the best there is, that it's a compliment."

"Yes, sir."

"Dismissed."

When he finds Corporal Catchpole again, the Sergeant says, "The Major insists you're the best for that duty. It's a compliment."

Catchpole smiles weakly. Bullshit, he thinks. Pure fucking bullshit.

From his position, he has a good view down the road. There is nothing unusual in this. The Camp must be protected, at all costs, and his rifle is loaded. Occasionally, the guards' vigilance is tested in mock-attacks, and Corporal Catchpole has never been found wanting. Maybe my being here *is* a compliment, after all, he reasons.

The Camp is sometimes put on the highest level of alert. Armed vehicles and tanks are put through their paces, and Catchpole feels the vibration of the tanks' treads, as they damage the road surface, ripple through his whole body. This makes him more observant than ever.

"How many out?" barks the Sergeant.

"Thirty-five, sir," replies Corporal Catchpole. "Ten tanks, twenty-five armed vehicles."

"Thirty-six, Corporal Catchpole," corrects the Sergeant.

"No, sir," insists Corporal Catchpole. "Only thirty-five, sir. You can't fool me, sir. That's why you put me here: to do a good job."

Corporal Catchpole sees that he has passed the test on numbers, but is nervous about the next question.

"How many infantry tanks?"

"Five, sir."

"And the others?"

"Cruisers, sir. I'd stake my life on it."

"You cocky bastard, Catchpole, but you're right."

"I do my best, sir."

The Sergeant is unable to tell if Corporal Catchpole is being arrogant or sincere. There is certainly no obvious clue in Catchpole's face.

"At ease. Very good. The Major wants a detailed report on today's exercise, and I shall let him know how well you've done."

"Thank you, sir. Much obliged."

The Sergeant is walking away when he hears this.

"Don't overdo it, Corporal Catchpole. There is still time to catch you out. You have set the bar high, and the Major's disappointment at any failure will wipe that smug grin right off your fucking face!"

* * *

The rain falls incessantly, and in a fallow field water collects at the lowest level. Trilby suddenly stops the car. Through the gate, he can see the streams, like stretched, silver worms, wriggle down the slope.

He tries the gate, and unties the knot keeping it shut. His smart clothes are getting soaked, and he is irresistibly drawn into the field. Water runs off his hat, and his turn-ups sag. The field's ridge has no distinctive landmark, such as a tree or bush. The enemy is beyond that ridge, no more than half a mile away, he guesses.

The water rushes into his shoes, and there is a squelching noise as he steps through the long brook that has formed at the foot of the hedgerow. The mud below the water sucks his shoes into it, so that very quickly he finds it difficult to walk. He needs to get to the ridge to see what is on the other side. The men look to me for hope, of which there is scant evidence in the ranks, he reminds himself, and I will show them that victory is possible with accurate intelligence.

Dorset is ever thus during and after a protracted period of rain. The lanes flood, bubble and gush, and when the water recedes, there is a quilt of mud washed from the fields. In time, it dries, leaving a crust that eventually cracks and is blown back onto the fields.

Trilby is staying at a guesthouse, just outside Bridport. The man and his wife – owners of a farm that welcomes visitors to west Dorset – like him. He makes his own bed, and always goes outside to smoke. If he says he would like breakfast at 8.30am, he arrives in the dining room at 8.29am. His manners are impeccable, and he smiles.

"What, may I ask, is your line of work, Mr. Bates?" asks the farmer, after placing a plate piled high with eggs, bacon, sausages, mushrooms, and fried bread in front of him. One of many names assumed, over the years, Bates is derived from an army doctor, who met his end on the western front.

"I'm a botanist," replies Trilby.

The farmer is none the wiser, so Trilby elucidates.

"Plants, wild flowers, that sort of thing. There are plenty of specimens along this coast."

"And what do you do with them?" asks the farmer's wife.

"I catalogue them. I'm planning to write a book about them."

The farmer and his wife have had a variety of guests – fossil-hunters, hikers, even couples pretending to be married – but never a botanist.

"Well, there's something!" declares the farmer.

"There's something, indeed!" echoes his wife.

Trilby is so convincing that he even gathers a few specimens for the farmer. Naming them confidently, he wants, when he departs on the day of Operation Sandstorm, to leave behind only wilting, delicate flowers, and his signature and comment in the guestbook:

Thanks for a lovely time. Everything a botanist could wish for!

In the middle of Trilby's stay, the farmer's wife says to her husband, "Why does he wear that hat, all the time? And isn't a tie a bit formal for a man who climbs up and down rocks? He spends hours in the undercliff at Lyme, he tells me."

"I've no idea," replies the farmer. "Leave the man alone. As long as he pays his bills, he's fine by me."

But his wife is suspicious. The accommodation is advertised in Bridport, Dorchester and Lyme Regis, but a lot of bookings are passing trade, as in the case of Mr. Bates. It is rare, however, they receive an enquiry, never mind a booking, from a single male botanist.

"Do you have a wife?" she asks, out of the blue, one day.

"You shouldn't ask personal questions," chides the farmer.

"It's all right," forgives Trilby. "It's a natural enough question. The fact is that I *had* a wife, but she died."

The farmer's wife wishes the earth would open up and swallow her.

"Oh dear, I'm sorry if I've upset you."

"Not at all. I imagine you wonder why I should pass my time in such solitude."

"And may I ask what she died of?" persists the farmer's wife.

The farmer rolls his eyes in disbelief.

"My wife took her own life."

The farmer's wife puts her hand to her mouth, horrified.

"I'm so sorry."

"I found her hanging from the end of a rope in the orchard."

The farmer ushers his distressed wife out of the room.

"She should never have pried. Please forgive her," begs the farmer. "It only opens up old wounds."

"There is, you might say, emotional shrapnel," admits Trilby.

The farmer leaves him alone to finish his breakfast. Trilby leans over his plate, and sees his wife in the morgue. On her neck are fading red marks where the rope has bitten. "Don't try and stop me," she says to herself. Then, to her husband, "I must do it. A bullet would lock you up for the rest of your life, at best. At worst, see you hang, too." The doctor had said that she had two or three months to live. Trilby has killed so many men that one more death cannot affect him.

By the fifth day of the week there, the farmer's wife confines her conversation with Trilby to domestic matters. Would he like more toast? More tea? Trilby tries to play his part in restoring the easy relations of the first few days, before the order to attack arrives. Men try to snatch sleep, an hour or two, ten minutes here or there, except on duty, when if bullets from the enemy do not keep you awake, the prospect of a hastily convened court martial, after which you are shot, certainly will.

So he spends as much time as he can away from the farm, and finds himself in a field, zig-zagging, as far as the sodden ground will allow him, towards the ridge, beyond which the enemy is reported to be dug in. His eyes flicker left and right. The sky is a slab of dark grey granite. Behind him, at the foot of the hill, his men are watching him in admiration, not dread. Soon, they will be ordered to engage the enemy.

The first shots whistle past Trilby's head. He knows to avoid movement in a straight line. Where are those bullets coming from? he wonders. Then, when he is high enough up the hill, he spots a copse, in which there must be snipers. In a moment of pure abandon, when he invites death, he charges towards it. He cries to his men to charge, and they emerge from their trench. A bullet grazes his helmet, and his ears ring, but God is with him. He shoots when he sees the strangely sleepy, German machine-gun post, and only the best shot in the Army could manage to kill all three lookouts.

He looks down on the bodies. Eighteen? Nineteen, at the most? But they are the enemy, undeserving of sympathy, in the middle of a war that invariably takes the young. One German twitches, so Trilby puts him out of his misery. On the other side of the ridge, he sees the enemy's trenches and barbed wire. His men arrive, and look, too. The defences suggest an overwhelming superiority of numbers.

"Shit!" Trilby curses, knowing they will have to fall back till reinforcements arrive. Then a shell bursts nearby, and the men look to him. "Fall back!" he yells, and they slip and slide back down the hill. In the trench, they eventually settle to waiting again, each second stretching to what feels like an hour.

Back at the guesthouse, he takes off his muddy clothes. Fortunately, he has spare hanging up. He is shaking, and his ears still hurt from the exploding shells. Four fallen soldiers were recovered from the hill. All good men. When things calm down, he will write to their next of kin, emphasise their bravery and sacrifice.

His car seat will need wiping. It has been a long time since he has experienced such a flashback. The episodes are almost always when he is in Belgium. You would think that all battlefields look the same, but they do not. The fields around Ypres have their own special hues and sounds. It is to one of the battles there, mostly to Passchendaele, that he usually returns.

Trilby deals well with his timeshifts. To the best of his knowledge, no one else sees him scared and demented, and he always recovers. He takes a long hot bath, and the gunfire fades.

In clean clothes, he is ready to face the biggest challenge of his career. The thing he most fears is getting the angle wrong. If his car is immobilised in a collision with the Brough, he and Peters are in trouble, stranded.

He goes downstairs. There is always apple cake and tea at half past four. The farmer's wife smiles, and does not flinch when the loud report of the gun is heard. Trilby dives onto the floor.

"Why, 'tis only my husband shooting at crows!" explains the farmer's wife.

Trilby takes a few seconds, then returns to his seat.

"I'm sorry," he whispers.

The farmer's wife understands, and says, "Put your muddy clothes in the basket. I'll soon have them clean."

"Thank you," says Trilby. "I appreciate that."

The farmer's wife would recognise it anywhere, has seen her brother behave in the same way. She knows it can strike any time, anywhere, and the shaking hands will never be still again.

She goes down to her husband, and speaks earnestly to him. He listens, nods affirmatively, and the crows can breathe a sigh of relief that the onslaught is over for the day. The farmer looks up towards his house, knowing he is one of the lucky ones. Trilby watches her link her arm with her husband's. A good woman, Trilby thinks.

It is nearly time, and he hopes that the day's episode will be the last till Operation Sandstorm is over. Deep within him, he knows it *will* be – one way or another.

CHAPTER TWENTY-ONE

The woman's cottage is cold. The air feels damp, and there is an odour of absence, neglect, and old, frayed upholstery. She opens the window, glad to be back from her sister's, in Somerset, where she has been to escape the pressure the Major has placed on her. If she had stayed at home, and reported Lawrence's every movement, she would have been complicit in the plan to bring him down. The fact that Lawrence wants her to do what they ask, so that he can learn more about their plans, means that she must distance herself from the whole situation. She feels used by both men.

Her sister was kind. All that she was told was that there is a man at the heart of the woman's misery. Her sister sympathises, as she herself has had a similar experience.

"Men!" her sister had exclaimed. "Don't we just love them! Drop him, dear. There are plenty of fish in the sea."

The woman confirmed that her days of fishing were very much over, and that she will take up embroidery, or find another job. She has not touched a penny of the money in the envelope the Major gave her, the last time he saw her. She thought it was her wages, paid up to the day they finished her in the kitchens. Instead, she has lived on the money received from her father's insurance.

She tidies up the cottage, then goes to let Peter know she is back.

"Anyone been asking for me?" she asks.

Peter has forgotten Lawrence's visit, and answers, "Not that I know of. It's been pretty quiet round here, apart from the tanks."

They talk about this and that, and Peter does not make a great effort, so she goes home. Soon, she runs out of things to do. All the time she is washing her clothes and sweeping the floor, she is putting off going to see Lawrence, to let him know that, during her absence, she has come to realise that she wants the chance of an ordinary life. Living with ghosts, Lawrence cannot possibly be the husband society – and, yes, she, too – expects her to have. The Major and Lawrence want too much of her, and she will not be intimidated.

Firstly, she returns the generous sum of money to the Major.

"I have decided I have found myself caught in a web with two spiders," she explains.

The Major pushes the money back across the desk, and says, "Keep it. I can't have you back in the kitchens. But there is a question I must ask. Does he know I have spoken to you?"

"I have returned to put an end to us, if ever there was an us."

"But does he have an inkling?"

"He is not stupid, and yes, I told him."

"Then say no more. I am sorry to have implicated you. It was rather hasty of me. We'll say no more about it."

The Major stands, and offers his hand, but the woman, leaving the blood money on the desk, leaves without any valediction.

When she goes, he comforts himself with the thought that it is her word against his. He knows Lawrence is a formidable strategist, and that he will now be aware that he is under the scrutiny of the Army. If what the woman says is true, that their relationship is over, then he is relieved that his mistake – poor judgement – has, so far, had no consequences. "I am a stupid bugger!" he curses. "I'm getting too old for this. I never thought of myself as a spider." Looking down at his long, thin legs, he adds, "But maybe I am, after all."

She does not put off her visit to Clouds Hill any longer. The officer on duty bars her way, and says, "Good morning, Madam. I'm afraid you can't come onto the property."

"Why not?" she asks.

"Because you can't."

What has happened? wonders the woman.

"Is Mr. ... Shaw at home?"

She remembers, just in time, that Lawrence uses the name Shaw; the officer might become suspicious if she asks for Lawrence instead.

"Is he expecting you?"

The woman thinks. The answer she really ought to give is yes and no, but she suspects that is unlikely to hasten her entrance to Clouds Hill.

"If I can't come in, ask him to step outside. He knows me."

"Slowly, put your hands in the air, and leave them there till I've patted you down."

"I'm not having a strange man grope me!" she cries.

The guard manoeuvres his gun into a more threatening position without actually pointing it at her.

"That won't be necessary," calls a voice.

It is Pat, who happens to be going for a walk. The officer waits, annoyed that he is now unable to exercise his authority as he wishes.

"Do you know this person?" he asks Pat.

"I do. She is a friend. Let her pass."

The officer, who knows that Pat has a key, and visits the cottage regularly to keep an eye on it, stands aside, and assumes his previous expressionless face.

The woman follows Pat, whom she has seen before. Pat invites her in.

"I'm Pat, Lawrence's friend."

"I thought so. He's spoken of you. I've seen you together before."

"Oh dear."

"He speaks highly of you."

Pat blushes and says, "You are a friend of his."

"Was. Am, I mean, but it's complicated."

"It always is with our mutual friend."

"Quite."

"He's not here, at the moment. He's gone away for a few days."

"Oh," says the woman.

Now she cannot tell him that things between them have changed. This is not something she can pass on via Pat.

"To be honest, he said he'd be back by now. I'm a little concerned."

Pat does not tell her about the sealed envelope he has promised to post if Lawrence is absent longer than he says he will be. In fact, Pat has only just remembered that it is in the dresser drawer. The name on the front is not one he knows.

The woman takes a deep breath. It takes real determination to pull herself from Pat, now that he has identified a possible problem. Though she has wasted enough time on Lawrence, she still cares for him.

"I expect he'll come back when he's ready."

"The guard is necessary. Did he … ?"

"You came just in time."

"I'll let Lawrence know you called."

The woman says, "Thank you." At her sister's, she made up her mind to sell her cottage, and move to Bridport, but does not impart this information to Pat.

Pat loses the motivation to resume his walk, and retrieves the letter when the woman has gone. Is he too late already? Lawrence trusts him with his life, so Pat goes to post it, and when it is out of his hands and in the mailbag, he is not sure whether he is doing the right thing or not. He knows that he promised to do it, but the responsibility of keeping him alive is one he never thought he need consider seriously, that it was an example of Lawrence's hysteria.

"Damn you, Lawrence of Arabia!" he shouts. "Will you never be free of this curse? You now put your life in my hands, and all I do is go along with your game. I swear this is the last thing I'll ever do for you."

The letter arrives at The Times, addressed personally to Geoffrey Dawson, Editor, and he reads it. He soon sees it is not the usual sort he receives. There is no explanation why Lawrence begs him to publish, as soon as possible, the second letter in the envelope. But Dawson, as well as the nation, needs him to make the case for peace to Hitler. This is the least he can do for him, in return.

"Never mind that it ought to go in the Personals," Dawson barks at his sub-editor. "Put it in Letters. Oh, and in Personals, too. No questions. Just do it."

What is Lawrence playing at? wonders Dawson. He has asked this as a personal favour, and who am I to deny him?

* * *

Smith is sitting in his brown, winged, leather chair, reading The Times. As a rule, he does not read the letters, but the day has been long, and he will do anything to lock out thoughts of Operation Sandstorm, which is now only a few days away. Alexander has not been in touch for several weeks, a sign that all is going well, that the original plan has no obvious flaws. Therefore, he does not resort to the gin and tonic he sometimes uses to block out the guilt he feels for his involvement in the eradication of a man who once saved his life. Besides, he needs to stay fit and healthy, think clearly.

There is a rant, a single paragraph, about the government's failure to do this and that: predictable ire and self-righteousness. There are one or two other letters on the subject of tensions in Europe, but it is the shortest that catches Smith's eye. It begins innocently enough, but Smith is trained to spot the unusual, the discordant. Quickly, certainly by the fourth line, he detects language denoting some kind of encoded message. By the time he has read it twice, his heart is racing.

This complicates matters, might even compromise him. He is sure that the message is meant for him, and can only have been written by one man. The author calls for a Mr. Sniper, who lives in Carrington, to make urgent contact with him, to discuss an important matter. The reply should be sent to Messrs Lawrence, Clouds, and Hill, Debt Collectors, Dorset.

He remembers The Times is my newspaper, Smith notes. He must be on to us, but does not know the extent of my involvement. Shit! He saved my life, and now he expects me to help him, maybe get him off the hook. Fuck! A very clever man, indeed. Well, he clearly knows Carrington is not dead, which is the official line he will have been told. If I do not respond, he will know there's more to it than me not having read his letter.

He should really tell Alexander, who will want to know why he has not been up front about his past with Lawrence. And that's me dead, certainly, Smith accepts. Lawrence's house is under surveillance, and I may have to manufacture a clandestine encounter elsewhere. Smith knows this calls for a forbidden gin and tonic, and it is during his second that he comes up with an idea to honour his debt. Then he changes his mind. I cannot go to Clouds Hill, he concludes. This is a ruse: he will put a bullet in my brains. He has discovered my treachery, and now he wishes to remind me that I am in a most uncomfortable place. He will not spare me.

Smith cannot help smiling, despite the seriousness of the situation. Lawrence has clearly not lost his sense of humour. However, Smith has been trained to suppress emotional responses to problems, and decides that, though he cannot compromise his role in Operation Sandstorm, he can let Lawrence know that, on this occasion, it is impossible to repay the debt. Sending a written reply, or even paying a visit to Clouds Hill, would certainly lead to his own assassination. He knows full well the risk Lawrence is perceived to present to the nation's security. Though Smith himself has a management role in the operation, he comforts himself with the knowledge that *he* has not taken the decision to eliminate Lawrence, and that *he* will not be involved in the physical taking of his life. This is just business.

So he decides to put a letter, in which he will encode his reply, in The Times. He knows that Lawrence has the ear of Dawson, so Smith must protect his own identity. He sets to writing. Lawrence will be looking for a swift reply. Smith has heard that there has been an enquiry, via several former serving officers, some now in the SIS, about his status, and that he has been declared dead. This will not fool Lawrence, who knows full well that all information in intelligence is deliberately unreliable. There is no easy way to let Lawrence down.

Smith is not totally satisfied with his letter, but it will have to do. How long must a debt exist before it is expunged from the records? And does the saving of a life necessarily carry a tariff payable when the debtor is least able to meet the obligation?

Dawson has Smith's letter on his desk. His sub-editor has brought it to him for his opinion.

"It's quirky," the sub-editor says. "We get them, from time to time, and they provoke others to write in. We don't want to damage the reputation of the newspaper."

"Oh, I don't know," says Dawson. "The odd cult following will do wonders for sales. You did right to bring it to me, though."

The sub-editor leaves, suspecting that there is more to this than meets the eye, but he has too much work to do to pursue it. Dawson is not stupid. This has some significance for Lawrence, he suspects, and so let not The Times interfere in the course of history.

Lady Astor fills her Plymouth house with so many plans and visitors that Lawrence feels he must return to Clouds Hill.

"But you have been here only two minutes!" exclaims Lady Astor.

"I must prepare for Williamson," explains Lawrence.

Lady Astor examines his face, and knows that is only part of the truth.

"A few days hardly constitute the rest for which you were looking," she argues.

"Pat will be worrying. I have gone beyond the length of time I said I would be likely to be away."

Lady Astor cannot hide her disappointment, but Lawrence is not her property, and she waves him off with a tear, and hopes that what she and like minds have set in train will come to fruition.

Lawrence pulls up at Clouds Hill. The guard acknowledges him with a strange movement of his head, and Lawrence opens the gate. Pat hears the sound of the Brough. A piece of pipe has sprung a leak, and he is mending it.

"Problem with the waterworks?" opens Lawrence.

"You're alive. I've sent the letter. I hope it saved your life."

Lawrence removes his goggles and gloves and drops them on the floor. Stretching energetically, he asks when it was sent.

"You had a visitor, a woman."

"I see," says Lawrence. "And did she say what she wanted?"

"She wanted to see you."

Lawrence stops his physical jerks, and snaps.

"For God's sake, Pat, don't beat about the bush. You know what I mean."

"You might catch her before she leaves."

Lawrence thinks hard, then rushes to the woman's cottage, but is too late. Another has deserted the sinking ship. My own fault. She deserves better. Might Peter know where she's gone? He hesitates, then returns to Pat.

"I'm off to Wareham," he tells Pat, who is lying on his back, testing the new section of pipe for leaks.

"Good – o," mutters Pat.

Lawrence heads for the library. The streets are busy, and the sun is bright. The librarian has kept copies of The Times for the last ten days.

He scoops them up and takes them into a corner.

"Is he a member?" the librarian asks a mouse-like colleague.

"Never seen him in here before, yet his face is familiar."

Lawrence is focused on his search, and ignores one or two articles on people he knows. The first three editions contain the usual sort of letters, then he comes across the one Pat sent on his behalf. Lawrence chuckles. As he reads, the letter sounds puerile, a bit obvious. Is he losing his touch? Then comes the frantic scrabbling for a reply, which he finds in the very last edition. So, just as I thought: he's not dead at all.

Lawrence assumes there is an encryption of the message from Carrington, and is not disappointed:

Sirs,

It has come to my attention that our national debt burgeons at such a rate, that the prospect of further costs, if war should again darken our land, brings me to only one conclusion: that some debts are impossible to repay. It is given that an Englishman's word is his bond, but these are uncertain times, where money is scarce, and life hangs by a thread.

Man and God are capable of making beautiful things, such as lace and the wren, but they face extinction soon if war is not averted.

Yours,

Thomas Haws-Ross

Lawrence takes the newspaper to the front desk, and asks, "May I keep this, please? I'm happy to make a small donation to the library."

"We were going to throw them away. We hold them for about ten days. You may keep it. Are you a member?" asks the librarian.

Lawrence feels the mouse looking at him intently.

"I regret to say, no. Another time?"

He places sixpence on the counter, tucks the newspaper under his arms and bids goodbye.

Outside, he reads the bad news again, and tries to come to terms with Carrington's inability to help. Saving a life counts for nothing, Lawrence muses, but I should hardly complain, given that I have taken more than my share. I have never liked hypocrisy, and detest myself.

Lawrence can think only about his own extinction. All that is missing is the where and the when, having known, for some time, the why.

CHAPTER TWENTY-TWO

Stephenson does not sleep. In his head are images he knows might lead to making a fortune. His contact acquires his information about Lawrence's trip to Plymouth from the intelligence officer who opens Lawrence's letter to Lady Astor. This deliberate leak is just the opportunity to try and discredit Lawrence. Armed with the news that Lawrence intends to go to Lady Astor's Plymouth constituency house, Stephenson waits for the fly to come into his web. Stephenson is battle-hardened, and long periods of surveillance are not the challenge they used to be, as he knows that, sooner or later, he will be rewarded.

At five o'clock in the morning, he spreads the photographs on his desk, composing aloud possible headlines to accompany them. He moves them about. Some are more newsworthy than others. There is one of Lawrence astride his Brough, goggles off. He is leaning back in a relaxed posture, and behind him is Lady Astor's front door.

"This is all right, I suppose, but the story is limited. Ah! This is the one I think will sell." He picks up another, and looks at it closely. "They were so engrossed in their cosy, little ride that they did not see me on the other side of the road."

Lady Astor's arms encircle Lawrence's waist, and her cheek rests on his right shoulder blade. She smiles. Bliss! is what she is thinking. Lawrence's head is turned slightly over his right shoulder, to witness the anticipation of a thrilling ride. There is everything in this photograph: the possibility of a liaison, two clandestine fascists making hay while the nation prepares for war.

While it is a strong contender, the one Stephenson picks up next is likely to be more lucrative. Lawrence is about to depart. Lady Astor has both arms round his neck, and is kissing him on the lips.

"I'm sure her husband will want to see that," says Stephenson. "Now, do I go straight to the editors, and sell to the highest bidder, or should I extract more from the two love-birds? It will be a fine judgement. Of course, blackmail, though potentially lucrative, is a serious crime, but the truth also can have serious consequences. I shall give it more thought, though I long for revenge, which will be all the sweeter for the delay."

Stephenson eventually decides that he will test the water with The Times. Dawson has bought one or two stories and photographs, over the years, and may just be tempted, having one of the biggest budgets. The American market would almost certainly bite his hand off, but revenge would taste better in England. His jaw still aches, a constant reminder that Lawrence needs teaching a lesson. If all else fails, he will offer them to Lawrence, believing that Lawrence has money enough to avoid a scandal involving Lady Astor.

Dawson sees Stephenson personally. Stephenson spells out the implications. Apart from the photographs of Lady Astor and Lawrence, there are ones of the other visitors. Dawson's face sets, and Stephenson knows he is waiting for the one of him arriving at the house.

"The one of you is safely under lock and key, where it will stay if you buy these," says Stephenson, smiling.

"What would publishing these achieve?" asks Dawson.

"Achieve? You would sell many more newspapers, I have no doubt. *You* make money, *I* make money. We are both happy. That's the world we are in, as sordid as it sometimes is or feels."

"Would I have exclusivity?"

Stephenson hesitates, gives himself away. To give one newspaper exclusivity on these particular photographs would not be bad business, or lead to the door being slammed in his face, the next time he has a proposition. But it might make enemies of former friends.

"That won't be possible. Do you realise how valuable these photographs are?"

"But what use are they to me if they appear simultaneously around the world? The Times is big. What figure are you looking for?"

Dawson is calm, once again.

"A hundred pounds each – cash. I've come to you first."

"And the one of me?"

"I can't promise anything."

"You have a nerve."

"I just take photographs, and write stories. I'm not breaking the law."

Dawson taps the desk with his over-long fingernails, to give the impression that he is actively considering doing a deal. But this is a charade, not the first time Dawson has been held to ransom.

"Give me forty-eight hours. I need to consult one or two of my people. Have you written the story to go with these? You know this newspaper's stance. We're straight down the line."

Stephenson has considered the story behind the photographs, and believes it could get too complicated. The last thing he needs is to fight a legal case. And the photographs have a high value.

"Make what you will of them. I'm not a greedy man," he says.

"Come back in forty-eight hours. If any of the ones you have shown me, or any of me, appears in any other publication before then, you won't get a penny."

"Understood."

They do not shake hands. Stephenson gathers his photographs, and leaves. Dawson remains still, says nothing, does not look at his visitor.

"Doris," he says to his secretary, "I want you to send a telegram." He writes, *Ring me urgently. Dawson.*

Lawrence thinks it is to do with a possible visit to Germany, and is upset to hear what Stephenson is up to.

"He was in Plymouth?"

"He has a couple of Lady Astor and you on your motorcycle."

"Does it look bad?"

"There is a kiss. It's what you make of it."

"What are you going to do? Can you go to the police?"

"I could, but no crime has been committed. It's a free country."

Lawrence sighs, frustrated. It is Lady Astor he is worried about. How did Stephenson know I was in Plymouth? It is a matter of public record that I used to work there, but maybe he followed me, or someone told him. Someone has been tittle-tattling.

"It's blackmail. Will you publish?" asks Lawrence.

"Can you see any advantages? You know, for our cause? He's got one of me."

Your cause, Lawrence wants to say.

"Does that bother you?"

"The Times publishes my photograph with a group of conspirators? Who would *not* be bothered?"

"It's me he's after," Lawrence tries to reassure Dawson. "The jaw. He must get tip-offs. How else would he find out where I was?"

Dawson knows Lawrence is Stephenson's real target, but suspects that if he pays a penny for the photographs, so he can destroy them, Stephenson will have duplicates.

"I won't touch them. Others might, but I won't. We could both find ourselves in another newspaper. He may try to blackmail you."

Lawrence laughs.

"If only I had enough money! Let him do as he wants. He may even be doing us a favour."

"It depends on the words that go with the photographs, and there are a few in my industry who would use it against us. They don't always share our views."

Dawson is more nervous than Lawrence, who has learned to take one day at a time. I should worry when they *don't* want to write about me, thinks Lawrence.

"You could, of course, offer him a penny for them," he suggests.

"No. I won't do that. I will not buy. Let him do as he pleases. I have principles."

Lawrence shrugs. If Stephenson does come to him, Lawrence is likely to take the law into his own hands. Down will come the scarecrow, at the top of the hill behind the cottage, and in its place Lawrence will tie, at gunpoint, Stephenson. All that target practice will be put to good use, at last. Then Lawrence will feed the corpse to the crows and buzzards, and Stephenson's skeleton will be hung from a tree, and his bones will rattle like macabre wind-chimes.

"Will you tell Lady Astor?"

"She knows already."

"And?"

"She laughed. 'Oh, *that* kiss!' she said. 'I do hope it is on the front page.' You know what she's like."

"I do, indeed," says Lawrence. "She's quite remarkable."

"Quite," agrees Dawson.

Dawson feels that Lawrence can barely contain himself.

"I've been thinking," says Lawrence.

Dawson is not sure if this is a good or bad idea, having learnt, over the years, that it is far better to deal in certainties than theories. But he is nothing if not open-minded, and encourages Lawrence to share whatever it is that has provoked the biggest smile he has ever seen.

"I've come to expect that of you. Go ahead. Be my guest."

Lawrence moves to the edge of his seat, as if what he is about to say might unlock the meaning of life, explain the origin of the universe. It is the sort of pose he used many times when trying to persuade military top brass and Arabs that a revolt against the Turks might be mutually beneficial.

"You would sell more newspapers if you published the photographs. Correct?"

"Correct."

"So publish, and interview me. It would pull the rug from under his feet. I could keep things light. I was visiting friends in the RAF, that we were exercising our democratic right to assemble lawfully. You see, Stephenson *wants* us to run scared. That's what keeps his price up. If Lady Astor does not mind, why should we?"

Dawson sees the logic in that, but fears it might damage their plan to send Lawrence to Germany. Williamson would certainly not approve.

"I suppose I could stick it on page five. Don't want to make too much of it. He'll only come back with more. Damn it, I just don't like the idea of dancing to his tune. My inclination is to tell him to shove his photographs where the sun doesn't shine!"

Lawrence frowns. The chance of a front-page appearance in The Times seems to be evaporating.

"But he'll only go elsewhere. Let's use it to our advantage. The public may just connect with our thinking."

"I respect your opinion, Lawrence, but I'm not with you on this. Stephenson will not get a penny from this newspaper."

The news, when Dawson delivers it to Stephenson, is not good.

"But you know there'll be others who *will* take them," argues Stephenson.

"Fine, but they're not for us. Not our kind of thing. Now, if you don't mind."

Dawson stands his ground. Stephenson hesitates, not really wanting to traipse round the other editors.

"If it's the price, we can negotiate. You can have them for seventy-five pounds each, but that's my best offer."

Dawson laughs, and thinks: he doesn't get it; he just doesn't get it.

"They're worth nothing to this newspaper. There's no story here. Now, goodbye."

Stephenson leaves, and Dawson picks up the telephone, and makes several calls. The editors at the other end listen. One or two can promise nothing, but others know Stephenson's game, and are sympathetic to Dawson's request to show him the door. By the end of the day, Stephenson realises that they have ganged up on him. Never mind, he tells himself. There is always America. The Establishment there is conspicuous by its absence, and people are really interested in how public figures brighten up their lives.

Lawrence is disappointed. Used to seeing his image on film and posters, he feels the suppression of Stephenson's photographs might ruin his last chance to slip into the limelight. There was always that difference in stance, to the exploitation of images, between the Arabs, particularly Faisal, and himself. They were the means to an end for Lawrence, but the Arabs were always suspicious of them, sceptical about what they could do for their cause.

Lawrence thinks up a plan. So far, he has not seen Stephenson's photographs, and cannot believe they are incriminating in any way. But what if Lawrence steals his thunder, and organises a few of his own? With the assistance of Lady Astor and the others, they could recreate the ones Stephenson was touting to Dawson. Why, there might even be a kiss or two! There would, of course, be a carefully constructed article to go with it.

"That is the worst sort of journalism," objects Dawson, shaking his head. "The Times does not publish to mislead the public."

"We would not be misleading them – just depriving Stephenson of a market."

"And what do we do the next time he comes with photographs for sale?"

"It seems you've made up your mind."

"I have. I'm uneasy about all this."

Lawrence says no more on the matter, and hopes that at least one other editor will publish. Can Dawson not see that if they do meet Hitler, it will be necessary to prove that their group's profile is high enough to be given serious consideration?

Back at Cloud's Hill, Lawrence is lying on his bed, leaning on one elbow, surrounded by books. Here is solace, a good connection with the intellectual life he craves but which is becoming ever more elusive. While he has his books, he has hope, and is untouchable.

It would, of course, be easy to permanently remove the nuisance that is Stephenson. Lawrence has executed men before, but it would be the slippery slope to add Stephenson to his list. I could not justify it, he thinks, but it would not hurt to make life a little uncomfortable for him, let him know there is a consequence to any action.

The idea makes him convulse from his semi-recumbent posture, and sit in his chair. As he writes, he laughs. It is a merry jape, and must seem authentic. Dare he try and get it into The Times? He will have to give it some thought. Of its own volition, his pen flies over the paper.

He copies the notice out three times, and posts them immediately, sure that they will have an effect, and prod their target.

In his flat that suggests a short-term occupancy, Stephenson sits and scans the newspapers, looking for a potential opening, still angry that his photographs have yet to find a home. Then he spots news of his own demise, his name in bold type, and rubs his eyes. There it is, under **Public Notices**.

"Good Lord!" he cries. "I appear to be dead!" When the absurdity of the announcement fades, he starts to shiver. His jaw still hurts; it is still painful to chew food. He chops whatever he eats into fine pieces. Soup is his usual fare. Then he mutters, as he reads quickly, "Suspicious circumstances, no fixed abode, amateur photographer, leaves seven children."

213

He knows he is meant to see it, that it is a warning. Not the hand of an editor, he is sure. But Lawrence: yes, only he could come up with something like this.

Lawrence wants him to come to Clouds Hill again. The police have already warned Stephenson about trespassing. This time, there will be direct action. This is war, and a photographer is no match for a true warrior. The Colt is fully loaded. It will be used in self-defence. He did not survive the war, only to be beaten by a hack. No one will find Stephenson. It will be as if he had never lived at all.

He imagines Stephenson's anguish at reading about his own premature death. If he knew, Pat would say to Lawrence, "Put your gun away. You can kill him a thousand different ways if you keep him alive," and Lawrence would know he is right.

Lawrence shakes his head in disbelief at his own stupidity. In the desert, did we not fight only the battles we could win? Why, we withdrew as many times as we advanced! he remembers. And the biggest battle is yet to be fought. Soon there will be a call to do my bit for the country again, and I shall be ready. My weapons are my words, my reputation. With such ammunition, peace can be won, but I must stay alive long enough to see it. I am weary of all this looking over my shoulder. If the world would leave me alone, I would be happy enough. But I fear the worst, smell the ammonia of threat.

He puts on music, balm despite the crackling. There is no conflict in the notes, just delightful combinations. Taking deep, slow breaths, he is beckoned into a world of dreams, and is soon asleep. Eventually, the record ends, but the absence of music does not wake him.

Even in deep unconsciousness, he becomes aware of a difference in atmosphere in the room. The visitor tries to tip-toe, not wanting to wake him, but Lawrence senses movement, and opens his eyes just a fraction, so that the visitor does not see that he is awake. The man has a gun, and is looking at him, as if not knowing what to do next. This has never happened before. Lawrence always locks the door. How did the man get in?

Lawrence thinks, is this what they had in mind? Lull me into a false sense of security, and then, when my guard is truly down, kill me? The Colt is too far out of reach. It is not possible to keep it by my side, as I did in the Army.

Then the awkward standoff is ended when the man whispers, "Are you awake, Mr. Shaw?"

Lawrence detects no hostility in the man's question. The gun is pointing at the far end of the room. Now is the time for Lawrence to try to overpower him. This is as close to death as he has been. He remembers his mantra: my words are my most potent weapon.

"Kill me. Get it over with quickly. I've had enough. All I ask is that you make it clean."

The armed guard frowns, perplexed.

"No, sir. You've got it wrong. My shift is done. My last shift, that is. I've come to say goodbye, sir. It's not been easy, us not being able to talk, but I'd like to say it has been a real privilege."

The guard's voice catches on the lump of emotion still swelling in the back of his throat.

Lawrence sits up, rubs his eyes, then stands.

"Is someone else coming to take over?"

"No, sir. Has no one told you? I imagine they've withdrawn the cover due to a lower level of threat. That's good news for you. Someone should have told you, though."

Lawrence accepts the offer of a handshake, and says, "Nice of them."

"The engine's running, sir. I'll have to go. Take care, sir. A real privilege, I can tell you."

The guard slowly goes down the stairs, as if savouring his last moments at Clouds Hill, and Lawrence hears the door shut.

Lawrence understands now that the world can see that they have done all they can to protect him. They have just been ticking the boxes, trying to lend an air of respectability to a plot that will reach its conclusion, suspects Lawrence, sooner than he imagined. He still has his Brough, and he could ride away on it, never be seen again. But Lawrence is not a coward, and exile is not an option he wants to take.

He picks up his trusty Colt, and the door remains unlocked, all night.

"I am ready," he says. "I am as ready as I've ever been. No regrets. In a thousand years, my name will be remembered, and Seven Pillars, if it continues to be published, will ensure that those who want me dead will be buried themselves with the millstone of history's retribution round their necks."

Secure in that knowledge, he begins to read The Mayor of Casterbridge, for the third time, as a homage to the dear friend he is certain he will meet again in an after-life every bit as fresh and green as the hills and vales of Dorset.

CHAPTER TWENTY-THREE

Lawrence places the ladder against the tree. The branches he selects are perfect, and he sets about chopping them off. Soon the sweat seeps through his shirt. There is a big, dark patch between his shoulder blades, and he looks, from a distance, as if someone has stabbed him, and the blood is spreading across his back. If he had not sold it, he might have used his Arabian dagger, but he wields instead his small axe, which does the job properly.

Seeing no need to consult his drawing of the frame he intends to construct, he makes one or two modifications to the usual Bedouin tent in which he has slept, in the past. He would not be Lawrence if he followed convention, but his design takes into account the fact that he does not have enough rope to be traditional.

With string, he ties together the poles in the appropriate places. The skeleton of the tent is placed on flat ground outside his cottage, at the foot of the hill. It is the best spot, and the tent will be protected from strong winds.

For some time, he has been thinking about building one. The cottage meets almost all his needs, but it does not put him in contact with the stars. A tent flaps and booms in a gale. It has no electricity, chairs or table. In a tent, if he wants, he can strip himself bare of all comforts.

In his garage, he has kept, for several years, two tarpaulins acquired from Bovington Camp. They were smuggled out by friends, so that he could cover his Brough, stop dust settling on it. Canvas does not have the vibrancy of colour found in Islamic art, but the sheets are all he has to reproduce a much missed experience.

"Damn!" he curses. "Not a great fit."

No matter which way he lays them, the sheets leave a gap, but they will have to do. He has an old rug from the cottage, and on that he will sit, eat, meditate, read, and sleep.

The box he takes from the garage makes a perfect table, on which he places a few candles. The nights are getting lighter, but Lawrence loves the shadows thrown by candlelight. There are no delicious, fresh dates, lentils, or flat bread to dip in olive oil, but he substitutes an apple and a fruit cake bought from Wareham.

When darkness falls, Lawrence sits on the rug, legs crossed, and lights the candles. There is, of course, no one to share the tent, no Faisal, smoking in fine, white silk, hand clasping his dagger. With whom can he discuss ideas and tactics? There are no other faces in dark corners, watching, mirroring the subtle and more obvious changes in mood. But he needs to recreate that environment, for his own sanity.

He breaks off a corner of a slice of the cake, and rubs it in the honey smeared on his plate. Eyes closed, he savours dates, sweetened coffee, goat's milk. In the tent, books and music do not intrude. He can hear an owl, and he thinks it sounds like the one he hears faintly from his cottage.

"I should have done this before now," he says.

If it rains, he knows the canvas will not keep him dry. In the desert, it has rarely rained when he has slept in a tent.

In his head, English words hold sway, whereas once it was full of the Aleppo and other dialects. It was not English that moved Faisal to revolt; it was Lawrence's command of the tribal languages.

"And as I do not practise them, they fade," he says, while eating his sweet cake.

He lights the fire, knowing he must ensure the smoke escapes, and lifts up the flap at the front of the tent.

It has been some time since he last wore his red, Arab head-dress. Then he had smiled as he looked in the mirror. Now he realises he has missed it, not just as a protection from the sun, but as a symbol of his solidarity with the Arabs.

He wipes up the cake crumbs, and reaches out to warm his hands on the flames. A night in the tent is not going to restore his purposefulness, his energy, but it reminds him of better times, which fired his imagination and sense of justice.

The owl screeches again, and he lies down, pulls a blanket over himself. Candlelight swims on the walls. The heat from the fire does not reach him. Nothing warms him any more.

* * *

Mills knocks on the Major's door. For days, Mills has been checking that the intelligence officers he has assigned to gate-keeping the roads into Moreton, on the day of the funeral, have sufficient resources. The Major has offered soldiers from the Camp, and Mills now comes to ensure that the Major understands what is expected. So the rap is sharp, and the Major looks up, not recognising the pattern of sounds.

He does not invite his visitor to enter. In fact, he has not been answering the door or telephone to anyone for a couple of days because he wants the space to study the map on which he has written the names of men he believes he can trust. It is May, and though the exact date will not be known till the day, he has to be ready.

The men already know they have been chosen to block a specific road in the event of an imminent hostile attack. They must erect a barrier at a safe distance from the Camp, so that no vehicle can pose a threat. Smith has liaised with the Major on that. At the funeral, they will simply block the major roads into Moreton instead, as they would in the case of an alert. The Major has personally supervised several rehearsals in the roads around Bovington Camp, to ensure that each team of eight knows exactly what it is doing. It has always been his intention to space the dry runs evenly, so that they do not arouse suspicion among the men. On those occasions, the roads were closed quickly and without hitch, and that is what worries the Major. Something is bound to go wrong, sooner or later.

Eventually, he calls, "Come!" Mills, who was admitted to the Camp on a special pass, enters. The Major sighs. Mills is the last person he wants to see. All those questions, all those what ifs …?

"Thank you for seeing me," says Mills.

"You might have given me more notice," moans the Major.

"You know the way things like this work."

"You mean spot checks."

"I mean we have to be sure things don't go wrong." The Major bristles, resenting the suggestion that the outcome depends upon just himself. "It's not personal."

"I'm sure it's not," says the Major.

After a long pause, Mills says, "If it's any consolation, *my* neck is on the block, too. Security cannot be left to chance. You know who's coming?"

"I can guess."

"Guessing is not good enough. Here."

Mills pushes a piece of paper across the Major's desk.

"Anybody who's anybody."

"What else did you expect?"

The Major is suddenly disgusted, and pushes the sheet away. He has met Lawrence, briefly. It is the hypocrisy the Major cannot bear. The hypocrisy of the whole operation.

"You all right?"

For a moment, the Major nearly tells him everything: that he is sick and tired of the Army. He has never minded soldiering, killing the enemy, but all this with Lawrence is sordid.

"The roads into Moreton will be controlled. The funeral will take place, and Churchill and the other big shots will be safe."

"If in doubt, deny access. Churchill and his wife have special protection, but we don't want to take any chances."

The Major knows Mills is talking sense, but he still feels that he has been dragooned into something with which he is totally uncomfortable.

"No, we don't. Look. Be assured. We know what we're doing, this end. Only *bona fide* mourners will get to the cemetery."

"You know the time?"

"He's not dead yet."

Mills takes a deep breath; the Major is trying his patience.

"Paper?"

He writes the time of the funeral on the sheet the Major takes from his drawer.

"Date?" asks the Major.

"Unknown."

"Why?"

"He might not die according to plan."

The Major begins to laugh hysterically, even makes Mills smile.

"What?" says Mills.

"People rarely do," says the Major. "I for one don't intend to."

* * *

Churchill feels agitated. All that he has come to value is threatened, and Clementine, his beloved Clemmie, wonders what this pacing and fiddling with books and pens on his desk signifies. During her long absence, their exchange of letters did much to ease their separation, and, occasionally, she spotted a telling, often throwaway, line that was a clue to his state of mind.

"You mustn't mind Germany too much," she says, from the other side of the room.

He glances at her, then walks over to the window. Where is he looking? she asks herself. Not Europe. Somewhere else. She knows him well enough to know that something has happened during her lengthy cruise. Several times, she has chided him for letting her go.

"Just a little," he eventually replies.

"Is there something else?"

She advances a few steps, and stops, thinking it best if she does not fuss so much.

"Should there be? Apart from all that happens in the House, there are *this* house's demands."

"Then slow down, my darling. This house will be here long after we have gone. Since I have been back, you've seemed preoccupied."

"I am sixty. If I slow down too much, I'll never get going again."

He opens his box of cigars, takes one out, and runs it under his nose. These are the gift Clementine brought back from Suez. She has no idea whether they are of good quality, but Walter Moyne recommended them.

"What is sixty?" she scoffs. "You've ten times the energy of men half your age."

"Clemmie, I appreciate your encouragement. I shall be as right as rain soon," he declares, suddenly snapping out of his dark mood.

"That's more like it," she says. "That's my Winston."

He sits and drinks with her, and his mood begins to thaw. Whatever it is will go, Clementine is sure. He always comes out of things on top.

When she is satisfied that she can leave him alone again, she makes the excuse that she must go and sort out dinner with Cook.

Churchill watches her close the door quietly. She is my rock, he admits. For a fleeting moment, he feels close to tears, and has to fight them. There is no turning back. In his heart, he rages that Britain has fewer planes than Germany, that Hitler boasts. But he himself has a plan, and must stick to it.

Sixty years, he reflects: time enough to learn to trust my own judgement.

When Clementine returns, the air is blue with pungent cigar smoke. She knows he will be annoyed if she wafts her hands as though clawing through dense fog.

"Why are you looking at me like that?" he asks.

"Like what?"

"As if you have caught me doing something I should not."

"I have been away for too long, it seems. I'm not aware I'm looking at you in any particular way. Is your article for the Standard finished?"

It is not. Black thoughts grip him, and he is rigid with misery. She is used to it, and recognises it now.

"I shall put the finishing touches after dinner."

She loiters, wants to help, but knows he must invite her. His letters to her detail his social life, but, from time to time, she asks about someone he has not mentioned.

"Have you seen Lawrence recently?"

It is an innocent enough question, but Churchill snaps, "No. He has his own secret life down in Dorset, in a tiny cottage. Strange that he should cower from his real name and life so."

"Is that what he does? That does not sound like him."

"Then you do not know him as well as you think."

Clementine takes that as a signal to leave him alone. Black Dog is out of its kennel, and must be left to bark till it slinks back in again.

* * *

There is little else for S to do but wait. He is experienced enough to know that one man cannot do it all. Even in his line of work, teamwork and trust are necessary to succeed. But the strain is telling on him so much that he needs some kind of release. He has seen too many intelligence officers disappear due to alcoholism, always a quick route to another country, on a one-way ticket, once it has been discovered.

In the early days of his search for a private corner in London, he was worried that a discovery would be the end of a promising career, but an associate recommended a club in Soho, even offered to take him there.

"You'll be safe there. They look after you well. You needn't worry. They know the score. There are more like you, and the club is a haven for a niche market like us."

S had been put out that his associate had considered them to have something in common, but gave it a try. He had signed in under the name of Trenchard, the name his associate had given the club. S had paid twenty pounds to see if he and the club liked each other. The rest, as they say, is history.

Now that Operation Sandstorm is just a few days away, he is so tense that a visit to see Pearl and Roman becomes imperative. What else can I do? he asks himself. This particular waiting is the worst he has experienced.

So, vowing to make this his last indulgence, he bathes and goes to Soho, which he considers his only vice.

He pays the driver, and alights from the taxi, several streets away from the club. Each time he goes, he chooses a different place to get out, and walks. This is standard procedure, second nature, whatever his destination. There is a spring in his step, all the way to the front door. He looks right, he looks left, but there is no response to his ringing the bell. The club is open seven days a week, he is sure. Patiently, he waits. It is unusual for the door not to be opened within thirty seconds, and S is anxious not to draw attention to himself. He is just about to go when the door opens, and a voice says, "Come inside, quickly." It is Pearl, and he obeys.

"Is something the matter?" he asks.

"You could say that," she replies.

She is not in one of her fabulous dresses, and the pearls look dull against the cardigan she is wearing. There is no one else, no background hum of conversation and occasional laughter. She does not take his arm, put a glass of something in his hand. There is no enquiry about whom he prefers, that day. All is flat.

"May I ask what has happened?"

He thinks cash flow problems. It has to be, but he cannot imagine why. The establishment has thrived for years is his impression. Membership is not cheap. In fact, the drinks are exhorbitant, but he has never been less than totally satisfied with the services provided.

"You can think yourself lucky you didn't come this time, last week. This place was crawling with the police."

"Why?" asks S, relieved he did not get caught up in whatever happened.

"The evening was going well, as usual. It was midnight. I remember the chimes of the hall clock. I took a guest to see Roman. The man was nervous. He told me, on the stairs, that he had never been to a man before. I said that there is a first time for everything. As I recall, he smiled weakly. We entered. At first, I thought Roman had slipped into the bathroom. The client saw him first, and I have never heard a man scream like that before. I followed where he was pointing."

"What had happened?" interrupts S.

"And there was Roman, on his side, eyes staring, bulging. Near him was his cut throat razor. Have you any idea how much blood we have in our bodies?"

He wants to tell her what he has seen in the war, that we cling to life by the thinnest artery.

"He did that?"

"Yes, I called the police. Assuming the murderer was still in the building, I locked the doors."

"Suicide," the officer thought. "Slit his own throat."

S wants to ask how they arrived at that conclusion, but he also wants to leave, distance himself from Pearl.

"Are they sure?"

"They've taken all the membership forms and the signing-in book."

Shit! thinks S. That's all I need. But here he is not Sinclair or Alexander. He is Trenchard. Think of a name, someone you do not like. Simple: Trenchard.

"I'm sorry," says S.

Forlornly, Pearl watches him go. He closes the door behind himself, and, as he looks up, a flash blinds him momentarily. S leaps at the photographer, who feels the gun in his stomach.

"Drop the camera."

The photographer does as he is told, and S rips out the film, and slams the camera onto the ground.

"All right," says the photographer. "It won't go any further."

"Down those steps by the entrance."

Now the gun is between the man's shoulder blades. Out of the public glare, S searches him. The man spreads himself against the wall, as ordered. He has seen my face, realises S. That is a pity. S steps back, fires, and the man falls to the ground. S picks him up, and dumps him in the adjacent dustbin. Routine, textbook stuff.

Then he retrieves what is left of the camera, and throws it in the Thames.

This is all I need, he curses. But I have not lost it. It had to be done, and I did it.

He walks quickly, looks for a taxi. There does not appear to be any blood on his coat, but he burns it on his fire, later. I am S, Michael Alexander says to himself. But he cannot remember whom he once was, no matter how he tries.

CHAPTER TWENTY-FOUR

The Major hates putting on a veneer for the Army. The men under him expect consistency and clear direction. They have been trained to take orders, and can count on the fingers of one hand the number of times they have seen him smile. With the burden of Operation Sandstorm weighing him down, he has, remark a few subordinates, little time for ordinary routines, with the exception of parade, where his profile and punctilious inspection have their usual impact.

He worries about not knowing who else knows that he is part of the operation. One slip from me, he calculates, and my career, if not my life, will be over. Fortunately, liaison with S is good. They have a direct, secure telephone line to each other, and the codes for dialogue are carefully agreed and changed.

The Major's failed attempt to enlist Lawrence's female friend is a sign that he does not understand women well enough to make good use of them. His wife rarely emerges from their fine house amid the officers' quarters. She would have advised him to leave well alone. There are few women, who truly love their men, that betray them for a few extra pounds a week. But he has sworn not to discuss security matters with his family. A firing squad may await such treachery.

The man the Major has assigned to keep an eye on Lawrence has a distinguished military career in undercover work. He is single, and prefers it that way. He has viewed life at a distance for so long that he cannot even entertain the thought of fully entering it.

"I want you to report to me once a week. The day and time will change, as will the venue. Does anyone at the Camp know or recognise you?"

The Major's man feels wounded that his exploits in France and Belgium have propelled him into obscurity, but this is not the time for petty squabbles about reputation.

"As you know, I've spent my best years in reconnaissance, working alone. My medals are in a drawer, in the past."

"Good," says the Major. "Then I can see no reason why you need a change of identity. Follow him. If he suspects anything, that's not the end of the world. He's well known. He has a sixth sense in these matters. If he catches you out, say you recognise him. Play up him being a hero. He'll like that. But don't get careless. He's clever."

The Major's man's lips tighten; he hates to take orders from anyone he does not respect.

"I won't."

"Let me know where he goes, whom he sees at Clouds Hill."

"I will."

"And if you see anything unusual, let me know straight away."

"I will."

The handshake is strained, functional. There is no love lost between them. The Major's man is about the Major's age, but has never risen to that rank.

At their first review meeting, the Major learns of Lawrence's trip to Lulworth Cove.

"You just bump into him?"

"No."

The Major assumes his man followed Lawrence.

"What was he doing?"

"Swimming."

"Swimming?"

"Swimming. I watched him go down onto the beach. I had a good view from the slipway. He left his clothes as a landmark for when he returned from the water."

The Major taps his pen on his desk.

"Are you sure it was him?" His man nods. "He confirmed it?"

"Yes."

"You spoke to him? That was a risk. Lawrence is not stupid."

The Major's man does not say that he secreted a note, bearing the date of Lawrence's dismissal from the RAF, for using the name John Hume Ross, into his pocket. He *wants* Lawrence to suspect he is being followed. There is no chase without a thrill. This method was never in the rulebook, in the war, and now, as then, the Major's man is determined to endow his surveillance with some good, old-fashioned risk-taking.

"Who would not speak to him, if they recognised him? It is natural. Besides, one can always gather more information by talking. He's polite, though cautious, not the sort to give anyone short shrift."

"And did you learn anything from the encounter? You've got balls, I'll give you that."

"No, I didn't, but he has visitors to Clouds Hill. Arty types."

"Names?"

"E. M. Forster, the writer. I'm an avid reader of his work. I recognised him the moment I saw him."

The Major's man waits for an expression of disapproval, but none comes, and that is because the Major, too, likes Forster's work.

"Anyone else?"

"Bernard Shaw's wife, Charlotte."

The Major is not a theatre-goer, but has heard of Shaw.

"Why would his wife visit alone?"

His man shrugs.

"Who knows?"

The Major is satisfied that Lawrence's visitors go there for social reasons, but is interested to know whom Lawrence visits.

"He goes to Max Gate, to see Hardy's widow."

The Major gets on well with Hardy's novels, which nourish his soul. His wife bought him The Trumpet-Major, and he found it so engaging that he read it four times before asking her to buy him Tess of the d'Urbervilles.

"Well, that is understandable. One never wants to admit that Hardy has gone, in a physical sense, that he has been dead for several years. His heart is buried in Stinsford's churchyard, you know."

"Apart from his forays to see Pat Knowles, his friend, he seems to lead a quiet life."

The Major does not reveal that Operation Sandstorm will try to thwart a plan to plead with Hitler. His man is surveillance, not strategy.

"Thank you. That'll be all," says the Major. "Oh, one more thing. Does your money come through all right? Don't want you to be out of pocket."

His man nods and leaves; he does not do this job for money. Is there no one in the British Army who understands that?

The next time the Major's man follows Lawrence, he is led a merry dance. It is almost as if Lawrence knows someone is tracking him, and has decided to make life as difficult as possible, now being highly visible, now accelerating sharply on his Brough, then disappearing down various alleys in Dorchester. All these little games are not to give his follower the slip, but to let him know that, whatever he does, Lawrence has the upper hand.

The Major's man welcomes this cat-and-mousing. It brightens up his day, and he sees it as a mutual acknowledgement of their obvious intelligence. Lawrence sits in the bright sunshine. That morning, he had rubbed his hands to warm them, but now the sun is in his face, and it is a pleasure to do nothing.

Dorchester is busy. It is market day, and people have come from far afield to buy and sell. Pheasants and rabbits lie on blood-smeared tables, and a man sits playing a fiddle. In his hat are one or two coins, but when he switches to his accordion, the hat fills, and one or two people begin to dance. Lawrence wants to add a penny to the musician's takings, but decides to buy a lardy cake instead.

This mingling with ordinary people boosts his spirits. He is not naïve enough to imagine they are all happy and without a care, but feels that the market binds them together, does not judge anyone, regardless of wealth or rank. I should come here more often, he tells himself.

Eventually, he makes his way to Maumbury Rings, across the road. The grass is long, and the sun has not yet dried it.

He enters the horseshoe of earth, and steps back into history. This leap of the imagination is, for him, rare in England. In Arabia, when recording archaeological sites was his focus, he became one of the long-dead citizens who lived there, centuries ago. He heard the sounds of trade and argument, smelt perfumes and spices. Now he is jostled by a ghostly throng waiting for the execution of a thief pleading for mercy.

"What say 'ee?" asks an old man.

"Let him live," urges Lawrence.

"A good man, 'ee, 'tis certain."

A young man and woman are strolling, hand in hand, planning, imagines Lawrence, their future: where they will live, how many children they will have. Two boys try to run up one of the sides of the amphitheatre, but struggle to make it to the top, and when they do, they tumble down, whooping, making warlike noises.

Soon, these people leave, and Lawrence stands in the middle. He turns full circle, safe from prying eyes. Over the centuries, the Rings, he has read, have served many purposes: to protect against invaders, marauders, to gather publicly for this proclamation, that trial and execution. It all seems so ordinary now, bereft of sounds and energy. There was no escape from justice here, but the keener sensitivities of moral progress have moved public execution to a more private place: prison.

The world has not changed much, believes Lawrence. One must do what one can. There is a law, increasingly disputed, that anyone who takes a life should lose theirs, and there are circumstances in which he has found himself fully supportive of it.

He finds himself faced with a man accused of murdering a fellow tribesman. Tears stream down the accused's face. There is no doubt that he is guilty. He has admitted the shooting. There are no mitigating circumstances, no claim of self-defence. He has committed murder.

Lawrence looks round the Rings. Arabs swarm like locusts to a position from which they can see the proceedings. A few carry their tribe's banner. Faisal and the others stand on a ridge, content for Lawrence to manage the situation. After all, Lawrence now wears the attire of an Arab, and is accepted by everyone.

Lawrence's instinct is to ask the distraught man if he has anything to say. This is because Lawrence is British, but it is a futile gesture. In the interests of inter-tribal harmony, Lawrence must dispense with western subtleties.

Determined that the convicted murderer should not suffer, Lawrence advances, to ensure his shots are clean. The man knows the moment is nigh, and raises his hands to the sky, in supplication, to Allah. A plea for mercy has never been so desperate. Lawrence, who has not yet taken his Colt from its holster, grabs one of the man's hands, and gently helps him to his feet. A gasp reverberates around Maumbury Rings. Is it possible that Lawrence offers forgiveness? What do these white westerners know of justice? Only Faisal knows that Lawrence intends no such absolution.

Face to face, the prisoner and Lawrence hold the attention of the crowd. Then Lawrence snatches his gun, and shoots the murderer in the chest. The man screams, and his blood spurts over his clothes. He is seized by spasms, and lurches towards Lawrence, who, trembling, shoots again, this time finding the man's wrist. The man rolls onto his back, calling to Allah. This is not what Lawrence wants, so, from close quarters, he fires a third shot into the neck, under the jaw. Lawrence swears that he sees a final attempt to move.

"Bury him here where he fell!" orders Lawrence to the crowd. "Bury this murderer, whose fate is that decreed by Arab tradition and justice, here where he met his ignominious end. Praise be to Allah for his wisdom and guidance."

A roar ripples round the Rings. Warriors raise their banners and guns. Shots are fired into the air, and Lawrence hears his name called. He slips his gun back into his holster. This is no time for celebrating the execution, but he raises his hand briefly in acknowledgement of their support. Faisal nods to him. Now the Arabs see that there is no need to be suspicious of Lawrence, who is truly on their side.

Lawrence does not watch the body being roughly dragged away to be buried. The soldiers disperse to their tents for a few hours sleep, before they move on. Damascus is a long way from Dorchester.

The policeman stops a few paces away.

"Everything all right, sir?" he asks.

"Fine. Why shouldn't it be?"

"It's just that you've been reported as behaving oddly by a member of the public."

Lawrence pulls himself together. What have I been doing? he wonders.

"Oddly? In what way?"

"Said you were waving your arm in the air, even shouted out words. You an actor, sir? They thought you might be. We don't get too many incidents like that reported."

"Something along those lines. I let my imagination run away with me sometimes."

Lawrence smiles.

"Then that's all right, sir, though you look as if you've had a bit of a fright. Your face is all pale."

"I'm fine," says Lawrence. "Just fine."

The policeman salutes, and does not know why. Back at the station, he describes his encounter to his Sergeant.

"You're going soft!" the Sergeant says.

"Soft or not, there was definitely something about him. Not an actor, but a man with a certain presence."

"Odd you should say that. The couple said he might have a gun, the way he was pretending to shoot."

Lawrence knows he is not fine. By the time he has returned to Dorchester town centre, his shaking has subsided but not gone completely. Not since he had dysentery, in the desert, has he felt so feverish. The flashback to the time he executed the Arab for murder is just one in a line of similar episodes. He contemplates seeing a doctor, but decides against it. What would such a man, who has probably no specialist experience treating ex-servicemen, know about the aftermath of war?

Max Gate or Stinsford? Lawrence opts for neither, and goes to Maiden Castle, where he knows there is solitude, the best treatment that can be dispensed. He attacks the slopes, and does not rest until he has reached the top. The wind buffets him, and he holds out both arms like a bird. Imagining that he can fly, he sprints towards the horizon, closes his eyes, and flaps his arms, but there is no upward lift.

"Such stupidity and vanity!" he shouts. "Bloody ridiculous."

In the very act of trying to fly, and then realising its absurdity, he laughs, and the last of the tremors go. He turns a full circle. The views are awe-inspiring, and fill him with hope.

"I might be safe up here," he says, "but in winter, the snow and ice would claim me instead."

An hour later, he descends to his motorcycle, an idea forming, and which comes to fruition, back at Clouds Hill. The poem, the one Florence knew was in the book – or did *not* know was there – the tribute Hardy wrote for Emma, his first wife, but did not finish, is at the heart of his thinking.

He sits down, the poem in front of him. Such a work is unfinished, it seems to him, but who is he to attempt its completion?

"A ludicrous idea!" he says. "Besides, Florence knows my handwriting. But I have a typewriter."

He drafts his poem by hand, and enjoys it so much that he believes writing poetry is the perfect sedative. Side by side, the poems are not identical but sit well enough together.

"How shall I deliver it to Florence? In a book, as she did to me? Or shall I leave it in a place, at Max Gate, to which she will eventually go?" he asks himself.

He types up the poem, which is short. Strange, he thinks, that poetry comes when I least expect it. Maybe it is not my inspiration, after all, but Hardy's.

"I flit from you so soon, my Florence dear.
No more nights you wait in silence drear,
and listen for the wheeze of welcome death.
Bury me, my love; I want no bier.

And when Max Gate seems like a gloomy crypt,
and your heart by grief is strongly gripped,
think not me gone for ever from this place.
Back I'll skip before the hoar has nipped!"

He waits for a third verse, but the pen fidgets, till he realises that all is said. It *has* to be Hardy. No such lines have ever come from him before. If he can bring some cheer to Florence, counterbalance the lines to Emma, then so be it.

It must seem to Florence as if Hardy has written it. Has Hardy a typewriter? Lawrence cannot remember; if Hardy has one, the typeface may be different from the typewriter in Clouds Hill. The voice of the two verses is unmistakeable. Florence will be comforted.

His first idea is to post the book in which he found the stanza to Emma, and also one of the others, in which, he can say, he found the two verses he himself composed. Florence may never have flicked through the others. The second course of action is simply to visit her, show her what he has found. There would be, of course, a moment of extreme embarrassment when she might break down at the thought that she was, after all, the true love of Hardy's life.

Lawrence wavers; he knows this is a conscious act of gross duplicity. But his verses came so easily that he cannot rule out the possibility that he is a conduit for those sentiments Hardy did not live long enough, or felt inclined, to convey.

Eventually, Lawrence decides to return it himself, not wanting the parcel to be lost in transit. He is reminded of Tess' letter, posted under the door, to Angel Clare, and missed by him. Such is fate, which turns upon its head the best of intentions.

Lawrence arrives unannounced, hopes that she will not be too suspicious when he apologises for being unable to stay for tea.

"I am returning two of the books you kindly gave me. Inside one is a letter and a poem seemingly written for your husband's first wife. In the other is a poem I think is meant for you."

He watches her reaction when he says *two*. So, Florence *was* saying, "Look at what I have endured since Emma's death!"

"I see," she says. "How strange! I had thought all his poems collected and published."

"Then you must add these to the others. A cursory glance, as is natural, was my only trespass upon their theme."

Lawrence begs forgiveness for dashing off, but must prepare for some work to be carried out on the pipes at Clouds Hill.

On his return, he feels uplifted that he has actually written a poem. He imagines her sitting in her chair, untying the string, and unfolding the brown paper. She takes out the poem she had placed in it. It is her responsibility again. She had hoped to be rid of it, that Lawrence would preserve it for posterity.

Then she finds the second poem. Hardy's promise that he will return to her has been fulfilled. In these two unexpected stanzas, he speaks to her directly; she recognises the tone and style, and smiles.

"Dear Tom," she begins. "How I miss you! This poem is like feeling your hand on mine again, at this fair hour, on this fair day."

Lawrence opens up the throttle. Let them do their worst, he thinks. I am ready. Tom, I now know, awaits me in eternity, and I long to see him again.

How the Brough surges!

"I am coming, Tom!" he shouts exultantly. On a straight piece of road, he reaches maximum speed. Briefly, he shuts his eyes, steers the motorcycle along the stretch he has memorised. "I am still invincible!"

Back at Max Gate, Florence busies herself, no regrets in her heart, only love and pride, which stem her tears. In her head, she hears the machine gun fire of Lawrence's Brough carrying him towards endless conversations, by the Spinner of the Years' fireside, with Thomas Hardy.

CHAPTER TWENTY-FIVE

There he is, astride his pedal bicycle, sporting a tweed jacket and flannels. His right hand is flat against the brick wall, and keeps him upright and steady. His bicycle clips grip just above the ankles, and a tail of hair hangs between his eyes. The sun is bright, and he squints, trying to look at the camera. His watch is showing, though he cannot see the time on it. There is his shadow. The man who took the photograph is Ian Daheer, a friend, who owns a boat-building business in Bridlington. Never has he taken a shot with such sadness.

"I do believe this is the last photograph that had my consent," Lawrence reminds himself. "Twenty-sixth of February, 1935."

He has not forgotten, of course, the thousands taken by the pressmen hanging about in the South Quay and his digs. Recalling with a shiver the Ozone Hotel, in which he lived with other airmen, he wonders how that triangle of land, resembling the prow of a ship pointing to the sea, managed to house so much pleasant company. The work sheds, too, need no photograph to jog his memory.

It is hard for him to believe that this snap is a souvenir of his final minutes of his last posting in the RAF. Is this a memento of my failure? he asks himself. But he has no regrets. He even retrieves from his box a copy of the letter he wrote to Air Chief Marshall Edward Ellington Trenchard, and rereads it. The letter confirms how happy he has been in the RAF, and asks that his file should close with this note that confirms he is sad to be leaving.

Even now, he is not sure if this request is an act of desperation, a seizing of one last chance to ensure he is not remembered as a spent, pathetic figure. It comes to us all, he reflects realistically. Who knows how to write the last page of one's working life? Yet he cannot find, in his box, one single letter from his friends in Bridlington. I have not been long gone, he explains to himself. They are busy, I am not. He has himself written several letters, but boat inspections, modifications, and repairs take precedence over his news. No one knows more than Lawrence how Britain depends on such hard work.

Lawrence has respect for Trenchard, who is no longer in the RAF, and the feeling is mutual. Among those of the highest rank, there is always the chance that their position becomes vulnerable, and that they feel obliged to resign. Lawrence wonders how Trenchard fares, and does not know that Allenby has contacted him, but it is clear that Trenchard has no knowledge of Operation Sandstorm. When the subject of Lawrence is raised by Allenby, on the telephone, Trenchard is cautious. As Metropolitan Police Commisioner, he has to be.

He is, however, happy to share his thoughts about Lawrence's love of London.

"Why, he would think nothing of leaping onto his motorcycle, in Plymouth, and riding the two hundred or so miles to London. He loved it here, you know. The bookshops especially."

This is not what Allenby wants to talk about. A direct reference to Operation Sandstorm to a man who knows nothing about it could have serious consequences, so he comes to the point obliquely, after a pause in which Trenchard, who does not contact him very often, suspects Allenby will elucidate.

"Is there anything you can do for him?"

Trenchard knows this is some kind of code. It cannot be a matter of money already. Lawrence has his pension, is known to live modestly, is not the sort to ask for financial assistance. However, Trenchard cannot decipher the code. What can he say?

"I am sure a man of his calibre does not need anything from me. I'm not sure I follow you."

There is genuine puzzlement in Trenchard's voice, and Allenby does not want to provoke him into asking questions elsewhere.

"I'm sure that, in time, the country will mark more formally his achievements. The way things are going, I fear that we may need him again."

Trenchard knows of Lawrence's sympathies with the likes of Williamson and Mosley, and the role of Metropolitan Police Commisioner requires substantial diplomacy. It would not do to become tangled up in a political web.

"We shall see," he replies laconically.

"We will, indeed."

The silence, longer than each wants, ends with Trenchard saying, "Well, nice to speak again."

"Yes."

The conversation is over. Allenby is none the wiser about the extent of Trenchard's knowledge about what faces Lawrence. However, no one can say that Allenby has not tried. Trenchard, still uncomfortable with what was not said in his telephone conversation with Allenby, flirts with the idea of ringing Lawrence, for old times' sake, but has enough to do, and, besides, Lawrence, he knows full well, is more than capable of looking after himself.

* * *

Pearl hears the gunshot, seconds after she closes the door. He, S, seems to her a nice man, generous, Roman had once told her. Those who look after her clients are allowed to keep their tips, and S is always appreciative. Pearl associates the gunshot with S, who must have witnessed whatever led up to or followed it.

Firstly, she sees a few fragments of the smashed camera on the floor. S has fled from the scene, has hidden his gun, two hundred yards away, in a bush. He will retrieve it at a later date, when any scene of crime investigation is finished. Pearl peers down into a well of space below her stairs, instinctively suspecting that she would find something there. There is blood on the floor and window, but no body. She does not scream, and telephones the police.

Let them find the tiny diamonds of glass, which are, she feels, connected with the gunshot. Pearl stands guard, nervously looking about her, in case the person with the gun returns, and she is relieved when the police arrive after fifteen minutes, and inspect the blood-stained area.

"Tell me again, slowly. You heard a gunshot. Take it from there," invites the officer.

"I'd only just shut the door, too. To think, I could have been caught up in that!" says Pearl with a shudder.

"Had you been out?"

"I'd only just said goodbye to one of the club members. He'd called and did not know that we had been shut down."

"What was his name?"

The officer's pencil is poised over his notebook. This is possibly a lead, though, as yet, there is no evidence of a crime having been committed. The blood needs, of course, an explanation, but procedure must have rigour, the officer has been taught.

Pearl slowly shakes her head.

"He could be any one of two hundred."

The officer is disappointed, and sighs petulantly. Any membership forms, she knows, would be of little use anyway. She has no time or resources to verify names and addresses, most of which are a complete work of fiction. Who in their right mind would leave such footprints?

Sloppy house-keeping! thinks the officer. What have we to go on?

Just then, one of his colleagues interrupts. There has been a significant development.

"We've just found a man's body in a dustbin. Dead. Shot. I've assigned Harris to safeguard the area, while we record it."

Pearl puts her hand to her mouth. A death so close to her establishment horrifies her, and she doubts her business will ever be the same again.

"Shot dead?"

"Is there anything about the man whom you saw go? Was he a regular?"

"He came, from time to time. Saw Roman, a few times, before Roman slashed his own throat."

The officer is confused, not being *au fait* with the history of the club.

"Who is Roman?"

"He looked after some of our clients."

The officer is no wiser, and asks, "Madam, what line of work are you in?"

Pearl wishes, even at this stage of her decline, to maintain her dignity, and replies, "We provide time and space, listen, offer massage, good company. We are – *were* – the best in town."

"And you say the man who left just before the shot used to see Roman?"

"Yes. Roman speaks highly of him."

"And do you have any reason to suspect that Roman's death is in any way connected with the man in the dustbin?"

"I've no idea. You'd know better than me. You're the police. I'm surprised you don't seem to know about us."

The officer begins to be frustrated. There are some leads, he is sure, in this curious sequence of events, but he needs Pearl to be less cryptic.

"Why?"

"Well, one or two of your chaps come here. 'Pearl,' one even said, 'anyone steps out of line, I'll have the full force of the Met come down on them.' Quite open, they were about their job. You see, they get privacy here. No one needs to worry that things will get out."

The officer scratches his head, and takes down a description of S. Pearl does not hesitate to lie about S's appearance. Who knows? When the business starts up again, Roman's client may well return. Alternatively, she considers that he might kill her as well as the man in the dustbin, so convinced is she that *he* shot him.

In due course, the body is searched, and there are various telephone numbers of newspaper editors in his wallet. The police correctly deduce – and it is later confirmed by one or two contacts – that he is a freelance photographer. Not too well liked, it appears.

"Looks like he tried to take one photograph too many, and it's my guess the man has a lot to lose," remarks the officer to a senior detective.

"Yes, find the film, and you may well find the murderer."

"I imagine so, but I expect the film has been destroyed. Has the dead man any relatives?"

"No, but he is known to us."

"How?"

"His name is Stephenson, and he once complained to the police that T. E. Lawrence, or Lawrence of Arabia, as he is commonly known, broke his jaw. It appears that, later, he tried to sell the photographs of him to a man called Dawson, Editor of The London Times, who wouldn't touch them."

"So you think the dead man is T. E. Lawrence?"

"Unlikely, as Lawrence lives in Dorset. We're talking about Lawrence of Arabia. Do you think such a hero would come to a place like this to be whipped, massaged, and buggered? It's unthinkable."

"Good work, though. We now have one or two possibilities."

"Good? Not yet. Dawson knows Lawrence, but we mustn't go there. Not a word about this, and that's come from someone high up in the Met. The dead man will be buried in an unmarked grave, and that's the end of him and our involvement. It has been made very clear to me that we should close this case immediately.

Tear up your notebook, there's a good chap. Let it go. There is always something else we can be doing. We don't want any trouble from above."

The officer follows orders to the letter. Whatever they have stumbled upon has rung alarm bells higher up the chain of command.

On his next visit to Pearl, he tells her, "East End gang biting off more than it can chew, but there's no need to worry. Soho is safe once more."

"Glad you got whoever did it. I didn't think the man who left just before the shot had anything to do with it."

Her change of mind on this matter is part of her adjustment to some semblance of normality. It does not matter that she does not know she was right; she is more than happy to be wrong.

"No. You'll hear no more from us."

Pearl trembles. Something makes her feel that she has not been told the truth, but if the police say the case is closed, then that is good enough for her.

* * *

The following day's edition of The London Times contains a sketchy report on Stephenson's death. Lawrence reads it with mixed feelings. The music to which he is listening is affecting his concentration, so he lifts the needle clumsily, and it bounces noisily. He curses, but there is no obvious scratch on the record.

When he finishes the article, he feels that Stephenson had it coming, and regrets that he himself did not kill him. It does not take long for Lawrence to realise that Stephenson was pursuing someone of importance in Soho. Shall I phone Dawson? he asks himself.

Later, he does call Dawson, who is reluctant to reveal any of the circumstances that were relayed to a reporter via a routine police statement: a pressman called Stephenson has been shot in Soho. It does not happen all the time, but sometimes reporters ask one question too many.

"Has anyone been to Stephenson's house? I imagine he keeps all his photographs, including the ones taken in Plymouth, there," points out Lawrence.

This is a chance for them to be retrieved and destroyed, and Dawson understands what Lawrence is implying.

"That is a matter for the police," says Dawson, realising that this is too good an opportunity to miss.

"Are you sure?" persists Lawrence.

Dawson thinks carefully, and says, "Call me tomorrow, same time. And, by the way, you'll be hearing from Williamson, any time."

"I'll look forward to that," says Lawrence.

Dawson rummages through his drawers for Stephenson's card, and when he finds it, there is his address. The reporter he assigns loves a challenge, is experienced, and not averse to using unorthodox methods to obtain a story.

He flashes a fake ID card to the landlady, and she shows him into Stephenson's rooms.

"You're a bit late, though. The police have beaten you to it," she says. "Took away everything he owned in boxes."

The reporter does a quick search, thanks the landlady, and reports back to Dawson, angry that he has been beaten to the tape.

Then I must speak to the Metropolitan Police Commissioner, says Dawson to himself, and Trenchard is sitting calmly, studying intently the photographs in front of him, waiting for the call that will surely come.

CHAPTER TWENTY-SIX

Williamson rises early, dispenses with his usual routine, and makes straight for his writing desk. There he sits, and starts his letter to Lawrence. His first few words displease him, so he crosses them out, and begins again, moving straight to the purpose of his writing: to request a visit to Clouds Hill on the matter of national importance they have discussed. Williamson does not refer directly to a proposal to make arrangements to visit Hitler, knowing well that his own letters, too, are being monitored by the SIS, at the behest of persons high up in the organisation.

He reads his message aloud, and makes one or two changes to punctuation, but it is the tone, above all, he wants to get absolutely right. Lawrence should feel that he is the all-important figure in this venture, and Williamson thinks that his draft is too informal. His second draft is better, and he leaves it at that. There – it is finished, and he posts it.

"Yes, it should arrive by the eleventh," the assistant says, in answer to Williamson's question.

"Good," says Williamson. "Then it is done."

The assistant finds that an odd expression, but attributes it to the fact that Williamson is a writer, and writers are wont to use such dramatic phrases.

When the letter arrives at Bovington Post Office, it is taken to the Major, who sees that it is addressed to T. E. Shaw. As he reads it, his heartbeat flutters, and the hand holding the letter shakes.

He quickly places the DO NOT DISTURB notice on the outside of his door, and, using a direct telephone line to S, dials.

S lifts up the receiver, and waits.

The Major says, "There is a chill in the air here."

S pauses and says, "Where?"

"The Camp."

"Go ahead," says S.

"Williamson has written to Lawrence. He's coming to Clouds Hill to finalise their travel arrangements to Germany. Do you want me to read the letter to you?"

"Yes. You'd better."

S's palms are moist, and his mouth dry. Please let there be nothing in it we have not thought of, he prays.

The Major reads it. S looks up at the ceiling, knowing that this moment would arrive.

"Thank you. Is there anything else?"

"No. It will be delivered to Clouds Hill on 11th May, unless you say otherwise."

"No, that's fine."

"Then this is it?"

S will not say. One can never be sure that no one else is listening.

"You did right to ring me," he says, then hangs up.

The Major sits, feels dreadful, and knows that, with that call, he has set in train a sequence of events in which he wants no further part. He has seen too many fallen soldiers to want to add to that total.

S pulls himself together. All that he has planned for must now take place. I am experienced, he tells himself. I am as cold as ice.

The room must be emptied. What few documents there are he puts in his briefcase. There are no personal possessions to remove. Then he suddenly stops, and thinks mathematically. If Lawrence receives the letter on 11th May, he will have to reply on Monday, 13th, it being a weekend.

"He must never leave these shores again," are the words he recalls from his final briefing. "The future of this country depends on it."

The man making it clear to S splutters on his cigar, then hangs up.

S vows to stop him. We shall be ready for him from the moment the letter is delivered to Clouds Hill. He will need to reply by telegram. Monday is the likely time he will send that.

He checks the code he will give to his team, and their designated responses. When do I make the calls? he asks himself. It must be first thing on the morning of Friday, 10th May. They need to get to Dorset. S knows he cannot worry about their state of preparedness. They were told it was in May, and to be ready. Once the calls have been made, the lines will be cut, and the taxi company will no longer exist.

* * *

The woman rents a terraced house in Bridport. There is plenty of work available in the town, her landlord tells her, but this is the last thing on her mind. She is more concerned with shedding her memories of the loss of her father and Lawrence.

The house needs airing. Though it is spring, there is a damp patch in one corner, and it has the fusty smell of lack of occupation. The furniture that comes with the house is basic. In time, if it becomes clear that she wants to buy a place there, she will fetch her own, which is currently being stored under tarpaulins, in a farmer's barn.

Her first night there, in the dark, is troubled. She leaves one side of the bed free for Lawrence, by sleeping towards the edge, and imagines him next to her. For what purpose, now that she has put some distance between them, she cannot say. On his motorcycle, however, she knows he can be with her quickly. But this is nonsense. They have no future together.

Her sister's advice rings in her ears, and the woman knows that Lawrence can never be with her in a conventional sense.

There is something truly romantic, she thinks, when her spirits are lifted by joining the real world at Bridport market, about never exchanging goodbyes. Her head still contains possibilities. Who knows? Perhaps, I can write a story, one day, when the mood takes me, about an elusive man whose past prevents him from ever settling down. I will have to give us different names, of course. He would never forgive me if I revealed our true identities. What is he doing now?

Lawrence receives her letter, in which she includes her new address. There is no explanation why she has moved to Bridport, simply information he could use if he ever wants to see her again. He reads it, not expecting to hear from her. There is no strong emotion in the letter, no exhortation to come and join her, and he wonders if her writing is a show of independence.

He puts it next to the typewriter. There is no need for him to rush into a decision about whether to act upon it. After all, it was she who went away. Yet there is a growing desire within him to put all aspects of his life in order. He is certainly not looking for a wife, and does not wish to raise her hopes, but there are loose ends, in their relationship, that need tying.

Hands shaking, the woman opens his letter. She recognises his handwriting, and her heart leaps in anticipation of hearing his voice again. In her head, she hears her sister's warning, but her life feels so empty that she is prepared to see how things go with him.

The opening two lines are vague apologies, then she sees that he would like to visit her, in two days time, on Sunday, when he suspects she will be free. If ten o'clock suits her, there is no need to reply; he will just arrive.

She scrubs the house from top to bottom, throws open the windows to let in fresh air, and wears a long, flowing dress, to hide her figure. Can he remember her naked? And she spends a long time on her hair. In the mirror, she looks well, but does not risk a complacent smile. Will he notice?

Lawrence brings no flowers. His eyes dazzle her, and she feels faint. She has to sit down, and Lawrence pours her some water.

"No sherry?" he says, in a pathetic reference to the last time they were together at Clouds Hill.

"I'm sorry," she says. "I don't know what came over me."

She looks up at Lawrence, and watches his facial muscles twitch with a thousand questions.

"Don't worry," he says.

"Did Pat tell you I'd called to see you at Clouds Hill?"

"I genuinely can't remember. It may have slipped his mind, and mine, too."

"That's me all over: just slipping people's minds."

Lawrence hears the edge in her voice, knows it is meant to cut him.

"I haven't come to go over the past."

"Then what have you come for?"

"You sent me your address. I assumed you wanted to see me."

The woman takes a deep breath, and says, "I sent it in case you wanted to see me."

This is not what Lawrence wants, this skirmishing. He sees she is different from how he remembers her: fuller faced, longer hair, more remote.

"I'm here."

His attempt to be conciliatory is cut short when she purses her lips.

"Will you take tea?" she asks.

"Yes, please."

Her absence from the room gives him time to plan his exit. This tension is unbearable. Neither has an obligation to the other. He will stay an hour, then leave.

Tea arrives, rattling on a tray. The woman tries to make small talk, which Lawrence assists, but he feels something more important is close to expression, and, when it comes, he is ready.

"We left things in the air," she states.

"Yes."

"What now?" she rushes, anxious to bring the subject to a head.

"You have a new life here."

"Yes, I suppose I have."

Her nausea returns, but she manages it.

"I'm not sure what these next months will bring."

"Then you'd better go," she snaps, standing up.

Lawrence needs no further pressing, and goes.

The woman cries, "Oh, God!"

For Lawrence there must be closure. For the woman, there is the unknown.

He starts to tremble again as he rides towards West Bay. A weight has been lifted from his shoulders, and he decides to treat himself to a coastal run. As he makes his way through Burton Bradstock and Abbotsbury, he relishes the challenge of the bends, climbs, and descents. The curvature of Earth is visible, and the sunlight becomes polished silver plate on the indigo water beneath it. Below stretches golden Chesil, and in the distance looms Portland, long and dark, in the haze and cloud.

The sorry 'interlude' – *his* words – is, however, one in a line of episodes that make him think of himself as the 'nearly man.' He always sets his mind to do something, and he starts well enough, but his ventures end in failure or disappointment. Clouds Hill is a real success, he is sure, but, prior to that, he had bought and sold Pole Hill, in Epping Forest, intending to turn it into a place where fine books are produced. In the end, he sold it for what he paid for it, so that he could buy Clouds Hill, but, every now and then, as he hurtles towards the outskirts of Weymouth, he thinks what might have been at Pole Hill. The views over London, the tranquillity, and his friendship with Vyvyan Richards were all promising, but none came to fruition in the way he wanted.

Back home, he thinks about writing a short story called 'The Nearly Man', but it is not yet time for him to damn his own life. He has the Germany project to think about. How he would look if Williamson were right about him being the man to speak to

Hitler! Then he would not be 'The Nearly Man'. No one would think that of him then.

Williamson's letter does not leave Lawrence much time to prepare Clouds Hill for him. Such a man ought to be accorded some special attention. It takes Lawrence several readings to be sure of its message, and the quandary in which he finds himself is not due to lack of self-confidence but an appraisal of the proposed course of action. It is, at best, a shot in the dark. It is not us Hitler abhors, he is convinced, but the only authority I have is given by the power of argument I bring to the table.

There is no time to send a letter, on the Monday. Only a telegram will do, so he decides to go to Bovington Post Office when he has done one or two domestic chores. Clouds Hill is not a palace, and he does not want to live in one, but he wants Williamson to think that the man on whom he is pinning his hopes lives respectably.

The telegram is brief. Bovington Post Office is empty when he lets the Postmaster have his message: **Lunch Tuesday wet fine cottage one mile north Bovington Camp. SHAW**. Lawrence does not wait but bids good day, pleased that he has provided clarity for Williamson.

When Lawrence leaves, the Postmaster calls the Major, who reads the message. Is there any point in ringing Intelligence? They already know of Williamson's plan to visit, but this confirms the day when the two plotters will meet.

The Major rings S, but there is no response. It is too late. There is no dialling tone. Their private line is dead. Operation Sandstorm has begun. No news of a telegram can impact upon it.

S reads the message when it is handed to him by an Intelligence Officer. They are underground in a basement of a grey building near to St James' Park, London.

"Well done!" praises S, looking at his watch.

The intelligence officer is unmoved, and leaves, knowing that she has never failed to intercept a telegram, when asked.

S picks up his phone with the intention of making three calls, after which he will leave the country for a month. His favourite destination is Jersey, and he already has his ticket for the boat. In the Lion d'Or, Mr. Green will have all the comforts he needs. In previous guesthouses, he has assumed various names and professions. Other holidaymakers take him as one of them, and he ensures that he immerses himself in the life of the island. He goes to the beach, eats Jersey cream teas to his heart's content. It is the perfect place to be safe. It is up to the others now.

The phone rings but no one picks it up.

"Answer, for God's sake," he says impatiently.

Then he hears a voice, which sounds like Trilby's. Trilby has been asleep. This is the call, he knows.

"Yes?"

"There is a sandstorm in the offing," says S.

When Trilby replies, there is genuine relief in his voice that the time for action has come.

"But it will soon be over."

Calmly, S replaces the receiver. So far, so good.

Trilby nudges the man who will torch the black car. There is no need for words, and they set off, all that both need already loaded.

Mills is next. S repeats his opening, and, for a moment, Mills' mind goes blank. He has obeyed the instruction not to write down any of the phrases. There is a lengthy pause in which he tries to keep calm and think clearly. S suspects what is happening, and says nothing. Surely, the whole plan will not founder at the second hurdle!

"But it will soon be over," says Mills, at last.

He did that on purpose, thinks S. I'll have him when this has all blown over. So help me, his career is now hanging by the slenderest thread!

"One to go," says S, trying to keep things in perspective. It would not be a job without one or two snags.

Smith is polishing his shoes. Three times in the last twenty-fours has he done so. It takes his mind off things. When the phone rings, strangely, he is in control of his nerves, and he picks up the receiver.

S's breathing is short. He starts to wonder if he has dialled the correct number. Get a grip man, he tells himself. Then he speaks.

"Operation Sandstorm is in the offing," he says.

Smith does not reply. These are not the agreed words, yet the voice is definitely S's, despite it being slightly strangulated. He cannot ask him to repeat the code. That would jeopardise the operation, so he waits, hoping that S will himself realise his mistake.

Smith's lack of response puzzles S. At first, he wonders if Smith has forgotten his words. Unlikely, he thinks. Then it occurs to S that he himself might have given an incorrect opening.

"Shit!" he shouts.

He tries to think logically: if I phone back and repeat the phrase, it might work, it might not.

He calls again, and Smith says, "Alexander? Is that you? What happened?"

S says, "There is a sandstorm in the offing."

Smith replies, "But it will soon be over."

S puts down the phone, as does Smith, who says, "Then the old bird is fallible, after all!"

"Thank God!" sighs S.

Sandstorms are unpredictable. Firstly, the wind gets up into little eddies, then, in a rage, sucks up sand and makes progress impossible, and all those who have experienced one know that one must wait for it to die. In the desert, a man is always at the mercy of kismet.

CHAPTER TWENTY-SEVEN

In May, the days are hot in Majorca. Arnold, Lawrence's brother, is sitting under a parasol, a book on Roman ruins by his side, and reading a novel, a rare treat for him. His academic work in Cambridge dominates his free time, so he finds The Moonstone a welcome escape from the rigours of university life.

The shimmering heat haze has built up enough to break up the landscape, and Arnold takes frequent sips of iced water, his constant companion. Then, when concentration melts, he closes his eyes, and lets his mind wander. It is not a bad life, he admits. Many would swap with him.

However, he regrets the fragmentation of his family: Thomas Edward, let down by the government and living at Clouds Hill, a hermit's cottage in Dorset, and his mother, in old age, floating around China with Montagu, his older brother. There is something wonderful about that, he acknowledges, but also idiosyncratic, odd, lacking roots, even dysfunctional.

Just before sleep lures him away from such thoughts, he decides that he will make more of an effort to see Thomas Edward, his famous brother. It is, as a fly lands on his nose, and the cicadas increase the volume of their incessant chatter, a shame that it has turned out rather badly for Thomas. No wife, no job to speak of. But he has a fine mind, and has planted Seven Pillars of Wisdom, as an immovable edifice, in the treacherous sands of time. His legacy is assured, despite the fact that his value on the world stage seems to have dwindled.

Soon, Arnold falls asleep, and awakes only when the sun has moved enough to start to burn the tender skin of his exposed feet.

* * *

The Yangtse carries Sarah Junner Lawrence, Lawrence's mother, and Montagu Robert, her son, on a short cruise. It is peaceful drifting, during which Sarah has time to really think about her separation from England. So different is life in China that she gives herself up to it spiritually, feeling that it would not matter if she never returned, knowing that Montagu's work at the Missionary Hospital is recompense enough.

"I could end my days here," she says.

Montagu looks at her, and smiles. She is no longer young, and Montagu wonders if she worries about her health as much as he does.

"Our lives will end somewhere, but I can think of better places," he says.

She looks at him. He is not old enough to really appreciate what she means.

"Yes, I shall be content to live to a ripe old age and die on this very river," she repeats.

"I hope you shall stop this musing and live to however long it is decreed. Don't be morbid, dear."

Sarah smiles. Dying to one who feels so well is a remote concept.

"Indeed, I think I shall live for a few more years. And so shall you, and so shall Arnold, and so shall Thomas, now that he has done with fighting. There have been many times when I've expected a knock at the door and a telegram to be handed to me, informing me that he has been killed in action. But he has come through it all, thank God."

Just then, a powerful wave from a bigger vessel slaps their boat, and the movement makes their stomachs lurch.

"Just when I was enjoying this little excursion!" Sarah cries. "Now, what was I saying? Oh yes, I believe Thomas, too, will live to a good age, even if his abode is a poky cottage lost somewhere near Wareham."

"Why wouldn't he?" asks Montagu. "The Turks couldn't get him, and now he's back in Blighty."

After a lengthy pause, during which she feels unsettled, she replies, "I don't know. I have no idea. Forgive me. I'm just a silly mother who wants to protect her children. Now look over there! See how the sun sets ablaze those terraces."

Montagu looks at his mother, then the terraces. How we are scattered! he reflects. Why, we are almost strangers in our own land.

* * *

Albert Hargreaves wakes up with strong sense of adventure in his heart. The day is fine enough to go looking for nests. He and Frank Fletcher, his friend, have talked about starting an egg collection, but Albert's father has said that it is a sin to disturb nests, in spring. Instead, there is always the prospect of going on a bicycle ride somewhere.

Albert climbs slowly out of bed, despite his joy at being only fourteen. His father has told him all about the many acts of heroism in the battle of the Somme, and Albert is proud to live on Somme Road, Bovington Camp. He is an errand boy for Dodge and Company, and values his time out in the snaking lanes of Dorset.

Frank is already waiting, riding in circles, when Albert wheels his bicycle out into the road.

"What shall we do?" asks Albert.

"Go for a ride to start with. Look for a few nests."

"I'll get shot if my dad knows I've been nesting."

"Who's going to tell?" asks Frank.

Albert follows Frank's circles. Frank slows down, and Albert wobbles. This contest continues till Albert loses his balance.

"Let's go to Waddock Cross," he suggests.

"Why?" asks Frank.

"Why not?"

So they set off, side by side. They talk about this and that, and Frank points two fingers at a squirrel twitching across the road.

"Missed," he says.

"I got it, straight between the eyes."

Frank laughs; they are up and running. For both boys, the day always needs something to propel it into excitement, and today it is a squirrel, and, for the next five minutes, each boy shoots at birds, shouting, "You're dead!" or "Got you!" or "Yes!" The boy from Somme Road shot thirty-five Germans before he and Frank heard the sound of a motorcycle behind them.

* * *

The Major sleeps fitfully, and his wife escapes his restlessness by moving to one of the other bedrooms. Each time he turns over in the bed, he switches on his lamp, and checks the alarm clock he has set for 04.00 hours. On this of all days, he does not want to overlay, as he needs to ensure that the road closure exercise he has organised goes to plan. This will be the third time in the last two weeks it has taken place. The men wonder if a hostile attack from Germany is imminent, but the Major calms nerves by saying that one or two improvements can and will be made. The men accept this. It is far better to be doing things than sitting around, kicking heels.

However, this is no rehearsal, but they do not know it. They will leave the Camp to go to their designated places, and establish road closures, and any vehicle wishing to pass will be turned around and sent back down the road. No one should be able to access Bovington Camp and the immediate vicinity. What the men do not know is that they will remain in place for the rest of the day.

The Major marches confidently towards the line of vehicles, in which temporary barriers are stored. Seeing this, his men fall

258

in, and notice something different about him. They see his brisk pace, and he is ten minutes earlier than expected. He calls them to attention, and addresses them.

"You will leave when I give the signal. It is not yet fully light, but be ready from the moment you are dismissed. This is an important exercise. It is vital the Camp is protected from an invading enemy. You are its first line of defence. If we control the roads, we have every chance of repelling an attack. Let no one pass, under any circumstances. Anyone taking this exercise lightly will be on a serious charge. Now, go to your vehicles, and prepare. Dismiss."

The men do not speak but follow orders. One or two exchange puzzled looks, but do not venture a guess. The Major watches them closely. How he hates lying to them! This cover – that the exercise is a routine defence of the access roads – should rouse no suspicion.

He walks over to the lorry standing alone near the gates. The driver is in his cab, and has been told he will go before the others, to make sure the main road is clear.

"You will leave on my signal."

The driver is fresh-faced and alert, and his salute is crisp. To show that he is willing and focused, he grips the steering wheel, and stares straight ahead. This is a soldier who would go over the top for his country, thinks the Major, and he bloody well deserves better than this!

The Major looks at his watch. There is nothing else he can do but wait for Corporal Catchpole to send for help.

* * *

Corporal Catchpole is at the camping ground, where he has been on duty for several weeks. His powers of observation are cited as the reason for him being a daily fixture there, and the Army has taught him to accept orders without question. The only highlights in his shift are when military vehicles pass. Occasionally, the drivers acknowledge him with a smile and a wave. Then he feels important, as if he is giving them special permission to leave and return to Bovington Camp.

As days pass, he becomes more vigilant, and stands closer to the fence. Sometimes he even stands to attention, to make clear that he takes his duty seriously. Soldiers see this, and some snigger, while others remark that he is merely doing his job to the best of his ability. He takes to saluting as vehicles pass, whether the occupants are of a superior rank or not. Over time, he becomes someone who is regularly on people's tongues, a sort of minor celebrity. People go out of their way to look at him, to talk to him about why he is so punctilious. But he never refers to his demeanour. Deep within him is a conviction that he is there for a special reason beyond his ability to observe, for what seems a permanent assignment there.

In his proud pose, he listens to the blackbirds. Somewhere in the middle of this choir is a song thrush. He would know one anywhere, and then he hears something totally different. His eyes look left, and he spots the source of it. The roar is deafening, but not that of a tank. This is the throaty growl of a motorcycle.

* * *

Lawrence is pleased that his telegram has gone. Of course, he does not know that it triggers Operation Sandstorm. His spirits are raised by the prospect of welcoming Williamson to Clouds Hill, to discuss a possible meeting with Hitler, and maybe literary matters, which always give him a lift. Lawrence has shoved to the back of his mind what Allenby has told him. Has he not lived with death lurking in every vast, waterless plain of Syria, behind every ridge that protects Turkish snipers? The one thing that stops him thinking about his own mortality is hurtling down the road on his Brough Superior. It has never entered his head that his favourite mode of transport might harm him.

He starts his motorcycle, and listens to its tone like a violinist tuning a Stradivarius, and when the engine is pitch perfect, he moves forward. Having owned several Broughs, he knows its reliability, its power, and, on local runs, feels that a helmet is an unnecessary encumbrance. The result of his laxity in this respect is castigation by one or two friends. It is an expression of arrogance to ignore advice about personal safety, and arrogance is not an attractive quality, even to Lawrence. But it is exhilarating to feel the wind ruffling his hair, to hear the engine answer his request for greater speed. This is his means of escape. Why, has he not raced a Sopwith Camel biplane? Does he not believe he can go faster than a train? There is no challenge he cannot meet on his Brough.

He is tempted to have some fun, and opens up the throttle. There is no time to think through the sequence of bends. The motorcycle gathers speed. There is no better feeling for Lawrence.

"Faster, my beauty!" he cries, and thrills to the vibration that judders through his whole body, like the first rattlings of an earthquake.

This is not merely a mode of transport. It is part of him, and he loves it more than any human being.

* * *

The black car is tucked out of sight in a gap in the hedgerow. Earlier, Trilby had lifted the rope, tied to the gate, from the post, and swung the gate back into the field. The ruts made by a tractor give the wheels a firm grip. The car is out of sight, but its windows are down, and Trilby and his accomplice can hear the birds and a cow or two. When they hear a powerful motorcycle, they will emerge from their hiding place. They have already seen Lawrence tear past, on his way to the post office, and know that it will not be much longer before they are called into action.

The other man checks the two cans of fuel are still in the boot. They are, and the interior of the car reeks. He has already looked several times, to be sure. In his pocket is a big box of matches. The place where he will torch the car is a wood just outside of Dorchester. This he will do when he has dropped off Trilby at the railway station. Both men will then go their separate ways, take a holiday.

"Check you haven't left anything in the car," reminds Trilby, who looks again to see if his gun is fully loaded. It is.

"I haven't," says his accomplice. "You all right?"

Trilby tries not to let him see his hand shaking.

"It's just this waiting. It reminds me of the minutes just before the off, in the war. I half-expect to hear the dreaded whistles, down the line."

His mate understands. He has blown up so many train lines that he expects to develop shell shock, any time. Every so often, they both think they hear an engine.

"Please, God, keep the cows out the lane!" says Trilby. "The last thing we want is an obstruction."

They look at each other. Is it possible that Operation Sandstorm will be scuppered by a herd of Red Devons? Then Trilby and his assistant laugh. Where does this strange sound come from? It is more than a release of tension. It is an acknowledgement that even with scrupulous planning, there are events that cannot be controlled.

Suddenly, Trilby grips the steering wheel, and starts the car. His accomplice stares straight ahead, and has not heard what Trilby has. Trilby has not only ridden a Brough Superior but has memorised its sound, in Nottingham. It is unmistakeable.

"Here we go," says Trilby. "Hold tight."

The car edges forward. Trilby looks both ways, and moves into the lane. Now they can both hear what they have been waiting for so nervously. A huge surge of adrenalin delivers a new level of consciousness, and Trilby visualises how it will be.

His accomplice has never worked with him before but knows that Trilby is the best.

"For King and country," says the passenger.

"For you and me," corrects Trilby.

* * *

Not far away, Pat Knowles, who constantly nags at Lawrence to wear his helmet, is weeding. In the garden, there is luxuriant growth. With his hoe, he loosens the roots, and rakes up the weeds, which he will put on the compost heap. He is watched by a robin, waiting for him to expose a worm or two.

"What are you looking at, my friend?" asks Pat. "Let's see if we can find you a little delicacy."

He rummages in the soil with his fingers, and slowly extracts a worm, which he tosses to the robin.

Pat enjoys these quiet moments. In Dorset, it is easy to commune with nature. Then he hears a fearful revving of a motorcycle changing gear, and stops. There follows a profound silence. It is as if he has been deafened. Something does not feel right. He drops his rake. No bird sings. The robin disappears. Pat tries to make sense of this new atmosphere, and will never forget the feeling that the world will never be the same again.

CHAPTER TWENTY-EIGHT

Lawrence is flooded with adrenalin when he sees a black car on a collision course with him, and there is little time for either vehicle to slow down. Occupying most of the narrow road, the car forces the motorcycle off its intended line. Corporal Catchpole advances to see it fly past the car, but does not spot the two cyclists, out to do some nesting, so close to each other.

By the time Trilby sees Frank Fletcher and Albert Hargreaves, he is already committed to hitting Lawrence.

"Oh fuck!" Trilby shouts. "Where did they come from?"

These kids are not what he expects or wants to kill. Their mouths are wide open, and they can see what is happening, and, therefore, can describe it. So he tries to avoid them; they are not as robust or dispensable as Red Devons.

Frank is in front of Albert. They veer left to make more room on the road, but their efforts are futile. There is no space left.

Lawrence breaks hard. Tyre marks are scorched into the road. The boys close their eyes, expecting to be hit, and Lawrence catches Albert's back wheel.

In his rear view mirror, Trilby sees Lawrence somersault over his handlebars, and land, in a sitting position, against a tree.

Catchpole hears a crash, moves quickly to see the Brough contorting wildly, and bouncing along the road.

"Oh no!" he cries.

He raises the alarm, and runs as fast as he can down the road.

Albert is lying still in the middle of it, and Frank picks himself up, and limps to see if his mate is all right.

"Albert?" he says, kneeling. "Wake up. Are you all right? Speak to me. Please don't die."

Frank has cuts and grazes that do not yet hurt him, has not lost consciousness, but is badly shaken.

Albert does not move or reply. Frank then spots Lawrence, and the blood flowing from Lawrence's nose and head frightens him. He looks from one to the other. This is going to put an end to the day's nesting, and he wonders what he should do. Run to get help from the Camp? But he is fearful that if he leaves that spot, Albert will die.

While Frank is bending over his friend, Trilby and his accomplice run to Lawrence, who is yards away from his Brough and where Frank fell.

Trilby takes out his gun, seeing that Lawrence's skull has a long wound serious enough to permanently damage the brain.

"No," says Trilby's man. "It's not necessary. A bullet will blow apart the operation as well as his skull. He's not dead, but his brain is a mess."

He feels for a pulse on Lawrence's wrist; there is too much blood on the neck to find one in his jugular vein.

"Anything?" asks Trilby.

"It's faint. He hasn't got long. No one can recover from this."

"Let's go, then. Leave the boys."

Calmly, the men return to their car, and head for Dorchester. Frank is so worried that his friend might be dying that he does not even see it pass them on its way.

Corporal Catchpole arrives, panting, notices the blood on Lawrence, and makes him his priority. The handkerchief Corporal Catchpole takes from his pocket is clean, and he tries to wipe the blood away to get a better look. It does not occur to him that he has deserted his post, but, in the circumstances, his action is justifiable; the noise of the crash drew him irresistibly.

Then he recognises Lawrence. Many times he has seen him at the Camp. People always point him out. But he has never seen him in this dire state. Corporal Catchpole feels sick, but stems his nausea. I am on duty, he reminds himself, and I must be professional. The Major would want that.

Pat walks briskly towards the Camp, and Trilby slows down as he approaches and passes him. No point in drawing attention to the car. The light dappling its windows hides the two inside. Pat stares hard, to see if he can discern anything pointing to the cause of the awful noise he has heard, but he cannot, not even the distinctive hat Trilby wears.

The Major sends the lorry by the Camp gate to sweep the lane, and it quickly comes upon the carnage. Corporal Catchpole helps the driver to lift Lawrence and Hargreaves into the back, and Frank's teeth are chattering in shock.

There is nothing to cover Lawrence's body. The driver sees that the blood-soaked man shows no obvious vital signs. The victim does not look like Lawrence at all. The driver wants to ask Frank what happened but does not want to distress him further. Albert is still breathing, so getting to hospital is crucial for survival.

The lorry driver sounds his horn continuously, to alert the Camp, and the Major hears it, and opens the gate.

"Accident, down the road. One, I think, is dead, and a lad is unconscious and needs to get to the hospital."

"You see what happened?"

"The motorcyclist swerved to avoid the two boys, I think," says Corporal Catchpole.

"Hospital. Now," urges the Major.

He does not mention anything else. Not that he has ever known the full plan for Operation Sandstorm. No one in the SIS ever gets to know any plan in its entirety. That would be far too dangerous. The Major knows that, though he is involved and at the sharp end, he must, to a large extent, live by his wits, for the moment.

The lorry reaches the hospital. The doctor is there, waiting, on edge. Immediately, he sees that Lawrence is not dead, but that nothing can be done. Two other doctors join him, and agree with his assessment.

"Do we know who he is?" asks one of the other two doctors.

The first doctor says, "Yes. It's Shaw, or Lawrence of Arabia, as the world knows him."

"How the mighty are fallen!"

In the operating theatre, they do what they can, but their furtive glances at each other confirm their original prognosis. The break in his skull is measured at nine inches, the severest part of the wound being on his right temple.

The Major cannot confirm anything to S. Communication is impossible now. The police are informed, but they seem to know already, and are sending two detectives to be with Lawrence.

"We had a call," the Inspector at the other end says.

The Major is resentful that he has had his authority undermined by S – no, one of S's minions, as S is an organiser, and rarely a doer – and knows that it is pointless asking difficult questions. It is clear that there are measures to deal with all outcomes, including Lawrence's survival.

It is not long before reporters flock to the hospital. They are given a simple bulletin. Questions are not taken. Among themselves, they discuss the accident, but are not in possession of the name of Corporal Catchpole, who has been ordered to remain in the Major's office, and not to speak to anyone. Outside the office, a grim detective guards the door. No one must get to Corporal Catchpole before the Major has gone through what happened.

When Albert awakes and gives his name, the doctor sends for the detective who has asked to be told when the boy comes round.

The Major is informed by the doctor that Albert is conscious, and that a detective is with him.

Detective? thinks the Major. Then these detectives that have descended upon us are not local; the constabulary does not have the capacity to respond in this way. They are SIS, he is convinced.

"He remembers nothing," says the doctor.

"Did Shaw hit him?"

"We'll wait and see. Shaw, even if he survives, is so brain-damaged that it is unlikely he will ever speak or move again."

"No one deserves that," mutters the doctor.

"No," agrees his colleague.

It was not supposed to be like this. The boys were not envisaged. The Major has executed his part of the plan, and there was nothing else he could have done.

"Keep me informed, won't you?" he asks.

The doctor says, "He has only a day or two. If this had happened at the Third Ypres, you'd put him out of his misery."

The Major agrees. Indeed, he has ended the suffering of several soldiers in a similar condition. He thinks about his next press release. Phrases such as 'in a serious but stable condition' and 'suffered trauma to the head' present themselves, and he will keep to the facts. There must be no speculation. It is important that those responsible for Operation Sandstorm are kept up to date, one way or another, even though there is a theoretical news blackout.

Meanwhile, Corporal Catchpole waits, and, when the Major enters his own office, stands and salutes. The Major smiles weakly, feels even humble in the presence of a soldier who will provide a clear picture of what happened.

"Sit down, Corporal Catchpole. There are one or two questions I want to ask you."

The interview lasts an hour. As it progresses, Corporal Catchpole becomes more worried. After half an hour, the Major calls for a detective, and asks Corporal Catchpole to repeat his account, which he does, almost word for word. He minds that, by being asked a second time to describe what he saw, he might have made a mistake in the first version. The detective listens carefully, watching closely Corporal Catchpole's body language.

"There was a lot happening: you heard a motorcycle roaring, then a crash. You say a black car passed. What sort was it?"

Catchpole replies, "I don't know."

"You don't know or you don't remember?"

"I don't remember."

Corporal Catchpole realises that, by giving that answer, he opens the door for the veracity of the rest of his report to be questioned.

"How many people were in it?"

"I don't know. It was going too quickly."

"I put it to you that you did not really see a black car."

Corporal Catchpole shakes his head emphatically, and says, "I *did* see it."

The Major wants to avoid a confrontation, at all costs, so says, "Sometimes, these things become clearer in time."

Corporal Catchpole does not like the insinuation that he made up his account.

"I know what I saw, sir."

The Major does not want to be bullied by a Corporal, and reminds him that he, and everyone else at the Camp, is bound by the Official Secrets Act, that he is forbidden to talk about the incident.

"You understand?"

"Yes, sir. I understand."

"Good chap," says the Major.

The detective leaves, frowning. The Major now suspects that the car was central to Operation Sandstorm, and is puzzled why they did not simply shoot Lawrence and dispose of him. Corporal Catchpole must remain where he is.

When Pat discovers what has happened, he recalls various conversations with Lawrence, suspects that this was what he feared: an attempt on his life. Pat knows Lawrence would want Clouds Hill protecting, so returns and lets himself in. However, it is not long before two detectives arrive to protect the cottage.

"We need to keep the press out," explains the older one.

"Do you have identification?" asks Pat.

"Special Branch," replies the other.

Pat understands, but has a key and comes over regularly.

The detectives accept this, not wanting to raise further Pat's level of concern. Pat himself thinks about hastily rifling through Lawrence's papers, and taking anything controversial away, but the detectives would surely ask him what he is doing, and he does not want to get into trouble. So a tacit truce is called.

The Major takes Corporal Catchpole a cup of tea and some sandwiches. The detective has made it clear that in any written statement, there should be no mention of a black car. The Major knows that Corporal Catchpole is a man of integrity, and would not want to lie – for any reason. But the Major must see this through now. He is too deeply entangled to do otherwise.

"Here, you've had a long duty."

"Thank you, sir," says Corporal Catchpole.

The Major watches him wolf his sandwiches.

"Now," says the Major. "I'm going to have to take a written statement. Can you write?"

"Yes, sir, but my handwriting's not the best in the world."

"Do you want me to write as you speak, and then you sign?"

Corporal Catchpole is suspicious, and reaches for the pen.

"That won't be necessary, sir," he says.

The Major pushes a sheet of paper and his own pen towards him.

"Take your time."

Corporal Catchpole begins. The Major reads the account, which is dated and signed. So, he is sticking to his version, notes the Major.

"Sir," says Corporal Catchpole, when he sees the Major has finished. "Will he die?"

The Major answers truthfully, wants no charade.

"The doctor says he is likely to."

"He was going too fast – sixty miles per hour, at least."

"But you haven't put that in your statement."

Corporal Catchpole takes back his statement, and adds the extra observation. As it comes after his signature, the Major thinks it might look as if he has been forced to add it, rather than gently prompted. Ah well, thinks the Major. It's as much as can be done, at the moment.

* * *

The King learns of Lawrence's injuries, and is so affected that he sends the best surgeons he knows to see if anything can be done, but they return to give him the worst possible news. Smith does not contact the Major. The SIS agents are in place at the Camp, at Clouds Hill, and the hospital. The motorcycle, only slightly damaged, is retrieved. So Trilby messed up, assumes Smith, and Lawrence's coma is worse than instant death.

Smith examines the location that is cordoned off after being officially denied passage by the roadblock.

"Who is in charge here?" Smith asks. "Special Branch."

"ID?" asks the Sergeant.

"Don't they teach you anything at the Camp? We don't carry ID. Now, I know you're following orders, and that is to your credit, but if you contact the Major, he will not confirm anything about me. May I remind you that you are bound by the Official Secrets Act, and that if you speak to him or anyone else about my presence, you may never see the light of day again." Smith smiles, and looks at his watch, adding to the pressure he has already exerted. The Sergeant stands aside, then Smith drives through the roadblock.

The soldiers look at the Sergeant, who pre-empts their questions with, "No bloody comments, none of you. No one says a word about this."

When Smith arrives at the cordon, he has a word with the commanding officer, who points at various places in the road. On his hands and knees, Smith makes his way slowly in the direction Lawrence was thrown. Occasionally, he picks up fragments of

Lawrence's clothing embedded in the macadam, and pockets them. Then he draws a simple map showing what happened and where, for future reference.

He saved my life, reflects Smith, and I could not do the same for him.

"Let's hope he lives," says the officer.

"Is he alive?"

Smith has been told that Lawrence has been killed.

"Apparently so. The word is he's in the Camp hospital."

Smith looks ghastly, his thoughts turning to the difficulties this presents. This is not looking good, he thinks. What the fuck do I do now?

* * *

Mills is a great one for lists, and inserts two things he must now do into an already long one. The first is to obtain the number of Cambridgeshire Police, and ask to speak to the Chief Constable. The conversation is initially a master class in caution, then, when each is confident that his interlocutor is genuine, becomes more open.

"Works at the university, does he?" says the Chief Constable.

"He does. I think he has something to do with archaeology, but I'm not sure. You will be able to speak to him? It's important he gets here as soon as possible. His brother has been in an accident, tell him."

"We'll do our best."

"He's to report to Bovington Camp."

"And where might that be?"

"Dorset. The camp is near Wareham and Wool. He'll have been before, I'm sure."

Unfortunately, Arnold Lawrence is on holiday in Majorca, explains a man in the Archaeology Department.

"Can he be contacted?" asks the Chief Constable, irritably.

"I'll see if anyone has a number for him."

"Please stress we need to see him urgently."

Fortunately, Arnold has left contact details, so the Chief Constable, realising the importance of the call to be made, takes it upon himself to deliver the bad news.

"Surely not," whispers Arnold, in shock. "Not this way."

"I don't know what your plans are, but if you could get yourself to Bovington Camp, they will give you more details."

"I'll come as soon as I can," says Arnold.

That is another box ticked, Mills says to himself, suspecting that the family will want some say on matters relating to the church service, the headstone, perhaps an inscription. Arnold will witness the quasi-transparency of the funeral arrangements, and will be made to feel he has himself made the key decisions.

The cable to Lawrence's mother and brother in Shanghai is less trouble, writing having greater scope for clarity and precision than the spoken word. Sarah reads it nervously, and feels the life draining from her. All those miles away, she reflects. We shall never make it. If only he hadn't gone back to that wretched Clouds Hill!

She sheds tears, but the distance between one side of the world and the other dilutes their saltiness, restricts their flow. Once more she reads the cable, to make sure she has understood. She has. Now she must explain to Montagu, her son. She is sure his faith will support him, but doubts herself. He is strong, while I, in my old age, only think I am. And I shall neither kiss him one last time before they nail his coffin lid shut, nor sprinkle soil on it. A son should not die before his mother. If I could swap places with him, I would, but I cannot, she laments.

"And we must go home?" asks Montagu.

"We must, though by the time we arrive, he will be buried. There is no hope for him, apparently. I recall that our last conversation about his precious Clouds Hill was not the ideal valediction, and I must live with that."

She holds Montagu tightly, to be certain he is still alive.

"We should prepare ourselves for the worst," he says.

"I know," she replies. "They would not send a cable if … "
"We shall go home, but tonight we must rest."
The next day, they pack a trunk, and leave for England.

CHAPTER TWENTY-NINE

On the hour, a doctor takes Lawrence's pulse, and records it on a card. The agent guarding Lawrence watches closely, tries to gauge the patient's progress, but the doctor avoids eye contact. The doctor draws a screen between Lawrence and the agent, as a smashed skull is not something anyone should see.

The agent understands fully when the doctor explains his insistence on privacy. Slowly, the doctor lifts the gauze pad covering the wound. The blood has congealed, and the doctor sniffs, detects the onset of putrefaction. Wondering if he should continue with the injections, which maintain Lawrence in a state of unconsciousness, he lifts the upper eyelids. His bright light pierces the pupils: no response. Then, after taking Lawrence's temperature under the armpit, he notes the downward trend of the readings, and, though he knows it will make no difference, he sends for two more blankets.

The doctor nods to the agent before leaving. In the quiet of the room, the agent tries to hear Lawrence's breathing. Temptation gets the better of him, and he stands with the intention of placing his ear next to Lawrence's mouth. He is one foot away from Lawrence's head, smells, too, something pungent, a mixture of antiseptic solution and decaying flesh, and recoils. When he is sitting again, he takes his handkerchief from his pocket, and places it over his nose and mouth. Soon he heaves, and vomits into the sink. When it is over, he rinses his mouth, and leaves the tap running.

"How much longer?" he asks the wall. "There is surely no God."

Twice a day, the three doctors meet to discuss Lawrence's deterioration. They are frank with Arnold Lawrence, when he visits, and Arnold thanks them for what they are doing to save his brother, but they emphasise that all they are doing is managing his condition.

"Given who your brother is, he has round-the-clock supervision," says the doctor.

"Is that the same as protection?" Arnold asks quickly.

The doctor does not comment. Arnold can see that the agent is not there in a clinical capacity, and has an uneasy feeling. His brother, always a risk-taker, knows how to look after himself, has thousands of miles on the clocks of quite a few Broughs. All Arnold knows is that his brother has sustained life-threatening injuries when he swerved to avoid two young cyclists. No one is able to add any more details, and it is hard to understand how his brother, who has faced extreme danger many times, can be so careless – Arnold can only assume that is the case – on his own doorstep.

"The boys are injured?" Arnold enquires.

The agent, ever vigilant, is eavesdropping, and suspects that Arnold might conduct his own investigation.

"There will be an inquest, when all the details will be made public," explains the agent.

Arnold's jaw drops.

"But he is not dead," he points out.

The doctor comes to the agent's rescue with, "It is unlikely he will survive the trauma, and, even if he does, he will be robbed of speech and movement. I'm sorry to have to be so frank. You should prepare yourself for the worst. There has been a gradual deterioration in his vital signs."

The agent adds, "I really meant that the full details of what happened have yet to be ascertained. The two boys in question are themselves recovering, and you should not approach them, no matter how much you want to get to the bottom of it. Do you have an address where we can contact you? By all means, stay with your brother a while, but we will contact you if it looks as if the end is near."

"I'm staying at his house, up the road – Clouds Hill."

Arnold kisses his brother on the hand, and thinks he feels the slightest of reactions, a movement. Again, he kisses the hand, but, this time, there is nothing at all.

* * *

Smith is not sure how he should approach the two boys, who are being kept separately at Bovington Camp. Visits are made to their homes, and their parents are reassured that their sons are in no danger. It is explained that close family members can come to the Camp but cannot see them immediately as a few questions about the accident need to be put to the boys.

"They are, however, no way responsible for the accident," says the Sergeant.

The parents are relieved, and are given a lift to the Camp, where tea and biscuits are provided. Hours pass, and no one comes to the room. No information is given. Mr. Hargreaves asks where the toilet is, and the guard points to the door facing. Soon, they begin to speculate. There is more to this than meets the eye, something they are not being told.

Smith notices that the boys are on the cusp of early manhood, and thinks this might make his task easier, but he is wrong. Their voices are tremulous, and their fearful eyes wide open.

"Does my dad know I'm here?" asks Albert.

"You can go home soon. Your dad is waiting for you in another room, but I want you to tell me what happened, exactly as you remember it."

Albert sees that Smith is poised with pen to write down every word, but a question burns so fiercely in Albert's mouth that he has to spit it out.

"Is he dead?"

"Who?" says Smith.

"The man who came off his motorcycle."

Smith thinks carefully, does not want to distress Albert by being specific about the prognosis.

"He's badly injured. Now then, tell me, in your own words, exactly what happened."

Albert begins, and there are bits about which he is not certain. Smith does not put words in his mouth, but encourages gently by nodding strategically.

"We were riding our bikes when we heard this great noise behind us. The road goes up a bit of a hill and narrows. Suddenly, this black car appears out of nowhere. It looks as if it might hit us, but it's the motorcycle that swerves and catches my back wheel."

"And?"

"The man flies over his handlebars, and lands near a tree."

"What does the black car do?"

"I … don't know. I was too dazed. I looked for Frank. The man was covered in blood."

"Did the black car stop?"

"I can't remember."

"Are you sure there was a black car?"

"Yes, definitely. It forced us all to the side."

"Did it hit Lawrence? I mean, the man on the motorcycle?"

"I know who he is, sir. We've seen him before in the lanes. He drives fast, sir. My dad says he's a hero, and that he's killed lots of men."

"Well, I don't know about that," lies Smith. "Now, before I see your friend, is there anything else you want to add?"

"I think there was a van that passed, too."

"A van?"

"Yes."

"After the crash?"

"I can't remember."

"Did it stop?"

"I don't think so."

"Was it coming from the Camp?"

"I can't remember."

Smith smiles briefly, and leaves. The black car: it must have been Trilby, and not even he could have predicted that two bicycles would arrive at the same time as him.

Frank confirms Albert's version of events, more or less, except there is no mention of a van. Smith pushes him on the black car. Yes, Frank saw it, thought two men got out of it and went to the motorcyclist, before driving off.

"Which way did they go?" asks Smith.

Frank thinks hard before admitting he cannot remember.

"Sorry," Frank says.

"Best not to mention it again," says Smith. "You know, if you're asked and can't remember."

Frank looks down at his hands, close to tears. All he wants to do is to see Albert again and go home.

* * *

The air reeks of acrid smoke, and the farmer picks it up before entering the wood. He's out to shoot a pheasant or two, and does not notice any tyre mark on the footpath. Then he sees what remains of a black car, which has rolled down a crater among the trees. There is a badger sett, and it is a wonder the badgers have not been roasted alive, given their proximity to what must have been quite a blaze.

The farmer examines the car at close quarters, and his first thought is: stolen. Then he wonders why the thieves have gone to such trouble to hide it. The two empty fuel cans are hidden in thick undergrowth, twenty yards away.

"What have we here?" the farmer asks his spaniel.

The dog sniffs excitedly at the car. Then the farmer remembers why he is there, and, when he hears the croaking of a pheasant, he suddenly points his gun and fires. The dog goes on command,

and the farmer decides to report his find to the police. He himself has heard nothing about a spate of such incidents, and there is no way he will pay for it to be salvaged.

He takes the bird from his spaniel's mouth, and says, "Good girl, Ava."

When he finally gets round to reporting the burnt out car to the police in Dorchester, they send a lorry to pull it out of the dip, and the farmer hears nothing more about it. Funny, he thinks, how whoever did it chose the spot where the flames would not be seen.

* * *

Williamson speaks to Lady Astor on the telephone. When he hears her voice, he assumes she has called to run over what they have discussed many times: the visit to Germany. But she has not. She sounds as if she has a heavy cold, and Williamson comments that he cannot hear her well enough. Then she asks him if he has heard any news about Lawrence.

"I'm waiting for a reply to my request to visit him at Clouds Hill," he says.

"Then you don't know? He's been in a terrible accident on his motorcycle. He's not expected to pull through, and I shall not know how to bear it if he dies, Henry. Truly, I won't. And you really didn't know?"

Williamson feels numb, that all is lost. Everything is now on hold, and all the time he suspects that the government is preparing for war.

"No, I did not. This is terrible news, the worst kind. Oh, I don't know what to say. How awful! And is there no hope?"

"The report is brief. No doubt the government has put a D notice out to all the editors. I've tried phoning the Camp, to speak to someone in authority, but all I get is a stone wall."

"Can Churchill help?"

"I doubt it, and I suspect his hand in all this."

All that day, she speaks to friends and associates. Charlotte Shaw listens without interrupting, cannot say anything even if she wants. Then the ramifications of Lawrence's death begin to dawn upon her, and one in particular: no more clandestine visits to Clouds Hill.

"And will he die?" asks Bernard Shaw.

"It is predicted."

"Will you go, before it is too late?"

"I won't. Apparently, he is unconscious."

"Then let us remember him as he was."

He rests his hand on her shoulder, and she shudders. It has been several years since he has touched her, but she knows he understands how she feels.

"You are right. Let us hope the end comes quickly enough if he suffers."

Charlotte stays in her room, and waits for further information. Food does not interest her, and every time there is a knock on the door, she fears it is Bernard come to deliver the worst possible news.

At Max Gate, Florence Hardy puts on her coat, ready to go into Dorchester. The house oppresses her, and she needs to keep in touch with the real world. She has nothing in particular to buy, but has money in case anything takes her fancy.

She walks past The King's Arms, on the right of the hill. As usual, she touches its façade, in acknowledgement of its significance in The Mayor of Casterbridge. No one recognises her, or sees her gesture. And it is better this way, to stay anonymous.

By the museum she sees a poster in a stand: LAWRENCE OF ARABIA IN SERIOUS CONDITION. She picks up a newspaper, and pays the vendor. Trembling, she reads the brief headline. This is not what she wants out of the morning. This is a day when she needs her dead husband, though is acutely aware she must free him of obligation to be always there for her. Now Lawrence is on the verge of joining him, and the feeling of exclusion from their association returns to hurt her.

Little news about Lawrence finds its way into the public domain, and there hangs in the air a heavy expectation of his inevitable death. The doctors are honest with Arnold Lawrence, who wonders whether he should see his brother again. He would much prefer to remember him as he was.

The room has no windows, and is dimly lit, except when a lamp is switched on during examination. The agent assigned to make sure there is no interference with Lawrence no longer watches him for any sign of recovery. He and another agent work shifts of twelve hours. The doctors carry out their duties with not even a glance at them. The agents are invisible, which is how they prefer it.

They swap over at 06.00 hours, confining their salutation to a grudging, "Morning." The one beginning his shift knows that it is a disciplinary matter to fall asleep on duty, but when the doctor has recorded his observations, the agent shuts his eyes, and dozes. The doctor, however, communicates his concern about Lawrence to a colleague, and they jointly decide to place a nurse at the bedside.

The agent awakes to see her holding Lawrence's wrist. She has been there long enough to know that the agent snores.

"I didn't hear you come in," he says.

The nurse does not reply, but concentrates instead on the spluttering pulse. Then, suddenly, she rushes to the door, and calls for the doctor, who comes running. No words are exchanged. It is as if they have agreed she would fetch him when there was no heartbeat.

The doctor seizes Lawrence's wrist, and, after what seems an endless minute, gently releases it. He takes a stethoscope from his pocket, and listens to Lawrence's chest. There is no sound. Lawrence is dead, and the doctor looks at the clock on the wall before recording the time of death as 08.00 hours. He suspects the clock is slow, but a minute or two do not matter. Not in the grand scale of things.

The agent thinks to ask the obvious but does not, and must stay there till Smith instructs him otherwise.

The nurse pulls the sheet up, covers Lawrence's head, and resumes her seat. That is what she has been told to do, and she is the best nurse in the whole military hospital.

Smith tells the Major the news. The Major's desk is free of clutter, as if he has cleared it for the last time, as Lawrence did, the day he left Bridlington for Clouds Hill.

"I suppose they've had their way," says the Major, quietly.

His reference to the architect of Operation Sandstorm in the plural does not go unnoticed. Smith has been here all too often to think about the politics of his work. Therefore, he does not respond to what the Major is implying. There are still things to do. Mills will now take over; better late than never.

"This is my last day here," says Smith, matter-of-factly.

"I wish it were mine."

The Major sounds defeated. He would never appear so to his men, but this is his only chance to show those behind Operation Sandstorm that there are more victims than Lawrence.

Smith says, "Well, I'll say my goodbyes, then."

Shaking hands is not appropriate. Both men know that obeying orders is obligatory, everything.

Smith leaves, establishes eye contact with Mills, who walks with one hand on the trolley taking Lawrence to the mortuary. It is all rush now for Mills: an inquest, then the funeral. It will all be over in a day or two.

Alone, the Major cuts a sad figure. Then he sits up, shrugs off his moroseness. Damn it all, he concludes. The job is done, and I shall leave the moral judgement to others, as all with the responsibility for the nation's security must do.

CHAPTER THIRTY

It is a long wait for S. Finally, he receives from an unnamed official, allegedly from Whitehall, the news that Lawrence is dead. All that S hears is that the sandstorm is over. He reads, of course, the basic details in the newspapers. What went wrong? he asks himself. Trilby is the best; it clearly went smoothly after the assassination attempt faltered; and all that is left to do is bury Lawrence. It's up to you now, Mills, logic tells him, and Mills is as safe as it gets. But why should S worry? He is out of the country, probably not where he said he would be. In two months, he will return, fresh, but, at the moment, he feels he has had a lucky escape, which he has.

Arnold is told of his brother's death, and arrives at the hospital mortuary to identify him.

"Will you give me a moment or two alone?" he asks the agent on duty.

"I'm afraid I can't, sir."

"Why not? I want to say a few words to him, personal stuff you don't want anyone else listening to."

The agent is tempted but knows he cannot. There would be time to tamper with the body. Though photographs of Lawrence naked have been taken for the SIS, showing every scratch, gash, and graze, Smith has given the strictest instruction not to let the body out of sight.

"Those are my orders. I do understand your position, but your brother is not just anyone."

"And?"

"I could search you, of course, make sure you have no hidden camera, but you would be offended."

"You think I would take a photograph of my dead brother, to make money? That is an insult!" shouts Arnold.

"Please, Mr. Lawrence, lower your voice. Use your imagination. You're a university man, clever. You know why I must stay, however much that deprives you of privacy with him."

"Will you go in the corner, out of hearing? Turn your back?"

"I cannot. Now, this is all so unseemly in front of your brother. Will you stay on my terms or will I send for you to be escorted from the hospital?"

Arnold approaches the corpse. There is little to see of it. The sheets are now pulled up to the neck, and tucked in tightly. The lint covering the wound is still in place, and Lawrence's skin has no wrinkles. The lips are slightly apart, and the eyelids open. His eyes are still pale blue, and they stare, in an unfocussed way, into eternity. Arnold can see there is no life there, and that releases his tension. He can tell that it is his brother – but only *just* his brother. It is now pointless to persist in wanting to talk to him; the waxy death mask has set.

"I understand. But the funeral: I need to make arrangements. My mother will not make it back from China in time. Do I have to see someone here? I assume you will not release Thomas."

Arnold does not know why he uses his brother's first name. Lawrence has no more conscious use for it.

"Go to the Major's office, and he will introduce you to someone who can help. My deepest sympathy to you and your family."

"Thank you," says Arnold, leaving.

"Down the corridor, and out the building. It's signed from there. Ask someone if you get lost."

Arnold leaves. A simple funeral, he decides. Thomas would want that.

On his way to the Major's office, Arnold is challenged three times, has to show the pass bearing his name, and is glad when he is there. He knocks, and a man in plain clothes opens the door slowly.

"I've been sent here by the man sitting with my brother, Shaw."

The use of the name Lawrence adopted throws Mills momentarily, but he has perfected a mask of inscrutability, and proceeds as if he and Lawrence had served together in the British Army.

"Do come in. My deepest sympathies on the death of your brother." Mills spares any eulogy, suspecting that Arnold will identify it as the vilest hypocrisy he has ever encountered. "I am here as the liaison officer, and my principle task is to organise the funeral. I am sure, as a close member of the family, that you will want to have a direct say in the church service. Contact has been made with Canon Kinloch, and the service will be at half-past two, on 21st May, at Moreton Church. Do you wish to let him know of any particular hymns or readings you feel might be appropriate?"

Arnold sees that this consultation is merely lip service. However, he knows his brother well, what he himself would choose.

"No flowers, no long faces, no ostentatious mourning."

"I must make you aware that the inquest has been scheduled for the morning of that day."

Arnold, too, is capable of inscrutability, and smiles.

"Rather indecently close to the funeral, don't you think?"

"Forgive what may be perceived as my acute insensitivity, but your brother has been dying for several days. The human body..."

Arnold waves his hand as if to say, save me the gory details. It does not matter any more.

"He would not want any military trappings, no grand speeches."

"I am sure," says Mills. "Because of who he was – *is* – there will be only specially invited guests. Otherwise, the world and his wife would turn up. For the sake of public order, we can't have that."

"You realise your timetable will prevent my mother from attending."

"It is most unfortunate that she is so far away."

The state, knows Arnold, is immovable. There are forces he cannot resist. There is no point in he himself being crushed.

"Indeed. My brother knew – *knows* – many people. The public will want to pay their respects. They will come from far and wide," he points out.

Mills is ready for this, and knows it is true. However, it is not possible in the circumstances. There are people who may look to take advantage of a mass gathering, and this will not be allowed.

"The numbers need to be controlled. The church and cemetery are both small. There will be high-ranking members of the establishment and government there, and their security is paramount. They will want to pay their last respects."

Arnold feels their hypocrisy is almost beyond endurance, but causing a scene will not help.

"Of course. Will Winston Churchill be there?" he asks.

"I cannot comment on matters of security, not even to you. You do understand, I hope. We don't want anything to go wrong, on the day. Have you thought about the pall-bearers? I understand his circle of friends is quite eclectic."

"Everyone liked him."

Not everyone, Mills reflects. Though even there, he imagines that it is the threat Lawrence poses to the preparation for war that is disliked, not the man himself. Philosopher, writer, all round good egg. Puts us all to shame.

"I'll speak to Pat," says Arnold, preparing to leave.

"Pat?"

"Pat Knowles, his friend, who is keeping an eye on Clouds Hill. He'll be able to advise. A good man."

Arnold updates Pat as far as he can, and asks him if he would mind being a pall-bearer. Pat readily agrees, having assumed he would be involved. This is the one and only time the eyes of the world will be on him, and he can think of no finer tribute than to hold aloft, with others, the man on whom those same eyes have been fixed since his exploits were brought to the world on film and posters.

"I thought you would help me out here," says Arnold to Pat, at Clouds Hill.

Pat has made strong tea, which Arnold likes.

"Of course. I would be honoured. And the others could reflect the span of his life."

Arnold is delighted with this suggestion. There is Pat, leaning against the shelf above the fireplace, just as Lawrence used to. This pose is subconscious, adopted by seeing Lawrence assume it a thousand times.

"A splendid idea. Six, I believe, is the ideal number. His ordinary mates in uniform were just as important to him as his glory days with Allenby or Faisal."

Pat is thinking of W. Bradbury and Arthur Russell, from his time in the ranks, and Stewart Newcombe, Ronald Storrs and Eric Kenington, from the earlier years. The names mean little to Arnold, but Pat has met them all, or heard Lawrence mention them so many times that it feels as if he knows them.

"I am sure we will make a good team," reassures Pat.

"I'm sure you will. Will you contact them? I'm sorry to say but our lords and masters will want to know who will be coming."

Arnold forgets that Pat is all too familiar with the scrutiny Lawrence and his associates have endured.

"I understand. I'll confirm by the end of the day. Which big wigs are coming?"

"I don't know. It's hush-hush, I imagine."

Pat is certain that Winston Churchill will be there. There are things that Lawrence has confided in Pat that Pat dares not share. After all, Pat cannot win in any fight he might want to pick with those responsible for Lawrence's death. But Pat has shared the forebodings that plagued Lawrence after his return to Clouds Hill.

"You know, he felt they were all closing in on him. The pressmen swarmed around him like gnats on a summer's evening, and he had this idea in his head that those above wanted him dead."

"But why? He said nothing to me."

Pat feels a little guilty at having Lawrence's confidence. Have I said too much? he wonders. No. Arnold is Lawrence's brother, and has a right to know.

"It's not for me to say. I've told you all I can."

The next information Arnold receives about his brother is at the inquest. At first, Mills tells the Major that he does not want Arnold there. The Major, however, pleads, in the name of common decency, to let him attend.

"He may prove difficult," admits Mills.

"He may suspect more if it all happens behind closed doors."

Mills relents, but he wants all those attending searched. The general public will be limited, and there will be the key witnesses: Corporal Catchpole, Albert Hargreaves, and Frank Fletcher. The boys' parents have been told not to let their sons speak to each other between the death and the inquest. The last thing Mills checks with the boys concerns their seeing the black car and the two men.

"If you can't describe them, then to say that you saw them cannot be admitted as evidence," Mills tells them, separately. "You can see that, can't you? Only reliable evidence can be submitted for consideration."

Each boy nods. This is an important occasion, and they do not wish to let their parents down.

But Corporal Catchpole is less compliant. He knows what he heard and saw. After all, was not his power of vigilance the quality the Major identified as necessary for a witness to raise the alarm at the Camp?

The Major and Mills both lose sleep over Corporal Catchpole. Telling the truth in an inquest is one thing; trumpeting it *after* the inquest, to people prepared to pay huge sums for his story, is quite another. Corporal Catchpole must be posted abroad, decides the Major, who fears a later, frank testimony to the part he himself played in establishing that particular duty.

Mills checks the arrival time of the train bringing guests from London. The Major's plan to control the roads into Moreton is implemented from first light. The men are sent with a warning ringing in their ears.

"Some people may pose as official guests. Be aware. If they are not on the list, you should ensure they are sent away. This is not a state funeral, but it is important because of the man being buried, and important to those people coming to mourn. Understand?"

They do, all of them, especially the ones who know that Winston Churchill himself will ask them for entry into Moreton.

The inquest, thinks Corporal Catchpole, is a foregone conclusion, and, of course, it is. In the dining room, witnesses are interrogated, and the boys deny ever seeing a black car. Mills, who is present, breathes a sigh of relief, but seethes when Corporal Catchpole sticks by his version of events. He *did* see a black car, and nothing will persuade him otherwise.

Albert Hargreaves' father is perplexed. Why did his son change his story? But all Mr. Hargreaves gets, when the long day is over, and he asks for an explanation, is a shrug of the shoulders. So his father leaves him alone, and reflects upon how life's unpredictability can ensnare two teenage boys on their way to do some nesting.

The day is fine, and guests arrive early. Residents of Moreton swell the throng. There are young children, too, not old enough to appreciate the significance of the funeral. The air fills with joyful birdsong, and cow parsley trims like ermine the foot of the hedgerows.

As the time for the arrival of the hearse approaches, conversations become subdued. Mills drifts like a ghost among the crowd, and is satisfied that the funeral will not be disrupted.

The Major accompanies the hearse, eyes it nervously in case some one tries to steal the body, to prove a point. The journey from the Camp to Moreton is not a long one, but the Major is vigilant, and the armed escort surveys the land either side of the road. All are respectfully silent, their finger on the trigger of their gun.

The Major thinks the plain coffin small for such a great hero. Who will turn out for me when *I* go? he wonders. There will be no security, no SIS, no press, for I am a lackey, at the end of the day, a puppet dancing to the discordant tune of a demanding puppeteer.

The pall-bearers await the hearse. Speaking in almost a whisper, they share little stories, some actually amusing, but do not smile or laugh, though are sure that Lawrence would not disapprove. They stand apart from the ever-growing crowd, wondering how it falls to them to take him from the bier into the church.

Then there is a collective gasp, followed by silence. Some mourners stand on tiptoes, and others face the church, not daring to look as the coffin is carefully manoeuvred into position on the shoulders of the pall-bearers. Cameras flash and whirr.

Already inside the church are the special guests. Churchill and his wife, Clementine, look solemn. On their way inside, Churchill nods to polite well-wishers, looking at them from under the brim of his hat. The pews are full of poets, privates and politicians. And there is Florence Hardy, clutching a piece of paper on which is a poem she is sure was penned by Lawrence, her dead husband's literary friend. She is lost among the mighty and good, but feels closer to him than many there. The whispering in the pews reminds her of her dear Tom's funeral in Stinsford's graveyard. She thinks to herself: one lived long, the other is now taken young, yet both are writers of prose so burnished it dazzles its readers. She feels the sadness of the loss of Lawrence, and is engulfed by the long black coats.

Nancy Astor dabs at her eyes, sees Winston Churchill clearly. This is not the time or place for dwelling on differences but of saying goodbye to a true citizen of the world. Like so many others, she does not really understand Lawrence's retreat to Clouds Hill.

The service passes quickly, the coffin is placed on the trundling bier, and the mourners gather behind it. No one speaks, which amplifies the birdsong. It is a relief when they set off. Local residents line the route, remove their hats as a mark of respect. At his mother's prompting, a child tosses bluebells in front of the bier, and she says, "Good boy."

Winston Churchill moves purposefully, and has to check his stride. It is not good, even for a man with such responsibility, to appear to be rushing.

Pat comments that it has stayed fine for Lawrence to a man he has seen before but to whom he cannot put a name. Among those at the back, there is muttered small talk. Each person wants to tell their story about Lawrence, and they eye the cemetery with a mixture of suspicion and morbid expectation.

The grave is ready to swallow Lawrence, and the sexton and his assistant stand some distance away, in a corner, leaning on their spades.

"They're coming now," says the sexton.

Indeed, they are, and make their way to the back of the cemetery, fanning out as they run out of space. By the gate, the Major stops, and recognises her instantly.

"Thank you," says the woman, tearfully. "They let me through the checkpoint. My name was on the list, just as you promised."

The Major remembers his abominable treatment of her. Sod rank! he suddenly thinks, and offers his arm, which she takes. Nobody looks at them; no one there worked in the kitchen with her. The Major manoeuvres her into a position from which she has sight of the open grave, and she thanks him, then removes her arm from his. He does not feel absolved to any significant degree, but it is a first step to reclaiming his self-respect, which he knows he has lost. Gradually, he withdraws from the crowd, not bearing to look at the interment. He makes for the cemetery gate, where he salutes the guards, and they do not notice the pain in his contorted face.

Words are solemnly spoken about the shortness of our lives, and Arnold is first to sprinkle soil on the coffin, which has been lowered into the grave. Next, the pall-bearers, then Winston Churchill and his wife, Clementine. They bow their heads, and make way for others. Soon, small groups form and talk, relieved it is over.

Suddenly, among the hum of conversation, hooves can be heard clopping, in the lane. Mills and Churchill look up. Who in their right mind is exercising a horse on this of all days? The distraction becomes louder, then stops. The crowd turns towards the gate, through which slinks and rolls a huge camel, on which sits a young Arab. In his right hand, he grips a rein, in his left a cane. The camel is draped in a bright, coloured cloak.

With a light flick of the cane, the young man urges the camel to move forward. Most of the mourners have never seen such a creature, and are torn between fear and a desire to see it at close quarters. The visitor's brown eyes sparkle. In his Arab attire, he looks magnificent, as if he is ready to cross the desert to seize any city to which Lawrence points.

When it is clear that the camel will not stop, the crowd parts, exposing the unfilled grave. The youth calls out something no one understands, then repeats himself more loudly. The onlookers are too busy to notice what is happening, but, when they do, they gasp, and step backwards.

This time, the youth receives a response that provokes cries of disbelief and fainting.

"Dahoum!" exclaims Lawrence. "You have come for me."

Lawrence, in his full Arab dress, walks over to the camel, and strokes and pats its legs. It is a fine beast, one of the best he has seen. Dahoum looks older, has filled out more than when

Lawrence last saw him, but is still his protégé, the most loyal of Arabs.

"I have come for you," he says.

"Where will you take me?"

"You wrote your will across the sky in stars, and there we will go together."

Lawrence clasps the hand reaching down to lift him up. Now behind Dahoum, he takes the rein and cane, and, with the strangest, most blood-curdling war cry ever summoned, strikes the camel's haunch. The camel lurches, and Dahoum jabs his heels into its flanks.

With a brusque yank on the rein, Lawrence turns the camel towards the cemetery gate, and, as it picks up speed, Churchill hears a terrible whooping, as up into the air fly Dahoum and Lawrence.

"I am resurrected!" calls Lawrence to Pat Knowles. "I am truly in-vin-ci-ble!"

Then, three seconds later, Lawrence and Dahoum have gone.

Churchill looks at the others, who are drifting away. Trembling, he pulls himself together, and helps Clementine into the waiting car. She looks at him, senses he is badly affected. The funeral, she assumes. Churchill remembers that the dreamers of the day are dangerous men, for they may act their dreams with open eyes, to make it possible. Then, after a confident slam of the car door, he says, "Let's go," and they do.

Mills pays the grave-diggers, when they have replaced the soil, and leaves, too. He has played his part. Operation Sandstorm is over.

Alone in his office, the Major knows the dust will never settle, so, with a heavy heart, he signs the paper authorising the posting abroad of Corporal Catchpole.

Pat begins to fix security bars to the windows of Clouds Hill. At last, Lawrence is free, he reflects. Not even Clouds Hill can hold onto him for long. But we have not seen the last of him, and it falls to me to make sure this place is ready for him when he turns up out of the blue, for this is Clouds Hill, his eternal oasis, to which others will flock, in the hope of catching a glimpse of the great Lawrence of Arabia.